Library of
Davidson College

Withdrawn from
Davidson College Library

URBAN LIFE AND URBAN LANDSCAPE SERIES

PLANNING FOR THE PRIVATE INTEREST

Land Use Controls and Residential Patterns in Columbus, Ohio, 1900–1970

PATRICIA BURGESS

OHIO STATE UNIVERSITY PRESS
Columbus

Copyright © 1994 by the Ohio State University Press.
All rights reserved.

Library of Congress Cataloging-in-Publication Data

Burgess, Patricia, 1947–
    Planning for the private interest : land use controls and residential patterns in Columbus, Ohio, 1900–1970 / Patricia Burgess.
      p. cm.—(Urban life and urban landscape series)
    Revision of the author's thesis (doctoral—Ohio State University).
    Includes bibliographical references and index.
    ISBN 0-8142-0632-8
    1. Land use, Urban—Ohio—Columbus—History—20th century. 2. Zoning—Ohio—Columbus—History—20th century. 3. Housing development—Ohio—Columbus—History—20th century. I. Title. II. Series.
HD268.C7B87 1994
333.77—dc20   94-11234
                                                                                                                           CIP

Text and jacket design by Nighthawk Design.
Type set in Walbaum by Focus/Graphics, St. Louis, Missouri.
Printed by Cushing-Malloy, Inc., Ann Arbor, Michigan.

The paper in this book meets the guidelines for permanence and durability of the Committee on Production Guidelines for Book Longevity of the Council on Library Resources. ∞

9 8 7 6 5 4 3 2 1

CONTENTS

Acknowledgments	vii
List of Figures	ix
List of Tables	xi
Introduction	1
1. Middle American City	11
2. Shaping the City: Private Controls and Residential Development, 1900–1945	29
3. Planning and Zoning: In Theory and in Columbus	59
4. Standardizing the Process: Residential Development, 1946–1970	102
5. Planning and Property Values: Zoning in Columbus, 1955–1970	130
6. Zoning in the Suburbs: A Success Story?	160
7. Planning for the Private Interest	187
Appendix	205
Notes	211
Bibliography	239
Index	253

ACKNOWLEDGMENTS

There are many people I would like to thank who played some role in the development of this work, either in its present form as a book or in its prior form as a doctoral dissertation. My graduate committee at Ohio State University—Professors Austin Kerr and Richard Hopkins of the Department of History and Professors Jack Nasar (who replaced Oscar Fisch mid-progress) and Kenneth Pearlman of the Department of City and Regional Planning—gave me the freedom to research what I wanted to and a standard to aim for. Within that group special appreciation goes to Dick Hopkins for revealing to me the wealth of information contained in public records and Ken Pearlman for sparking an interest in the equity impacts of land use controls. Although he was not on my graduate committee, I also thank Mansel Blackford of Ohio State's history department for the interest he took in my work at the research stage and has taken since.

I must also thank the people who gave me access to their municipality's records and a place to dig through them: Margaret Henry (Columbus), Dorothy Pritchard (Bexley), Jim Blackburn (Grandview Heights), Joan Klitch (Marble Cliff), Jane Clark Wait (Riverlea), Margie Halk (Upper Arlington), Nancy Fischer (Whitehall), and Janice McNeel (Worthington). In addition, Jane McMaster of Ohio State University's Engineering Library provided relevant items from that library's special collections.

Conversations with friends in graduate school and with colleagues both at the universities where I have taught and elsewhere kept me stimulated and helped clarify my thoughts on many occasions—especially those with Marc Weiss and Robert Fairbanks. Moreover, the comments, suggestions, and questions posed by the series editors, Zane Miller and Henry Shapiro, and the outside reader were invaluable in transforming a dissertation into a book.

Both Richard Cole (Dean of the School of Urban and Public Affairs at the University of Texas at Arlington) and Eric Kelly (Chair of the Department of Community and Regional Planning at Iowa State University), who were my immediate superiors when I taught at their institutions, provided encouragement and support while I was revising the manuscript. And the typing and computer skills of two secretaries—Lou Howard at the University of Texas at Arlington and Gail Stecker at Iowa State University—produced a cleaner manuscript in less time than I could have. Ashley Logan, a graphic artist at Iowa State, produced the maps, and Marcia Campbell arranged for photographs from Ohio State University library collections.

My family also deserves thanks. When I was growing up, my mother, brother, and sister taught me not to put limits on what I might try to accomplish. When I was a nontraditional adult student working on a graduate degree (twice!), my then-husband and son were encouraging and tolerant of my papers, printouts, and time at the typewriter and computer.

Finally, if they were around, I would thank the early city planners and urban reformers who saw problems in deteriorating residential neighborhoods and tried to solve and prevent them, and the developers who platted a city I came to know literally from the ground up.

FIGURES

1.1	Study area	10
2.1	Number and location of subdivisions platted, 1885–1899	36
2.2	Number and location of subdivisions platted, 1900–1920	39
2.3	Comparison of subdivision size, 1885–1945	41
2.4	Comparison of subdivision density, 1885–1945	42
2.5	Number and location of subdivisions platted, 1921–1929	44
2.6	Number and location of subdivisions platted, 1930–1945	50
3.1	Percentage of requests for rezoning or variance by location, 1923–1930	89
3.2	Percentage of requests for rezoning or variance by location, 1931–1935	91
3.3	Percentage of requests for rezoning or variance by location, 1936–1945	93
3.4	Percentage of requests for rezoning or variance by location, 1946–1955	94
4.1	Comparison of subdivision size, 1945–1970	108
4.2	Comparison of subdivision density, 1946–1970	109

4.3	Number and location of subdivisions platted, 1946–1960	110
4.4	Number and location of subdivisions platted, 1961–1970	117
5.1	Percentage of requests for rezoning or variance by location, 1956–1965	142
5.2	Percentage of requests for rezoning or variance by location, 1966–1970	145
6.1	The seven suburbs	163

TABLES

2.1	Percentage and distribution of subdivisions by area and municipality	40
2.2	Subdivisions platted with setback restrictions, 1900–1945	46
2.3	Subdivisions platted with use restrictions, 1900–1945	46
2.4	Subdivisions platted with price restrictions, 1900–1945	47
2.5	Subdivisions platted with size restrictions, 1900–1945	47
2.6	Subdivisions platted with race restrictions, 1900–1945	48
3.1	Land use classifications of the Columbus zoning code, 1923–1954	86
3.2	Requests granted by council and the BZA, 1923–1955	88
3.3	Percentage of each type variance granted, 1923–1955	90
3.4	Changes to commercial use by distance from the city center, 1923–1955	90
4.1	Subdivisions platted with setback restrictions, 1946–1970	108

4.2	Subdivisions platted with use restrictions, 1946–1970	109
4.3	Subdivisions platted with price restrictions, 1946–1970	111
4.4	Subdivisions platted with size restrictions, 1946–1970	111
4.5	Subdivisions platted with race restrictions, 1946–1970	112
5.1	Land use classifications of the Columbus zoning code, 1923–1970	140
5.2	Requests granted by council and the BZA, 1956–1970	141
5.3	Percentage of each type variance granted, 1956–1970	143
5.4	Changes to commercial use by distance from the city center, 1956–1970	144
5.5	Number of changes requested by distance from the city center	150
5.6	Changes requested by area	151
6.1	Comparison of suburban zoning activity	169
A.1	Subdivision data variables and functions	209
A.2	Zoning data variables and functions	210

Introduction

In one sense, the seeds of this work were sown by a history professor's offhand remark. In the course of a class discussion on urban reform, he made the observation that there seemed to be many more histories of efforts to enact reforms than there were histories of their impacts. A thorough survey of the literature might prove otherwise, but at the time I thought he was right. Whether about Progressive Era efforts to defeat the bosses and break the power of political machines or Great Society attempts to fight social, political, and economic inequity, the stories often ended when new legislation was passed and the forces of good triumphed over evil. How well the reformers' goals were achieved, or whether the quality of life improved for their intended beneficiaries, was the untold "rest of the story." Certainly that was the case with the history of zoning.

My education as an urban historian had taught me about the squalid living conditions of lower income and working class people in America's rapidly growing turn-of-the-century industrial cities. I knew of efforts to improve those living conditions by enacting tenement house laws and similar legislation, and, when those proved insufficient, to control land use publicly through zoning. Zoning was to prevent slum formation by limiting population density and preventing incompatible land uses, such as the intrusion of factories into residential areas. Zoning would also, of course, limit the property rights of private landowners, and therein lay opposition to its acceptance. Still, there was legal justification for so limiting private property rights in the city's police power to provide for the public health, safety, and welfare. Consequently, in the passage of New York's pioneering comprehensive zoning ordinance in 1916 and zoning's legitimation in the U.S. Supreme Court's *Euclid* decision ten years later, one could see the triumph of the public interest over private profit. Cities in the future would be better places to live, especially for the poor.

My education as a city planner—to prepare for the urban future rather than explain the urban past—had likewise taught me the planning theory of zoning. Zoning would serve the public interest (i.e., protect its health, safety, and welfare) by directing future growth and development, determining land use according to an adopted comprehensive city plan. That education—as well as my own observation of a growing metropolitan area—also taught me that the zoning process often did not function as intended, producing criticisms of both the principle and the practice and prompting calls for its demise.

If the much sought after and struggled for reform was not doing what it ought to be, what, then, was it doing? Moreover, what was the result for American cities of seventy years of public land use controls? Jane Jacobs's *Death and Life of Great American Cities* all but castigated the city planning profession and blamed zoning codes for the socioeconomic stratification and racial segregation of residential areas. But historian Sam Bass Warner had found that those same conditions existed in cities before zoning. And zoning observers both pro and con had noted that the social and spatial structure of Houston, the largest U.S. city without a municipal zoning code, was much like that of any other south central American city.[1] How, then, had the adoption of zoning affected American cities?

From these observations and questions came the initial basis of this research. Roy Lubove had effectively described the conditions that prompted city planners and reformist lawyers to campaign for public land use controls and told of the struggle for their passage; *The Progressives and the Slums* ends on that note of triumph.[2] I initially set out to learn the rest of the story. What happened to American cities since and because of the adoption of zoning?

Early in the research I discovered another factor that had to be considered and that subsequently broadened the scope of the study. Zoning was to determine land use and shape the city's spatial structure. In doing so it would also affect the social structure, influencing who lived where by permitting or prohibiting some types of housing in some places. Also determining land use and residential patterns, however, were private land use controls in the form of deed restrictions. Restrictive covenants in the property deeds contracted between buyers and sellers appeared in American cities before 1900. They were systematically applied to some new residential areas by the late nineteenth century and used with increasing sophistication in the twentieth. Such covenants sometimes restricted land uses in areas subsequently covered by a zoning code. Thus I expanded the study to include examination of the application of private land use controls and residential development as well, to consider whether such controls effectively preempted the public sector or perhaps merely added another layer of regulation limiting property rights.

The ultimate purpose of the research, and the subject of this book, then, became to examine the role of public and private land use controls in shaping urban spatial and social structure. There were two simultaneous processes under consideration. One was the process of residential land development, which was an element of urban growth and had involved—sometimes—one private individual's imposition of restrictive land use controls on another private individual. The other was the application of zoning, the imposition of land use controls by a public body. The processes were parallel, and they interacted when both involved the same parcel of land at the same time.

There were also two primary sets of actors: one private, one public. Private property owners platted and subdivided for development land they owned. Through restrictive covenants they could control or determine the use of that land long after they ceased ownership and irrespective of whether it lay within a municipality. City councils and zoning boards, which were part of local government, passed and administered zoning codes governing land use only in their jurisdictions.

Moreover, each set of actors had a specific interest to serve. Land developers and the prospective homeowners who bought in their restricted subdivisions attended to their own individual interests, seeking to protect or increase the value of the land they owned or purchased. City councils and zoning boards were theoretically obliged to serve the public interest, promoting and protecting the health, safety, and welfare of the citizens as a whole, the public at large.

The two sets of interests were not mutually exclusive in theory. It is not unlikely that actions benefiting the citizenry as a whole would also benefit some private property owners within it. However, in serving the whole, actions might benefit some groups or individuals at the expense of others. Indeed, that was the hope of reformist zoning proponents. Zoning would serve the whole city, preventing the recurrence or expansion of slums, while improving the living conditions of lower income persons but at the same time limiting the potential profits of landlords and speculative developers. Thus, although they might sometimes tally, private and public interests could not always be equally well served.

This brings us full circle, back to the initial question, which then became a secondary purpose of the research. In examining the two processes—the application and impact of private and public land use controls—carried out by two sets of actors for two ostensibly different purposes, I would also be examining the effectiveness of zoning and learning what happened because of its adoption. This was important, for zoning has directly or indirectly affected the lives of many Americans. New York was the first, but not the only, large city to adopt a comprehensive zoning ordinance. By 1930 more than 80 percent of the urban population of the United States lived in zoned municipalities, and more than 65 percent of the zoning ordinances that regulated their land were comprehensive in nature. Even Houston, by 1990 the lone unzoned holdout among major cities, was considering a municipal zoning code.[3]

The most appropriate manner to determine the effectiveness of zoning was to measure its application against the stated goals of its earliest proponents, the city planners and reformist lawyers who pushed for its adoption and have been most consistently involved in its application for over seventy years.[4] Chapter 3 will develop the planning theory of zoning and explain those goals more fully, but they can be briefly understood in terms of the following questions.

First, has zoning been in accordance with a comprehensive plan? Although courts have given different interpretations of the requirement that provisions of a city's zoning ordinance conform to its comprehensive plan (the conformity provision), many observers have stated that the relationship between zoning and the plan is crucial. Uniformity or consistency of application would imply that the zoning ordinance is following a plan and thus being used to direct growth and development.

Second, did the actions produce or strive to produce a balance of land uses to meet the community's needs, allowing housing at various income levels and providing for commercial and industrial land in proportions appropriate to meet both employment and consumer needs? It was once quite common for municipalities to greatly overzone land for commercial use since such land had a higher potential market value and could produce higher tax revenues if so assessed.[5] If land was zoned for commercial use far in excess of the city's needs, the land might sit undeveloped for many years (since development for a less intensive use would not be profitable), and unmaintained vacant lots could have a blighting effect on the surrounding neighborhood. Underzoning for commercial land, on the other hand, could inflate the price of that land and thus determine the type of establishment that could locate in the city. The amount and location of land zoned for commercial or industrial use also reflected a city's expectation of future growth and the (sometime) desire to prepare for it.

Third, did the zoning actions prevent the intrusion of incongruous or potentially harmful uses? Uses appropriate to commercial or industrial districts could cause deterioration in residential areas, as Lubove's reformers observed, while the infrastructure of residential districts might be inadequate for business or industrial activities.

Finally, did the zoning actions, taken as a whole, serve *all* income groups equally well? Did zoning provide low income persons better quality, less dense housing, and some choice in location, or only preserve the sanctity of upper income enclaves? Slum conditions motivated Lubove's reformers and others like them. They realized that the poor lived in overcrowded, underserviced inner city areas because they could not find affordable housing elsewhere. The construction industry built single-family homes the poor could not afford in outlying areas while old dwellings in the inner city were subdivided to create more and smaller units. Some early zoning proponents hoped that zoning could do what the private sector on its own initiative would not, that is, allow for some moderately priced or multifamily housing in outlying areas to increase the residential options of low income persons. Others looked to zoning to provide the same sort of residential neighborhood protection from injurious incursions for the lower classes that the wealthy could obtain through deed restrictions and the housing market. Equal opportunity and treatment concerned them.

Collectively, these questions established the criteria by which zoning could be measured. These criteria, in turn, reflected the goals of city planners and reformist lawyers and were necessary for zoning to be both legally justifiable and an effective device for planning urban growth.

The most meaningful way to determine the role of private and public land use controls in urban growth and residential development was by examining their application over many years to the specific parcels of land affected. Some researchers had studied the use of restrictive deed covenants as an aspect of urban (or more often suburban) growth, but not in conjunction with zoning. Others had studied the process of zoning, both present and past. I was more concerned with the product; how had land use controls shaped the city? A detailed case study of a single city would provide answers to my questions. I could do one using the information contained in public records regarding individual land use actions and decisions, drawing implications for the city as a whole from the aggregate of those actions.[6] In the way that one completes a jigsaw puzzle, I would study the individual pieces, then assemble them to create a picture of the city that controls had shaped.

Having chosen an approach, I now needed a city to study. Three requirements—legal authority to zone, physical expansion after the adoption of zoning, and availability of past public records on zoning and development—determined my choice of Columbus, Ohio. The first was a given; I could not study the impact of zoning on a city that lacked either a zoning ordinance or authority to adopt one. Like many cities, Columbus adopted its first zoning code in the 1920s. The 1912 amendments to the Ohio Constitution, granting home rule powers to municipalities that adopted a charter, provided Columbus, which adopted a charter in 1914, the necessary authority. The second requirement was equally important. At its simplest, zoning was to direct growth and development by determining future land use. Zoning ordinances addressed density of development by limiting building heights and specifying how far structures had to be set back from the street or adjacent lots, but they were equally concerned with separating incompatible land uses. As a planning device, then, zoning's greatest potential was in determining the use and size of structures before they were built. Its effectiveness would obviously be limited in a city with little or no undeveloped land at the time of adoption or in a city whose physical growth was checked by natural barriers or adjacent incorporated municipalities.

Columbus was a most suitable candidate for study. The land area of the city in 1920, three years before adoption of the first zoning code, was 23.9 square miles; in 1970 the land area was 134.6 square miles. Annexations of unincorporated land, particularly in the 1920s and 1950s, had greatly expanded the city as that land was developed. Armed with the legal power, the city could theoretically determine its spatial structure as it grew. Moreover, the necessary public records still existed. The Franklin County recorder's and auditor's offices held subdivision plat maps and deeds telling how property owners had platted, subdivided, and restricted their land for development. The *City Bulletin*, published weekly, recorded all actions—zoning and otherwise—of City Council. Into the 1930s it also recorded decisions of the Board of Zoning Adjustment. Zoning board actions from the 1930s on were stored on microfiche or in files in the regulations division of the city's Development Department, as was the original zoning map. I could thus track development and examine zoning on an incremental parcel-by-parcel basis and see how controls and restrictions set and altered land use patterns as the city grew more than fivefold.

Columbus made sense as a case-study subject for another reason as well. This research was not to be a history of one city's growth or of city planning but rather a study of the application of land use controls, and I believe that the Columbus experience with both private and public controls was typical. Existing literature on historical patterns of urban growth and development, much alluded to or cited in the body of this work, indicates that growth in Columbus followed a fairly standard pattern. With the development of streetcars, "suburban" communities formed at the city's fringe. Often blessed with natural amenities and favorable wind and water currents, these communities were generally intended for upper middle and upper income residency. Most incorporated as independent municipalities early in the twentieth century, and the city responded in subsequent decades by annexing unincorporated fringe developments and trying to annex the incorporated ones as well (though it was rarely successful in the latter tactic).

Columbus developers used restrictive deed covenants much like their counterparts elsewhere. Moreover, the comments about zoning that city planners expressed at their annual conferences and in their journals from the 1920s through the 1950s and 1960s (also discussed in the body of this work) indicate that they faced and observed circumstances like those in Columbus. So what happened in Columbus happened in towns and cities all over the country, and the lessons are applicable elsewhere. Rather than being an anomaly Columbus seems to have been the norm. The interaction of public and private land use controls and their impact on urban social and spatial structure, illustrated by Columbus, also help explain the observations about cities, with their empty cores and segregated neighborhoods, made in the wake of the 1960s riots.

Given the size of the city, I clearly would not be able to examine every platted subdivision for restrictions and every zoned lot for changes in land use. But the portions of the city I would choose to examine would have to allow me to track its emerging spatial and social structure. The first decision was to focus on areas that were initially residential or developed primarily for residential use. This was not only because a major concern of zoning proponents was housing conditions and the formation of slums as residential neighborhoods deteriorated but also because developers most often applied restrictive deed covenants to residential subdivisions. I thus excluded from the study the core of the city, which was fully developed and mostly commercial by the 1920s.

To track growth over several decades I needed to examine those areas where development occurred first and continued longest. Like many cities, Columbus was fairly compact until the advent of the streetcar, then developed along the streetcar lines, which became major arterials with the increase in automobile use. By examining maps from several different time periods, I was able to delineate for detailed study six segments or corridors of the metropolitan area, each bordered by a streetcar line that became a major arterial. This allowed me to observe the advancing fringe of development and also to include all or part of seven separately incorporated suburban municipalities. Collectively these segments comprise the study area for the research. Figure 1.1 shows the outline of the corridors and their location in the metropolitan area, and the appendix describes their boundaries.[7]

I subsequently examined all zoning actions involving any lot or parcel of land within the study area, whether that action was taken by the City of Columbus or one of the included suburbs (all of which adopted zoning in the 1920s or upon their later incorporation). I also examined the recorded plats and deeds for all subdivisions platted within the study area that were beyond the urban fringe in 1920, irrespective of whether they were within or subsequently annexed to Columbus or one of the suburbs. Since platting sometimes preceded construction by more than twenty years, this included some subdivisions platted as early as the 1890s, when the use of restrictive deed covenants was just beginning in Columbus.

Consequently, I was able to examine the growth and residential development of the metropolitan area over several decades. In doing so I could consider how private and public controls on land use had shaped the spatial structure and affected the social composition of residential areas. In essence, I could learn who "planned" Columbus and whose interests were served.

The ensuing chapters contain two stories. Most obvious is that of the urban growth of Columbus, Ohio, and its environs, telling that a moderately sized state capital became the largest city in the state in both area and population and the center of a complex metropolitan area (though not the largest metropolitan area in the state). The other, and more important, story is of the application of land use controls—both public and private. I believe that the story of how those controls shaped the growth and development of the metropolis and its spatial and social structure could be told for many U.S. cities.

10 • Introduction

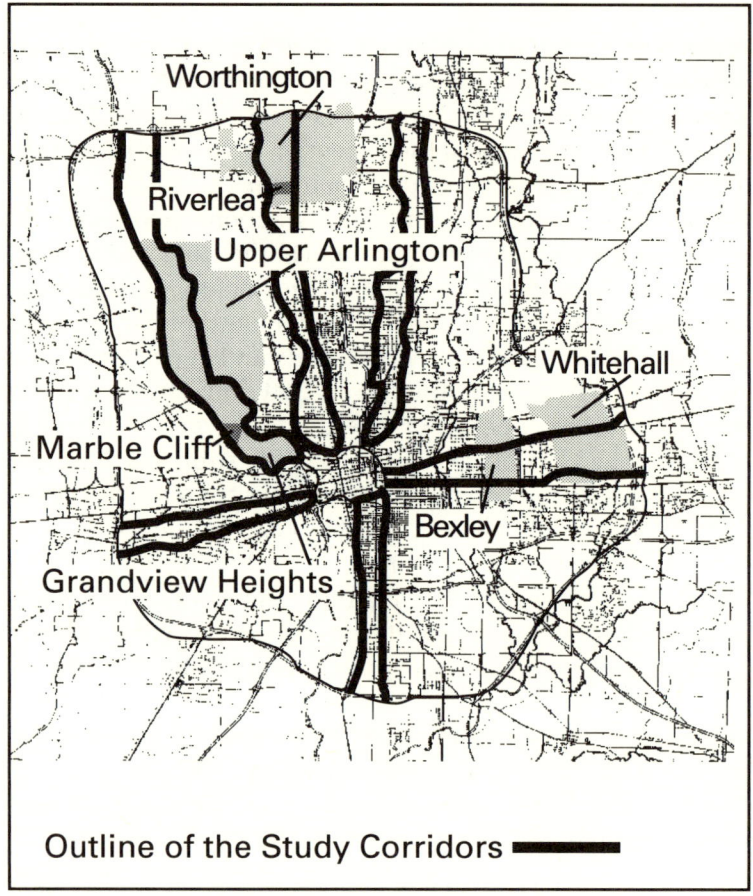

Figure 1.1 Study area

ONE

Middle American City

In 1970 Columbus, Ohio, was like many another American city. There were remnants of old industrial areas adjacent to a mostly commercial downtown, deteriorating neighborhoods housing blacks or whites (but rarely both), middle and upper income (largely white) suburbs, suburban shopping malls and office-industrial parks, and freeways to take one to or through town. Such a scene could not have been envisioned a century earlier. The 1870 city was a center of agricultural commerce and state government, a small backwater compared to her urban counterparts, Cleveland and Cincinnati.

How did the city of 1870 become the city of 1970? Was the growth an undirected process and the resulting form a reflection of thousands of individuals' incremental decisions? Or had the city been consciously shaped and planned with a specific goal in mind? If the latter, what was the goal and by what authority was it pursued?

In one sense, the "planning" of Columbus, Ohio's, growth is the subject of this entire work. To set the stage for that extended discussion, this chapter describes the city at both the end and the beginning of the process and considers the tools at the city's disposal.[1]

The Postindustrial City

Approaching Columbus, Ohio, from the north on Interstate 71 in 1970, one encountered construction of a suburban beltway that would surround the city and several suburbs. When completed, the outer belt I-270 would form a rough circle with a sixty-mile circumference. Looking at a map of the metropolitan area, one might be reminded of a rifle sight, with I-270 being the circle and Interstates 70 and 71 forming the cross hairs. Instead of intersecting in the center of the city, however, I-70 and I-71 merged to create a second, smaller beltway. This inner belt enclosed an area, more rectangular than round and two miles at its widest, that was the original walking city. At the center, where High Street (U.S. 23) met Broad Street (U.S. 40), sat the state capitol.

Like many other cities, Columbus had been founded on a river. At the northwest corner of downtown, the Olentangy River (flowing from the north) joined the larger Scioto (flowing from the northwest). Continuing south through the city the two thus formed a slightly cockeyed Y. Three miles east of the city's center a smaller river, Alum Creek, flowed through the area from north to south, and six miles farther east—almost to the outer belt—was a third watercourse, Big Walnut Creek.

By 1970 downtown Columbus was almost devoid of residences. The major retail establishments lined High Street while the major office buildings bordered Broad. Other downtown streets had their share of both retail and office commercial structures. A block west of the state capitol, a Greek Revival-style building with a domeless rotunda, stood the city's lone skyscraper. Rising fifty-four stories, the Leveque-Lincoln Tower looked like a scaled down Empire State Building.[2] A complementary group of light-colored buildings housing local, state, and federal government offices stretched along the east bank of the Scioto, and the state penitentiary, a crenelated fortification, sat just east of the Scioto-Olentangy confluence. Downtown Columbus had one other notable feature. A mile north of the statehouse on High Street stood Union Station. Chicago architect Daniel Hudson Burnham had designed the station in the 1890s, but its once impressive arcade of shops—lining both sides of the High Street viaduct over the railroad tracks—was now largely vacant and few travelers passed through its grand arch.[3]

Businesses and industries newly located in outlying areas competed with those in or near downtown. Remnants of some nineteenth-century factories that had been at the edge of the old walking city continued to operate alongside the inner belt. Others lay vacant, and still others had been wiped out by the freeway's construction. New factories and office-warehouse industrial parks were springing up along the outer belt. Regional shopping malls near Interstates 70 and 71 on the west, north, and east sides drew customers from the city, the suburbs, and rural areas well beyond the outer belt.

Although development appeared to have spread out like tentacles from the city's center, it was not evenly distributed. The north leg was the longest and I-270 farthest from the city center on that side. Two suburbs—tiny residential Riverlea and once-colonial Worthington—nestled just inside the outer belt's north rim. Located one-third of the way from downtown to Worthington was Ohio State University, home to fifty thousand students. The east leg was not quite as long but also contained two suburbs: grand "old" Bexley on the east bank of Alum Creek and prototypical 1950s Whitehall on the west bank of Big Walnut. The west leg was shorter still, less dense, and contained no separately incorporated suburbs. The State of Ohio owned a large parcel housing two public facilities on a hill about three miles from the city center on the west side. The parcel was comparable in size and distance to the north side's university but the occupants were much different; they were resident patients of the Columbus State Institute and the Central Ohio Psychiatric Hospital. The city's top-heavy development was accentuated by the northeast and northwest legs. Though it had developed sporadically and later than the north side, the northeast was almost as long. Its lone residential suburb, Minerva Park, was several miles from downtown. The northwest side, between the Olentangy and Scioto rivers, was entirely suburban—in character if not by legal incorporation. The municipalities of Marble Cliff, Grandview Heights, and Upper Arlington spread west and north from the rivers' confluence, but the City of Columbus had reached out around them and thus the new homes being built north of Upper Arlington were in the city proper.

Driving south out of town, whether on Interstate 71 or High Street, especially on a summer day, one quickly realized why the south side was much less developed. A variety of unpleasant smells assaulted the nose. Studies and reports completed at different times attributed the odors to various sources: the city's landfill, the sewage treatment plant, or the Mead Paper Company (located outside the city of Chillicothe, an hour south of town). The outer belt was only six miles from the city center on the south side—closer than at any other point—and there were no separate suburbs in that end of town. Still the south side had one notable feature. An area known as German Village was just south of downtown. Originally settled by German immigrants in the mid-nineteenth century, it had fallen on hard times by the mid-twentieth, when some residents of the area realized something unique was at risk. By 1970 many of the homes had been renovated or restored and neat brick singles and doubles fronted on neat brick streets. German restaurants and taverns, some in business for a century and others German only in menu and decor, served a growing neighborhood and tourist clientele and sponsored an annual Oktoberfest in the local park named for the German poet Schiller.

The south side notwithstanding, the overall impression of the Columbus metropolitan area in 1970 was one of growth and economic development. As the national economy began its transformation from one based on manufacturing and heavy industry to one based on commerce and service industries, Columbus could capitalize on the change. Though there were some factories, manufacturing had never been the city's economic mainstay.[4] Columbus was a center of government and, owing to the university and those facilities attracted by it, a center of research as well. It was also home to several national finance and insurance companies, and in 1970 the Borden Company began moving its national headquarters from New York City to Columbus. Others soon followed suit. Rather than sharing the hardships and economic dislocations of its rustbelt neighbors, Columbus was a green oasis of economic development—a postindustrial city.

The social geography of Columbus was like that of most American cities of the time in that residential areas were separated by class and race. There were differences, though, reflecting Columbus's later growth and lesser reliance on industry.

Although the slums of Columbus were not as great—qualitatively or quantitatively—as those of its contemporaries, the city had its poor. They congregated just beyond downtown on the north and east sides in older neighborhoods where once-fine Victorian homes had been subdivided into a multitude of rooming houses and apartments. As was the case elsewhere, some low income people had been displaced by freeway construction or urban renewal projects. They then moved into adjacent areas, increasing the concentration of poverty. Those displaced by the private renovations of German Village had moved into areas immediately east or south of the village, confirming in the minds of middle and upper income people in other parts of town that the south side was not a desirable place to live. Low income people lived on the near west side, too, but not in the chopped up former homes of the wealthy. The near west side was locally known as "the bottoms." Low-lying land on the west bank of the Scioto from which the "Hilltop" (where the state institute and psychiatric hospital were located) rose, the bottoms had occasionally flooded and its old row houses and other dwellings had not aged well.

Generally speaking, the farther one went from the city center, the higher was the income of the residents. This was especially true of the west, north, and northeast sides, where middle and upper income people lived in new homes in outlying areas. Though Grandview Heights was more modest than its neighbors, it had few if any really poor people, and the suburban northwest was entirely middle or upper income in residence. The east side's residential patterns were a little unusual, however. The area between downtown and Alum Creek was largely poor and largely black. Alum Creek then served to separate the poor, black near east side from the staid stone mansions of upper income Bexley as effectively as a moat protected a castle. The area between Bexley and Whitehall was less wealthy than Bexley but still middle or upper middle in income. Whitehall was a curious mix. There were very modest neighborhoods and apartments that had been built only to 1950s FHA minimum standards and exclusive areas near Columbus Country Club and Big Walnut Creek. The south side flipped the usual pattern since those "gentrifying" German Village generally had higher incomes than those who lived farther south.

As early as the 1920s the city's black population had been concentrated on the near east side. As was the case elsewhere, though, prejudicial actions both private and public had greatly restricted residential choice for the black population as it increased over the years. Alum Creek and Bexley had effectively stopped expansion due east. The east side black concentration consequently expanded straight north (to the near northeast side), then north and east into largely undeveloped outlying areas. An area of slightly less minority concentration extended south and east of the near east side and by 1970 there were also blacks in the bottoms. Highly visible because of their geographical concentration, blacks were 18.5 percent of the city's population (only 12.5 percent of the population of Franklin County) and they were the only ethnic or racial group whose presence was readily apparent.

There were few remnants of ethnic groups or ethnic neighborhoods because Columbus had not experienced the extensive late nineteenth- and early twentieth-century foreign immigration of many other cities. The city had fewer and smaller industries to attract immigrants, and its inland location, as neither a major river nor lake port, made Columbus a less likely destination than Cleveland or Cincinnati. German Village was evidence, of course, of a mid-nineteenth-century immigration, and German singing and sport societies still maintained an active membership. Evidence of a smaller nineteenth-century Irish immigration remained in the name of St. Patrick's Catholic Church but the church's congregation no longer lived in the surrounding near northeast side neighborhood. An even smaller concentration of Italians had long since disappeared from the near north side, where they had lived cheek-by-jowl with the Irish. A second small concentration of Italians, who had lived near and once worked the stone quarries across the Scioto River from the northwest suburbs, existed mostly in the memories of a few older residents of the unincorporated village of San Margarita. Jews lived in two parts of the metropolitan area, although not in large numbers. Those involved in business, or descended from the city's small nineteenth-century Jewish population, tended to live in Bexley, and the city's Orthodox and Conservative congregations met in or near that suburb. A Reform congregation, some of whose members had an affiliation with Ohio State University, met on the north side and was preparing to build in suburban Worthington.

Thus in 1970 Columbus exhibited many of the same demographic patterns as other cities, though in less extreme form. Disallowing the areas already noted, the overwhelming impression of the city was that it was largely white, native born, and middle income. Demographically the city thus better reflected the new, postindustrial economic growth and development than would an old manufacturing center.

Having reached out to surround its suburbs rather than being ringed in by them, Columbus was by 1970 the largest city in area in the state. The encircling outer belt's diameter was about sixteen miles and much of the land within it was developed. Of Franklin County's 833,249 residents, 539,677 lived in the city proper. Since growth would not be checked by either natural features of the landscape or resistant suburbs, Columbus could continue to expand and to capitalize on the changing national economic trends.

The Preindustrial City

Such an auspicious present would have been almost inconceivable a century earlier. Columbus was poor farmtown stepchild Cinderella compared to her thriving industrial sisters Cleveland and Cincinnati. And there seemed little likelihood of change.

The city of the 1870s was roughly cruciform in shape, with the north and east arms longer than the south and west. The state capitol and its grounds dominated downtown, where row houses and mansions were as prevalent as commercial buildings. Just under half (31,274) of Franklin County's 63,019 residents lived in Columbus. A few of the city's wealthiest lived in palatial homes on East Broad Street, but the urban area ended at Alum Creek, where the original state fairgrounds were located.

The north side was more extensively developed. Just north of downtown fine Victorian homes lined the streets around Goodale Park and on Neil Avenue, which led to the university. The university itself, a large part of the former Neil farm, had only one building, which served as both classrooms and dormitory. A few streets had been laid out north of the campus, but within another mile the area abruptly changed from residential to rural.

Schiller Park marked the southern edge of the twenty-year-old German neighborhood. It was very nearly the southern end point of the city as well. On the west side, streets and homes occupied less than a mile of the low-lying land west of the Scioto River and below the Scioto-Olentangy confluence. Farm plots large and small filled the remaining land between the west side neighborhoods and the Central Ohio Insane Asylum and the Idiotic Asylum, as the two state institutions were then called.

Though nothing remotely resembling a suburb existed yet, there were two small population concentrations north of the city. A dozen or so houses and shops comprised the unincorporated village of Clintonville two or three miles north of the university. Four or so miles beyond Clintonville was Worthington, a bit of New England set in the Midwest, with its village green, churches, and academy. Its founders had laid out the town on a large tract, allotting to each a one-acre town lot for his house on a street in the village and an eighty- to one-hundred-acre farm lot outside the village limits. Though some of the farm lots had changed hands or been subdivided, the little town retained its basic New England colonial form. All Franklin County's other villages, incorporated or not, were very small and none was within the area that would be encircled by Interstate 270 a hundred years hence.

The little city's economy reflected its geography. Its infant industrial district was split in two. Some factories had located on the east bank of the Olentangy north of the confluence and on the east bank of the Scioto south of it. A second industrial concentration existed around the various rail lines that met at the union depot, which adjoined the U.S. Army barracks at the northeast edge of the city. But the factories were fairly small and primarily served a central Ohio market, for in 1870 industrial development was just beginning here while it was in full flower in Cleveland, Cincinnati, and elsewhere.[5] Rather than being based on industrial commerce, then, the Columbus economy was based on agricultural commerce. Flat or very gently rolling farmland surrounded the city, and the area's minor rivers along with the National Road had for years provided an easy means for farmers to transport their products. The potential for state government or university-based research to become an economic contributor was not yet apparent.

Befitting its small size and early stage of urbanization, the city's population was much less stratified than it would become. The wealthiest lived in the East Broad Street mansions or the large Victorian homes on the north side, but there were modest single-family homes, doubles, and row houses on side streets in both areas as well. The city's most destitute resided in the county poorhouse. The population was more than 91 percent white, and the proportion of foreign born (18 percent in 1870) was steadily dropping, as was the percentage of "free colored."[6]

Thus in 1870 Columbus was, and would probably remain, a would-be metropolis. It was not likely that its industrial development would catch up with that of its larger competitors and there was little to attract growth. The city was a temporary home to state legislators when the legislature was in session, and only legislators and farmers had much reason to come to town and join the city's 31,000 permanent residents.

Planning for the Future

By 1900, though, the winds of change were stirring. The population had more than quadrupled to 125,560. Farm-to-city as well as foreign immigration expanded cities throughout the United States at the same time it aided and was aided by the increasing pace of industrialization. Columbus, Ohio, might not be New York or Chicago but it, too, was growing rapidly and city fathers thought it time to put a guiding hand to the process. By 1908 the city had a formal plan.

The story of the *Plan of the City of Columbus* of 1908 is typical of its era. The business community saw a need and promoted the idea; the resulting document showed how Columbus could become a "City Beautiful." What happened in Columbus is much like what happened in Chicago, but also in such smaller cities as Harrisburg, Pennsylvania, Seattle, Denver, and Dallas.[7]

Like many others, the *Plan of the City of Columbus* of 1908 had its origins in a parks commission report. By 1900 the Board of Trade, composed of the city's business leaders, recognized that the city's public works, particularly the water and sewer systems, were inadequate and that the state's capital city needed a larger and better park system. At the urging of the Board of Trade and the mayor (himself a former Board of Trade president), City Council in 1904 approved the appointment of a Parks Commission, whose eighteen members would represent different sections of the city. Council provided no funds for the commission's operation, however. With funds provided by the Board of Trade, the Parks Commission solicited advice on the city's park and improvement needs from three nonresident independent consultants. Based on their study, the commission prepared a report for council, requesting that the city appropriate up to "$5,000, by which to employ proper experts to come to Columbus to prepare specific plans." Encouraged by the Board of Trade, civic organizations, and the newspapers, council authorized the expenditure in 1906. The city commissioned the same three consultants who had previously served the Parks Commission and added two more. These five individuals, who would report to the council and the city's Board of Public Service, were formally designated the "Columbus Plan Commission."[8] They included Austin W. Lord, a New York architect, as chair; Charles N. Lowrie, a New York landscape architect; Albert Kelsey, a Philadelphia architect; H. A. MacNeil, a New York sculptor; and Charles Mulford Robinson, Rochester's famous civic adviser, as secretary.[9]

The commission's *Plan* of 1908 was a three-part report, with sections devoted to the city in general, the city's parks, and a proposed civic center. Part I, "The General Survey," described the city's layout and topography and noted that Columbus served a triple urban function. As the state capital it was a center of government, but it also was a center for commerce and industry as well as a center for education. The survey commented on what was good in the city—particularly Union Station and its arcade—and offered suggestions for improvement and future growth. The commission recommended that utility wires be put underground, that the placement of buildings and signs in the public right-of-way be restricted, and that public toilets and baths be provided. Careful attention should also be paid to the site and size of schools as the city grew. As general guidelines the report recommended that primary schools be within walking distance of their students and not be too large. Schools needed adequate play space and should ideally adjoin parks, while saloons should be prohibited from opening near them. Noting the relationship between a city and its surroundings, the report suggested conscious, formal interaction between Columbus and its infant suburbs so that the smaller communities not be allowed "to disfigure the outskirts of the city." It also recommended that Ohio State be explicitly integrated into the city's design and functioning since the university was a major presence. The university's large tract of land bordering the Olentangy River provided the city a "breathing space" and the opportunity to create a "noble" landscape. At the same time, growing enrollments and public attendance at sporting events presented a challenge the city could not afford to ignore. The plan's suggestions for schools, suburbs, and the university were fairly general, however, for the commission recognized that actions affecting those areas lay outside municipal government authority. Hence, cooperation—particularly with the school board and the university administration—was urged.[10]

The plan's middle (and largest) section was titled "Parks, Parkways and Recreation Grounds." Although this section was well illustrated with photographs and drawings of park plans, the commission here saw mostly potential, for the city's parks were few, inadequate, and underfunded relative to comparable cities'. The principal parks—Schiller, Goodale, and Franklin (which had replaced the original state fairgrounds on the east side)—were ornamental and provided little for the city's working people. The report noted that parks could provide an economic benefit: property taxes, like property values, tended to rise for parcels adjacent to a park and parks could attract a better quality labor force. The report then recommended a complete park system composed of four elements. First were playgrounds. These should be within a half-mile's walking distance of all the city's children and could use schoolyards, if appropriately equipped. Next should be neighborhood parks, like Schiller, Goodale, and Franklin; but the city needed more of them and to add some recreational facilities for the working classes. Third were large parks, one in each leg of the city's Maltese-cross configuration to serve the population of the corresponding north, east, south, and west sides. Finally, the report suggested outlying nature reserves well beyond the urban area. The report proposed that boulevards and parkways connect the various elements of the system, and said the city should effectively use its rivers and view the proposed and existing parks as an integrated system.[11]

City plans of this era almost invariably called for a civic center of some type and the Columbus *Plan* of 1908 was no exception. Indeed, such an element was viewed as more important here than in many other cities because Columbus was the seat of state government and the capitol was an ideal focus for such a center.

Addressing the "heart of the city," the report proposed a Capitol Park Mall between the Scioto River and the statehouse. City Hall and other buildings serving local, state, and national government purposes should form a Civic Court around the mall, along with an art gallery or music hall. The governor's mansion, beyond the capitol at the east end of the mall, would complete the picture. Like the parks section, the "Civic Center" was lavishly illustrated to show what could be accomplished, and photographs and references to European cities provided additional inspiration.[12]

The *Plan of the City of Columbus* of 1908 dealt only with the city's physical elements. There was no mention of housing needs, employment base, or the city's population structure, but that was characteristic of city plans (and city planning) in that era. Nor did it address water and sewer systems, for much-needed public works improvements were already underway by the time the Columbus Plan Commission began its work. Like its contemporaries the *Plan* was comprehensive only in that it considered the whole (albeit physical) city rather than just parks or a civic center.[13]

Underlying the plan was the premise that growth would continue in much the same manner and in the same directions as it had already occurred. The city should thus take the initiative and buy the necessary land for parks, parkways, and civic center before economic growth and development pushed up the cost. Although the *Plan*'s ostensible focus was aesthetic, which the illustrations accentuated, its text repeatedly emphasized the benefits to be enjoyed if the city should adopt and implement its suggestions. Sprinkled throughout were phrases like "beauty and dignity," "importance and destiny." Planning would provide for "convenience and commercial economy." Well-planned railroads and ancillary facilities, as well as other public improvements, would foster economic growth and prosperity. In parks citizens could be refreshed by the "song of birds" and the "scent of flowers" and have the opportunity to "build up again the physical strength so freely expended, day by day in factory and shop."[14] A plan would encourage the philanthropic impulse of individuals to make gifts of land to the city for street widening, parks, or schools, and civic beauty would be a positive influence on all citizens. A well-planned Columbus would have to play second fiddle to no other city and could achieve what its status as state capital implied.

Columbus and Home Rule

The Plan Commission had given the city a vision of what it could become, a goal to be pursued. And though the business community had provided the original impetus for planning the city's future, city government would have to take the action. The city's ability to do that, however, was limited, for Ohio had no provisions for municipal home rule. Like other cities, Columbus was subordinate in all matters to state government, which established the rules by which cities of different sizes could operate.

The twentieth century's first decade, which saw the preparation of many city plans, also saw the push for municipal reforms that would give cities the authority and flexibility to implement those plans effectively. At the national, state, and local levels progressives fought for a multitude of political, social, and economic reforms. And the same urban conditions that made apparent the need for those reforms and for cities to plan for their futures also spurred the push for municipal home rule. Cities had to be freed from their state legislatures so they could best solve their individual problems. In 1900 only four states provided for municipal home rule; Ohio was not among them.[15] By 1912, however, Ohio and others had joined the group.

Ohio's cities were at the forefront in the fight for municipal reforms. Cleveland and Toledo had reform mayors in Tom Johnson and Samuel "Golden Rule" Jones. In Columbus, Congregationalist pastor and nationally known exponent of the social gospel Washington Gladden was elected to City Council in 1900. An independent reform candidate, Gladden was known to support municipal ownership of public utilities and the adoption of city charters, so the signs were auspicious.[16]

Early in the 1901–02 session the state legislature began efforts to adopt a municipal code. The legislature examined several plans, some with home rule provisions, and discussed them at length. In Columbus, where the legislature was meeting, Gladden pleaded from his pulpit and elsewhere that legislators "give the people of the cities the rights and privileges that belong to them as citizens." Citing the principle of local self-government as the basis of democracy, he charged the legislature to "make it legally possible for the cities to govern themselves." The Republican majority was not ready to go that far, however, and although the municipal code they adopted provided some improvement over the existing situation, it did not provide home rule.[17]

A decade later things had changed. The Ohio Constitution required that a constitutional convention meet every twenty years to consider amendments to that document, and the years leading up to the 1910 call for a convention had been ones of growing progressive and reform strength. Voters elected delegates to the convention in November 1910. Although local municipal contests often overshadowed delegate selection, progressive and reform candidates did well generally. It was estimated that only one-quarter of the delegates—mostly from rural areas—were conservatives. The convention that assembled January 9, 1912, was thus split between conservatives and progressives rather than along party lines.[18]

Several prominent reformers played a major role. Cleveland's Tom Johnson, concerned about bosses and machine politics as well as other municipal ills, had laid the blame for their existence on the state constitution. Without home rule it effectively hog-tied those cities that attempted to solve their own problems. Washington Gladden and the reformist mayors addressed a conference of the state's mayors and other municipal officials that met to draft a home rule amendment to be submitted to the constitutional convention. The convention then passed the submitted amendment by a strong vote.[19]

Home rule was only one of many issues the convention examined. Delegates also considered the merits of proposals for initiative and referendum, the licensing of saloons, institution of the direct primary, and granting the vote to women.[20] Altogether the convention prepared forty-two amendments to submit to the voters for approval. Each would require only a simple majority for passage, and if passed would take effect January 1, 1913. Progressive and reform forces supporting the amendments, most of whom were Democrats or Roosevelt Republicans, were well organized, and the state's big city newspapers also supported most of the major issues. The voters of Ohio responded and approved thirty-four amendments—including the one for home rule.[21]

It was now up to the cities to exercise their newly granted power. Columbus lost no time, beginning discussions on a city charter in

February 1913. Ohio State University President William Oxley Thompson presided over the Municipal Charter League, which was created to draft a charter, and Washington Gladden served on its executive committee. Fifteen months later voters in Columbus approved a city charter containing many municipal government reforms. The charter provided for a seven-member City Council, with members elected at large, to be the city's legislature. The mayor, also elected at large, headed the executive branch of municipal government. The charter did not provide for a planning commission, but council had the authority to establish one if it felt the need.[22] Other cities were less eager to govern themselves. By 1916 only twenty-six Ohio cities had submitted home rule charters to their voters, and only ten of those charters had passed. Still, though the provisions were not fully utilized, Ohio's cities had more favorable home rule provisions than any other state's except California's. Moreover, a 1923 Ohio Supreme Court decision ruled that the home rule power of local self-government was self-executing: a municipality could act on its own behalf regardless of whether it adopted a charter. It need not ask the state legislature's permission. With its home rule provision, then, Ohio's 1912 constitutional amendments gave cities the impetus, opportunity, and authority to attack many of their long-standing problems.[23]

Annexation

Ohio's cities were not entirely free of the state's influence, however. Through its provisions regarding annexation, the Ohio Municipal Code governed how cities could physically expand.

The code clearly spelled out the procedures and requirements.[24] The county commission of the appropriate county had to approve all annexation petitions, and only contiguous territory, adjacent to the existing municipal corporation limit, could be annexed. Either landholders in the area to be annexed or the city it was to join could petition the county. If the former, a majority of resident adult freeholders had to submit the petition; absentee owners and tenants had no voice in the matter. After hearing arguments (if any were offered) supporting or opposing the petition, the county commissioners either approved or denied it. If the petition were approved, the city council of the municipality to be joined then voted to accept or reject the territory in question. But approval of the territory's landowners was not required if the annexing city initiated the petition. The city defined the territory under consideration for annexation, then petitioned the county commissioners, who approved or denied the petition after hearing any relevant arguments. If county officials approved the petition, city council still had to vote to accept or reject the territory.

The major limitation on a city's imperialistic ambitions—other than some owners' arguments before the county commission—occurred if the city sought to annex land within another incorporated municipality. If approved by the county, such an annexation required city council acceptance by both the annexing city and the city to be annexed.[25] In the 1920s, Columbus successfully annexed the incorporated Village of Linden Heights. Located on the northeast side, Linden's council voted to join its much larger neighbor. Columbus made similar overtures to the suburbs of Bexley, Grandview Heights, Marble Cliff, and Upper Arlington at the same time.[26] Citizens in those communities preferred to maintain their independence, however, and their councils voted against joining Columbus. Most annexations to Columbus, thus, were of unincorporated territory.[27]

Residents owning land in an area could also vote to de-annex (or detach) their property from a city and petition the county commission for approval. In 1903, landowners on the east side of Marble Cliff, then just two years old, detached their land from the village. A portion of the detachment soon became the core of Grandview Heights and the rest annexed to Columbus in the 1920s. Similarly, owners of two large parcels on Bexley's western edge detached themselves from that suburb and annexed to Columbus in 1910.[28] Generally, though, once joined to a city, territory remained there.

Once City Council accepted an annexation, residents of the annexed territory received all the "rights and privileges" of citizenship. This was their primary motivation for seeking annexation, for it meant they would receive city services—especially water and sewer lines. On rare occasions someone owning a parcel within a larger tract being considered for annexation did not want municipal services or the corresponding taxes. This most often happened if the owner did not intend to develop his land or if he lived on a lot so large that a well and septic tank adequately served his water and sewer needs. Seeing no benefit to being part of the city, such an individual could request exclusion from the annexation. Absent a compelling reason to do otherwise, the county commissioners generally agreed, which produced some annexations of very irregular shape. Even decades later there remained little islands of unincorporated land surrounded by a sea of city. Most landowners, though, preferred the benefits of municipal citizenship.

Provisions in Ohio's *Municipal Code* governing annexation thus served to facilitate land development while encouraging urban expansion. It became common practice for a land speculator or developer to buy one or more parcels of unimproved land just beyond the city limits where land costs were lower than for vacant land in town. He would then plat streets and building lots, file the subdivision plat with the county, and petition for annexation to the city. Once part of the city the lots could receive the water and sewer service desired by future homeowners, and the city would also be responsible for maintenance of the streets, which the developer dedicated as public rights-of-way when annexing to the city. While now able to sell "improved" building lots, the developer had not borne the cost of the improvements. For its part, the city expanded in area and tax base.[29]

Facing the Future

By 1915 Columbus was prepared. The city had a plan, and the city had the power to take whatever steps it deemed necessary to implement it as the city grew. Admittedly, that 1908 plan did not provide guidance for all aspects of the city's future but the fact that the plan existed indicated that some of the city's leading citizens were looking ahead. The 1914 City Charter was further testimony to that fact.

It seems reasonable to assume, then, that Columbus would continue to be forward looking and progressive in its approach to planning and growth. As the profession of city planning developed during the ensuing decades, plans became truly comprehensive in nature. They took into consideration a city's political, social, and economic characteristics and needs as well as its physical structure. City planners and reformist lawyers developed and promoted the concept of zoning—public controls on the use of land—as a device to implement those city plans, prevent the errors and problems of the past, and provide for a better future.

The municipal officials of Columbus could creatively and effectively manage and direct the city's own development as it grew from a city of 235,051 people covering 23.9 square miles in 1920 to a city of 539,677 covering 134.6 square miles in a larger metropolitan area by 1970. Alternatively, the public sector could abdicate its role and leave the city's future in the hands of hundreds of private individuals as they purchased and developed land for whatever purpose suited their needs at the time. What happened during several decades of residential development and the application of land use controls would indicate who actually shaped the modern American metropolis in Ohio's middle.

TWO

Shaping the City: Private Controls and Residential Development, 1900–1945

During the twentieth century's first half, Columbus real estate developers large and small collectively shaped the urban area. From 1900 to 1945 they experimented with various aspects of the land development process and eventually standardized it. The range of both development size and density decreased while the use of restrictions imposed in deeds for individual lots increased.

Through their choice of site and the nature of the restrictions they imposed, land developers established the city's social and spatial structure. They chose specific locations to develop upper income residential subdivisions and used deed restrictions to ensure upper income development, thus granting to certain areas an exclusive or desirable character and leaving other parts of the city for those less well off. Moreover, racial covenants in deeds, particularly between 1920 and 1945, limited nonwhite residency in new developments. Though not all developers were equally successful, two who operated on an exceptionally large scale had a major impact on the city's form.

In this manner developers established the character of newly formed suburban municipalities as well as the city itself. This was because development occurred irrespective of municipal boundaries. Real estate developers most often chose unincorporated land beyond the urban fringe. Whether a subdivision subsequently joined the city proper or one of the suburbs was determined by its location and the pace and direction of municipal growth, since only contiguous territory could be annexed. Because many developers operated both in areas that became part of the city and in areas that became part of the suburbs—and the process was the same in either case since most development involved land that was initially unincorporated—one can best understand the cumulative impacts of residential development if one examines the process in the metropolitan area as a whole, rather than studying the city and its suburbs separately. Viewing the land the way real estate developers did—as so much raw material before it became part of any municipality—one can more easily see how they shaped the area as they chose their sites, platted their lots, and restricted their deeds.

The Nature and Use of Deed Restrictions

Columbus land developers did not pioneer the use of restrictive covenants[1] in real estate deeds but they quickly caught on to the benefits gained from private land use controls. Though zoning and other governmental limitations on private property have been condemned for their erratic application or excessive restrictiveness, restrictive covenants, to which buyer and seller agree, have not. Yet, "If the controls exercised by public authorities over land-use in America seem excessively detailed and capricious, the controls happily adopted by private citizens are positively sadistic."[2] Why have American property owners so willingly accepted these limitations?

Deed restrictions have been used in American property transfers since very early times, but their application in their modern form to control large tracts of land being sold to many different individual lot purchasers is a fairly recent development.[3] The forerunner of the contemporary restricted subdivision was Riverside, Illinois, developed in 1871. As urbanization increased through the end of the nineteenth century and the first decades of the twentieth, the development of the restrictive covenant also increased. At the very time when land was increasingly changing from agricultural to urban uses, little of it was subject to any control. Municipal controls did not yet exist, and individual lot holders could control only their own lots. Realizing that acts on one parcel could affect the value and condition of adjacent property, owners of large tracts for development began to apply restrictive covenants to prevent waste (so that buildings would not be erected in a public right-of-way or easement), to stabilize or enhance land values, and to provide for various amenities.[4]

In the early stages of their application of deed restrictions, real estate developers used them primarily to prohibit nuisances. They conceived of a residential nuisance very broadly, including such things as the keeping of livestock or fowl, quarrying, maintaining a saloon or slaughterhouse, or operating a tannery. Restrictions might prohibit having a fuel tank above ground or erecting any signs or billboards.[5] Some even prohibited certain trees considered nuisances.[6]

Gradually developers became more comprehensive in their use of restrictive covenants. They inserted a blanket restriction prohibiting any business or trade, or designated only certain properties by lot number for commercial use. If a subdivision was to be entirely residential, developers specified that each lot contain only one single-family home or designated specific lots for doubles, row houses, or apartments.[7] Some even distinguished between duplexes and doubles, prohibiting the latter (which were easily identified as two-family structures) and permitting the former (which often appeared to be large single-family homes).

Developers also regulated construction of buildings, indicating where on the lot structures could be erected. They indicated a building setback line in the deed or the recorded plat to produce a more uniform street appearance or assure adequate light and air for all dwellings. In upper income subdivisions they often prohibited the erection of a garage before the residence, ostensibly to discourage moderate income owners from living in the garage until they could afford to build the house. Construction restrictions sometimes specified a particular building material, such as stone or brick, or a minimum construction cost, and the most restrictive required that the developer or his representative approve building plans.[8]

Developers' deed restrictions determined who could use the property as well as how by limiting alienation or occupancy. A few required the initial grantor's approval of buyer for all future transfers (the most extreme form of ownership control). In the 1920s deeds often prohibited ownership or occupancy by blacks or Asians or limited it to Caucasians, which generally excluded blacks, Jews, and Asians. State and local courts generally upheld this practice until the 1948 U.S. Supreme Court decision *Shelley* v. *Kraemer*.[9]

Developers had some difficulty deciding how to enforce the deed covenants or for how long. Being recorded in the deed, the covenants were part of the public record of the property. As such they were "binding upon subsequent holders" even if the deeds to those subsequent purchasers did not repeat the actual restrictions. However, courts sometimes refused to enforce covenants they felt were primarily to benefit the grantor rather than to develop a plan for the area. If there was a question as to the intent of the restrictions, courts tended to resolve it in favor of the free and unencumbered use of the property.[10]

Restrictions could be ended if a court decided the area had changed so much as to render the restrictions ineffective or their enforcement inequitable. Restrictions also ended when their stated expiration date (if one existed) was reached or if all the property covered by them were united under single ownership and the new owner chose to end them. Moreover, individual lot owners could mutually agree to release one another from the covenants.[11]

The duration of deed restrictions concerned both the length of time specified and the method for continuing them. In general, the more highly developed the subdivision, the longer the restrictions' duration. In Baltimore's Roland Park restrictions were effective for sixty-three years and in Cleveland's Shaker Heights for one hundred and one. However, restrictions examined in the 1920s showed a "surprising uniformity" of thirty-three years' duration. Developers had to set an explicit time limit lest the restrictions be held invalid as against public policy under the "rule of perpetuities,"[12] a common-law rule prohibiting perpetual restraints.

To effectively implement a developer's plan, restrictions had to remain in force long enough to set the character of the development. At the minimum that meant long enough for most lots to be sold and built on, as some developers felt the built-up area could maintain its own character. Others felt that to protect the purchasers' investment by prohibiting incongruous intrusions into the area, restrictions should last as long as the probable life of the originally planned use.[13]

Developers also provided for restrictions' extension and enforcement. In Kansas City's Country Club District, Jesse Clyde Nichols mandated automatic renewal of restrictions for specified periods unless certain procedures (such as a vote of a majority of the covered property owners) ruled otherwise. Others also used this technique, which has continued to be practiced.[14] Enforcement of the restrictions by the grantor had the disadvantage that his interest in the property decreased with the sale of each lot and disappeared completely when the last lot was sold. Municipal enforcement of deed restrictions, suggested by some developers, also posed problems, for the restrictions were part of the private contract between buyer and seller; the city was not party to the agreement.[15] Nevertheless, if an owners' association existed and if it were an active group, it could be a very effective enforcer of restrictions. It reflected the occupants' concerns, and the association's interest in the property—unlike the developer's—was permanent.[16]

Through the use of deed restrictions, the realtor subdivider was really planning cities, noted city planner and former National Conference on City Planning (NCCP) president George B. Ford in the 1920s.[17] Subdivision development meant not only platting the streets and lots but also preparing them for use, and the subdivider imposed his control by restricting the property when he sold it. Through his "planning," the subdivider tried to provide the maximal amenities that would create and protect land value. To accomplish a plan, a developer had to restrict an entire subdivision. Applying restrictions on a piecemeal, deed-by-deed approach sometimes tempted subdividers to make concessions for a particular lot or purchaser to enhance sales prospects. However, when uniformly applied, the restrictions and the plan had a reciprocal relationship. A plan would gain through the application of "restrictions that are drawn to its execution and the restrictions gain prestige in the courts when they are based on a plan."[18]

Court opinion legitimated the right to create deed restrictions. Although based on the right of free contract, that right was not unlimited. Restrictions could not be "contrary to public policy" or "unreasonable" (in its legal sense). They had to be rational and meet the standard of being what "the average man" would expect under the circumstances. Whether covenants could run with the land was determined by the nature of the covenant itself. If a deed restriction benefited only the seller, courts would regard it as a personal covenant binding only the original purchaser. However, if the covenant also benefited other land, such as adjacent lots to maintain the character or quality of the entire neighborhood, it could restrict the owner of any lot so covered — including subsequent purchasers.[19]

Developers assumed that deed restrictions increased property value, either by making the lots more desirable or because of the relative scarcity of restricted properties. Either way, the subdividers benefited. The lot purchaser's benefits were less clear. He or she wanted maximal amenities but did not want restrictions to be an obstacle if change in the area or local market made it profitable to alter the property's use. If deed restrictions ran too long, they would preclude such change and thus limit the potential profit. Developers saw restrictive covenants as a way to reduce the speculative element in land subdivision and sale, stabilizing both land use and value. Consequently the nature of the local market was very important, and the provisions and duration of restrictions had to be appropriate to local conditions. It was important for a developer to maintain the character of the neighborhood he was creating until he had sold most of the lots, for the first 75 percent of lot sales covered his development costs and only the last quarter of lot sales provided his profit. Thus restrictions had to be tight enough to make the lots desirable but not so tight as to hinder sales. Developers found restrictive covenants a very useful marketing device, as they could assure purchasers protection from undesirable neighbors or inharmonious uses.[20]

Deed restrictions established and maintained the character of some of the more exclusive residential areas in the United States. Roland Park in Baltimore was one of the first to systematically control an entire neighborhood, and the principal developer of Berkeley, California, also recognized their usefulness in determining a neighborhood's character. The developers of Kenilworth, Illinois, and Short Hills, New Jersey, paired restrictive covenants with design controls and picturesque subdivision site planning to establish their exclusive communities, while the developer of Wissahickon Heights (later St. Martins) in Philadelphia added ownership control to the deed restrictions. A speaker at the 1916 meeting of the NCCP noted that in the absence of municipal controls, deed restrictions had been used to help maintain the exclusive community of Shaker Heights, preventing the intrusion of incongruous uses and stabilizing land values.[21] Developers in Columbus, Ohio, were consequently in good company when they began applying restrictive covenants in the closing years of the nineteenth century and standardized the practice in the early twentieth, thus determining the social and spatial structure of the metropolitan area.[22]

Development before 1900

Although a few residential neighborhoods existed well beyond the urban fringe, at the turn of the twentieth century Columbus was essentially a walking city.[23] It was still quite compact, with only two small areas—one in the north and one on the west—extending more than three miles from the city center. There were no independent suburbs yet, as no outlying areas had incorporated.[24]

Although the fringe of development coincided quite closely with the city's corporate limits, a mile or more beyond the urban fringe some residential development had already occurred. In 1885 developers began platting subdivisions well outside the city, and by 1900 they had platted forty-one subdivisions (18.7 percent of the total platted through 1945) beyond what would be the 1920 fringe of the city. Moreover, they had laid the foundations of the suburbs; the twelve subdivisions platted in the northwest became parts of Marble Cliff and Grandview Heights, seven of the nine platted on the east side became part of Bexley, and two of the eleven platted in the northeast became the Village of Linden Heights. Developers platted only one subdivision on the south side and none on the west. Thus they began a trend that continued through 1970 (as illustrated in Figure 2.1).[25]

Real estate development was a small-scale business activity, so although there was considerable variation in size and density, most subdivisions and lots were not large. More than 35 percent of the subdivisions covered less than 10 acres, and 31.6 percent covered between 11 and 25 acres. The remainder ranged from 25 to 174 acres. These produced average densities of ten lots per acre for 20.6 percent, eight lots per acre for 20.6 percent, six lots per acre

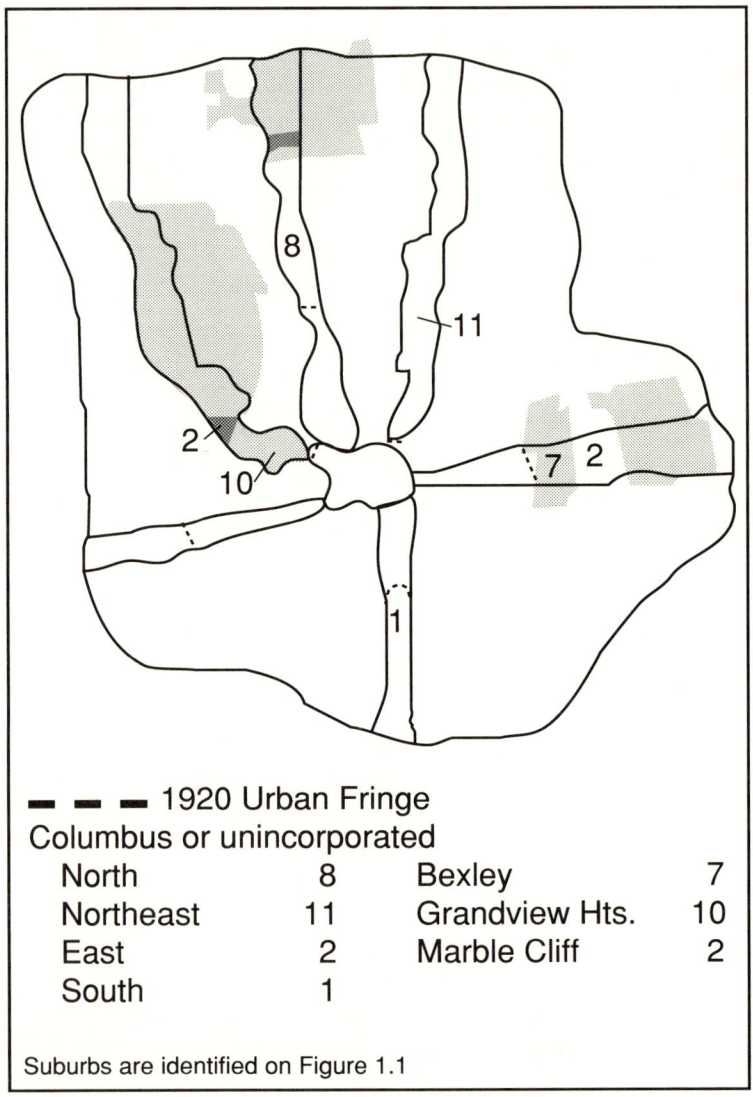

Figure 2.1 Number and location of subdivisions platted, 1885–1899

for 17.9 percent, and five lots per acre for 12.8 percent. The rest held between four lots per acre and two acres per lot.

Developers in Columbus, like those elsewhere, were beginning to realize the potential of restrictive covenants. Deeds for eight subdivisions placed a minimum value on the buildings to be constructed, and deeds or the plat for four established a building setback line. More important than the number applying restrictions were their location and the nature of the restrictions themselves, for their use helped establish the character of various communities. One Linden area subdivision on the northeast side set a ten-foot building line, while one Grandview Heights subdivision set a fifteen-foot line and a second Grandview development had a forty-five-foot line. A Bexley developer mandated a fifty-foot setback. Four subdivisions (two in Linden, one each in Marble Cliff and Grandview) set building cost minimums of $501–1,000. Two Bexley subdivisions and one in Grandview set minimums of $1,501–2,000, while another Grandview subdivision set $2,500–3,000 as the minimum construction cost, clearly limiting occupancy to middle and upper income persons. One Linden subdivision and two in Grandview had both setback and price restrictions. There were no racial or size limitations on any lots, nor did developers find it necessary to limit construction to housing, for such outlying developments as these were understood to be residential.

Thus, by 1900 developers had laid the foundation for the suburbanizing city. They began a trend of restricting land use by cost and location on the lot (with Linden the least select) which they increased during the next two decades.

The First Suburbs: 1900–1920

During the first two decades of the twentieth century, while residential development beyond the urban fringe increased, practices that shaped the city's form emerged. As happened in other parts of the country, residents of several areas voted to incorporate as separate municipalities.[26] Developers, meanwhile, expanded their use of restrictions and raised the standard of real estate development. They also began to limit occupancy on the basis of race. However, restricted subdivisions were not uniformly distributed. Although fewer than half the subdivisions platted in this era were in suburban municipalities, half the subdivisions bearing construction cost minimums were suburban, as were more than half the subdivisions with setback lines or use restrictions. As before, developers gave relatively little attention to the south or west sides of the city (Figure 2.2). Table 2.1 allows a comparison of subdivision development by municipality and section of the city through 1945.

As developers continued their activities, residents on the northwest, east, and northeast sides incorporated their communities. The Village of Marble Cliff, on a bluff above the Scioto River almost four miles northwest of downtown Columbus, was the first to incorporate in 1901. Two years later the village reduced its size by two-thirds, recording a detachment of territory with county officials. From that time on, its borders remained virtually unchanged. Almost half the land detached from Marble Cliff formed the nucleus of the Village of Grandview Heights in 1906.[27] Four small annexations during the next eleven years added to Grandview's size; then in 1921 the village more than doubled itself by annexing several subdivisions platted in preceding years by developers King and Ben Thompson.[28]

The pace of incorporation picked up in 1908, when residents formed the Village of Bexley, just east of Alum Creek three miles from downtown. Like Marble Cliff, Bexley also lost territory when two parcels totaling eighty-four acres were detached and then annexed to Columbus in 1910. It gained, however, when a 1917 annexation roughly doubled the size of the village and set its present boundaries. A second 1908 incorporation created the Village of Linden Heights, comprised of two pre-1900 subdivisions four and one-half miles northeast of downtown along the street railway line. Eleven years later the village annexed an area almost as large as itself. Then, in 1921, the entire Village of Linden Heights ceased to exist as a separate municipality, for it was annexed into Columbus.[29]

Upper Arlington was the final suburb to incorporate between 1900 and 1920. Located directly north of Marble Cliff and Grandview, on land between the Scioto and Olentangy rivers, Upper Arlington was a wholly planned community developed by King Thompson. Its four hundred residents petitioned for incorporation in 1918. In the 1920s the village almost doubled its size through five annexations—all of land developed by Thompson. Suburban incorporations and annexations meant that 45.4 percent of the subdivisions platted between 1900 and 1920 on unincorporated land would end up in the suburbs.

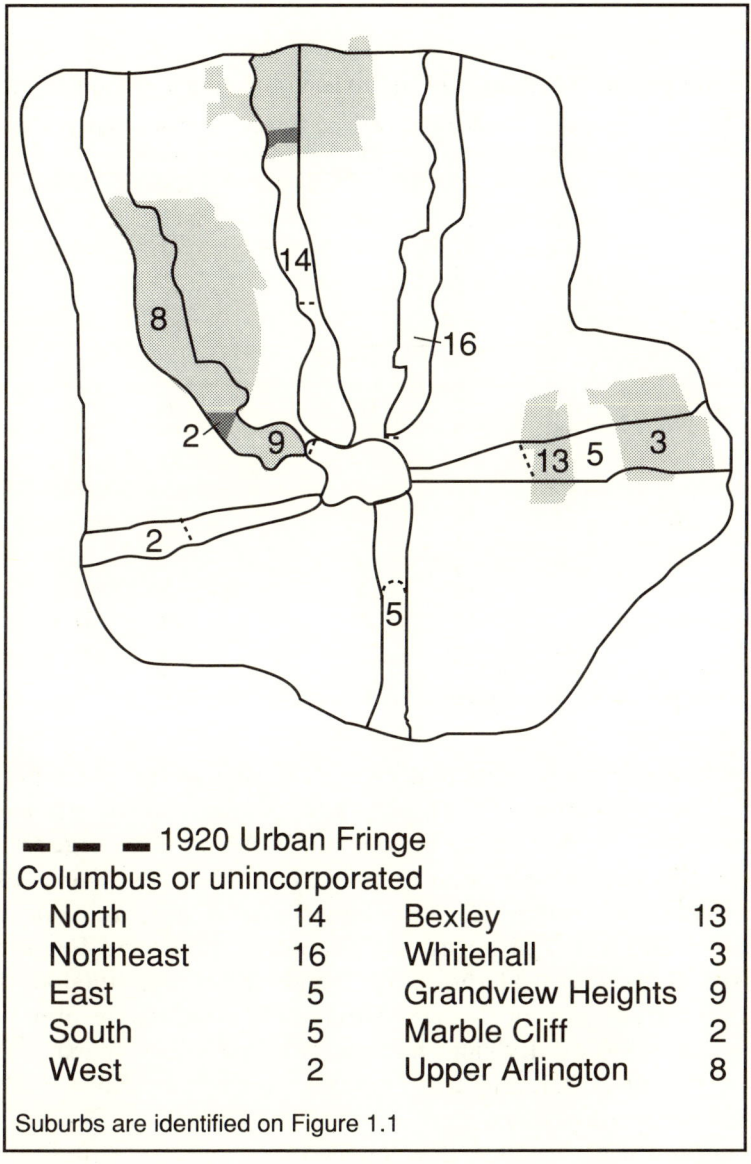

Figure 2.2 Number and location of subdivisions platted, 1900–1920

Table 2.1
Percentage and distribution of subdivisions by area and municipality

Corridor	1885–99	1900–20	1921–29	1930–45	1946–60	1961–70	1885–1970
North	20	18	20	32	13	15	18
Northeast	27	21	29	5	13	17.5	20
East	22	27	24	9	25	22.5	24
South	2	6	6		4		4
West		3	6		1		2
Northwest	29	25	14	55	43	45	31
Municipality							
Unincorporated		5	10		8	5	6
Columbus	54	49	61	5	17	25	39
Worthington			1	32	13	15	7
Riverlea			1				0.3
Bexley	17	17	6	5	1		8
Whitehall		4	6	5	23	12.5	9
Marble Cliff	5	3	1			2.5	2
Grandview Heights	24	12	5	5	8	2.5	9
Upper Arlington		10	8	50	29	37.5	19
(N) =	(41)	(77)	(79)	(22)	(75)	(40)	(334)

Note: Percentages may not total 100 due to rounding.

Although developments platted during this twenty-year period had a greater range of both size and density than their predecessors, they tended to be larger subdivisions with bigger lots. Where two-thirds had been smaller than 25 acres before 1900, fewer than half were that small in the next era, and one was between 200 and 225 acres while another was over 400 acres. Density figures reveal the same trend: fewer subdivisions had eight or ten lots per acre and the range of lot size was greater, with three post-1900 subdivisions having average lot sizes in excess of 2 acres. (Figures 2.3 and 2.4 compare subdivision size and lot density through 1945.)

Whereas prior to 1900 developers made only minimal use of restrictions, after 1900 they both used them more often and set higher standards. More than two-thirds of the subdivisions contained a building setback line, with twenty feet being most commonly specified. One subdivision required that all buildings be one hundred feet from the street. Price minimums were even more frequently imposed, with 77.9 percent containing such limita-

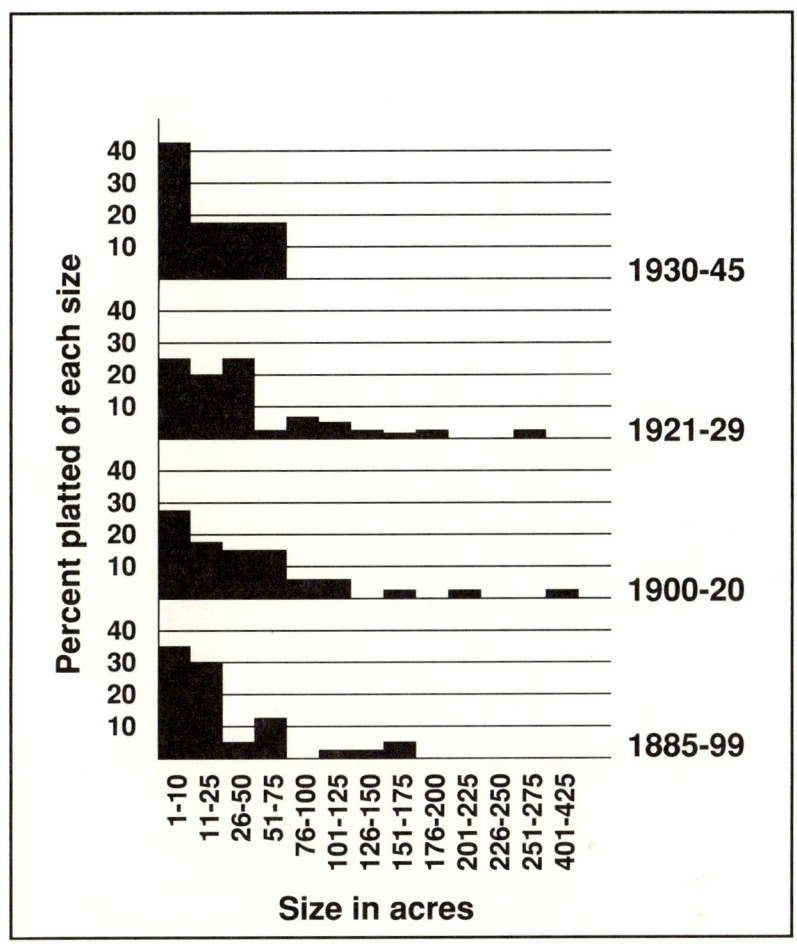

Figure 2.3 Comparison of subdivision size, 1885–1945

tions. Minimums ranged from $500–1,000 in two subdivisions to $7,001–8,000 in three. Almost half (44.2 percent) were between $1,501 and $4,000. Thirty-four subdivisions (44.2 percent) also limited construction to residential buildings. Twenty of these were in suburbs and permitted only one single-family dwelling per lot, while four other suburban developments permitted units housing up to four families.

Two other types of restriction made their appearance between 1900 and 1920—building size and race. One northeast subdivision required 501–750 square feet of floor area for a building, another

42 • Shaping the City

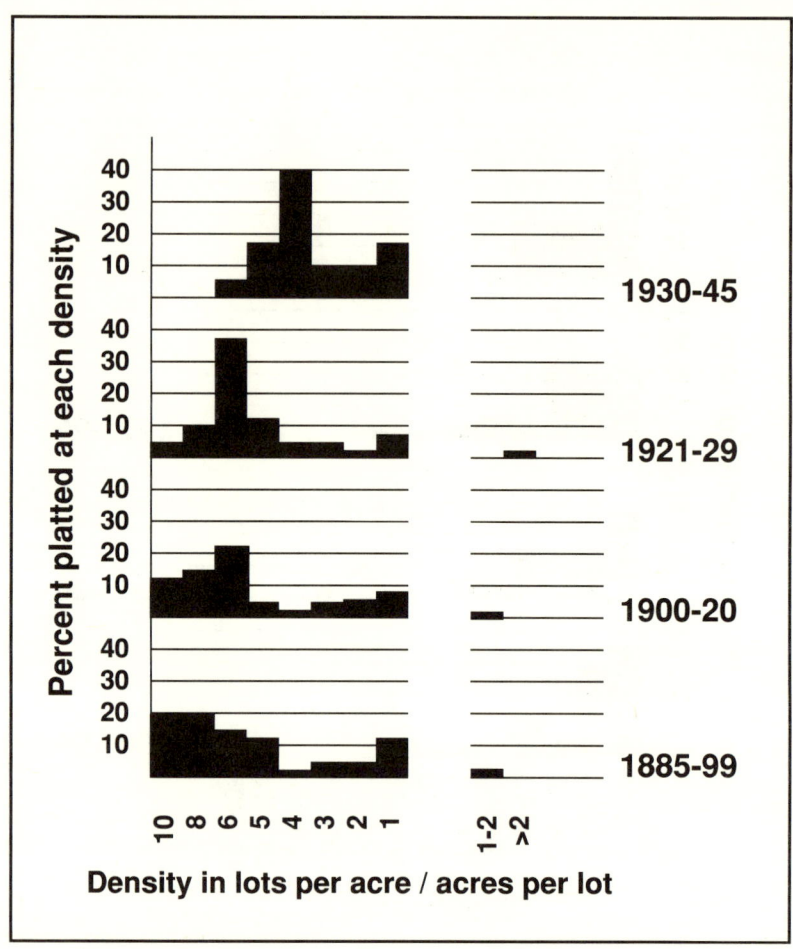

Figure 2.4 Comparison of subdivision density, 1885–1945

required 750–1,000 square feet, and three others had size minimums that varied with the lot. Race restrictions were more common, with one-quarter having such provisions. Nineteen subdivisions either limited occupancy to Caucasians (thus excluding blacks, Jews, and Asians) or prohibited it to blacks, and one (in Grandview Heights) prohibited persons of Italian descent. Ten of the subdivisions with a race restriction (eight in Upper Arlington and two in the northeast) did not apply it in the first deeds executed but added it to all deeds recorded in the 1920s.

The first two decades of the century were thus a time of increased activity and experimentation by developers. They expanded the scale of their operations and applied new forms of development controls. The larger lots and tighter controls appeared only slightly more often in the suburbs than in city subdivisions, although slightly fewer suburban subdivisions were platted. The groundwork had been laid for the development process to become standardized during the real estate boom of the 1920s.

The 1920s Boom

During the 1920s Columbus and its suburbs, like much of the rest of the country, experienced a boom in real estate development.[30] Real estate developers platted more subdivisions in nine years (seventy-nine) than in the preceding twenty-one years (seventy-seven). Although the south and west sides saw some land development activity, developers were not nearly as active there as in other parts of town, thus continuing the earlier trend (Table 2.1). And though the suburbs farthest from the city center continued to grow, much more activity occurred in the city proper or on land that never became part of any municipality (29.1 percent suburban versus 70.9 percent nonsuburban subdivisions). Also the more remote subdivisions would not join their suburbs until the 1950s. The city itself grew physically as well, even though it failed to acquire Bexley, Marble Cliff, Grandview Heights, and Upper Arlington. During the 1920s Columbus annexed 7,221.18 acres on the north, northeast, and east sides and another 427.52 on the west, thus growing out to or beyond some of the suburbs. Also during the 1920s developers standardized the process of bringing residential land to market, and this standardization occurred regardless of the location of development (Figure 2.5).

Although the range of subdivision sizes was almost as great as in the preceding era, developers clearly favored the larger sizes (Figure 2.3). Only 48.0 percent were smaller than twenty-five acres instead of 59.3 percent; and half again as many as before ranged between seventy-six and two hundred acres. The density range was also as large as previously, but this time developers platted only 3.8 percent of their lots at ten per acre and applied a six per acre size to 39.7 percent. They platted an additional 30.8

44 • Shaping the City

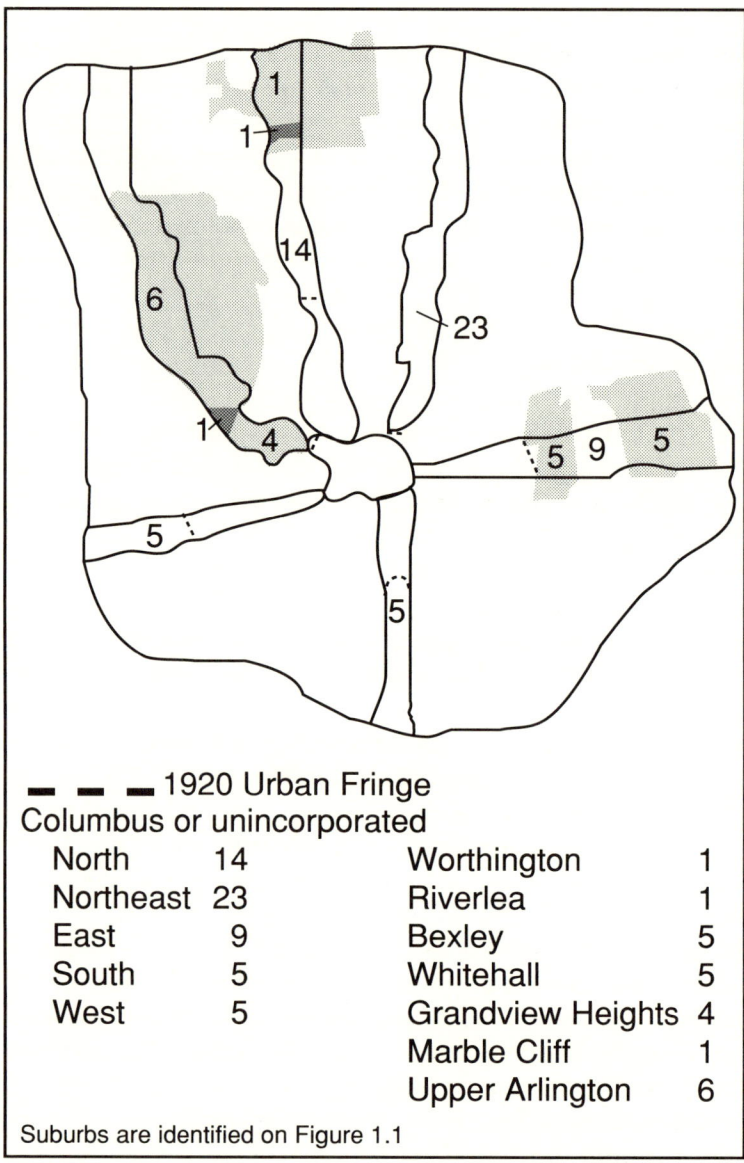

Figure 2.5 Number and location of subdivisions platted, 1921–1929

percent at three, four, or five lots per acre, but only one subdivision required two or more acres per lot. Thus they tended toward the manageable, marketable middle sizes (Figure 2.4).

The use of restrictions also became common. In the 1920s, only 7.6 percent of the subdivisions lacked a building setback line. As with size and density, the setbacks specified varied almost as much as previously, but middle values predominated. Forty-one subdivisions (51.9 percent) required buildings to be twenty, twenty-five, or thirty feet from the street. The use of size restrictions more than doubled (from 6.5 to 13.9 percent) but was still not common.

Specifying a building type, its value, and its occupancy was almost the norm. Thus real estate developers determined what kind of people would live where in the growing city. (Tables 2.2–2.6 show the number of subdivisions restricting setbacks, use, building price, building size, or occupants' race, respectively, in each suburb or section of the city and allow comparisons through 1945.) Altogether 70.9 percent of the subdivisions specified a minimum construction cost for buildings. These ranged from a low of $501–1,000 for one subdivision to a high of $15,001–25,000 for two. The most commonly specified value was $4,001–5,000, which appeared in deeds of 13.9 percent of the subdivisions; $6,001–7,000 appeared in 11.4 percent. The brackets of $5,001–6,000 and $7,001–8,000 were somewhat less common at 8.9 and 7.6 percent, respectively. Consequently, developers of 41.8 percent of the subdivisions were aiming at the middle or upper middle income market, and a few were going for exclusivity.

Reflecting racial concerns, 67.5 percent of the platted subdivisions had some sort of race restriction on ownership, occupancy, or both. Most common was the prohibition of blacks (41.8 percent), whom deeds referred to as "Negroes," "mulattoes," or "persons wholly or partly of African blood." Developers of an additional 15.6 percent broadened the exclusion to include Asians and Jews as well as blacks by limiting ownership or occupancy to Caucasians. Nor did all others have equal access. Deeds also singled out "Undesirables," "foreigners," and "foreigners of the Dago class" for exclusion (along with non-Caucasians), particularly on the northeast side of town.[31]

Developers also determined the use of much of the land they subdivided. Deeds for 74.7 percent of the subdivisions permitted

Table 2.2
Subdivisions platted with setback restrictions, 1900–1945

	1900–20	1921–29	1930–45
Columbus or County			
North	8	12	
Northeast	9	21	1
East	3	8	
South	3	5	
West	1	5	
Northwest			
Worthington		1	6
Riverlea		1	
Bexley	11	5	
Whitehall	3	4	1
Marble Cliff	1	1	
Grandview Heights	9	2	1
Upper Arlington	8	6	11
Total restricted	56	71	20
Total platted	77	79	22

Table 2.3
Subdivisions platted with use restrictions, 1900–1945

	1900–20	1921–29	1930–45
Columbus or County			
North	6	8	
Northeast	2	8	
East	2	8	
South		2	
West		5	
Northwest			
Worthington		1	4
Riverlea		1	
Bexley	10	4	
Whitehall		4	1
Marble Cliff	1	1	
Grandview Heights	5	2	1
Upper Arlington	8	6	11
Total restricted	34	50	17
Total platted	77	79	22

Table 2.4
Subdivisions platted with price restrictions, 1900–1945

	1900–20	1921–29	1930–45
Columbus or County			
North	9	8	
Northeast	9	13	
East	4	7	
South	3	3	
West	1	4	
Northwest			
Worthington			5
Riverlea		1	
Bexley	12	4	
Whitehall	3	4	1
Marble Cliff	1	1	
Grandview Heights	9	2	1
Upper Arlington	8	6	11
Total restricted	59	53	18
Total platted	77	79	22

Table 2.5
Subdivisions platted with size restrictions, 1900–1945

	1900–20	1921–29	1930–45
Columbus or County			
North			
Northeast	5	7	
East			
South		1	
West		1	
Northwest			
Worthington			
Riverlea			
Bexley			
Whitehall		1	
Marble Cliff			
Grandview Heights			1
Upper Arlington			
Total restricted	5	10	1
Total platted	77	79	22

Table 2.6
Subdivisions platted with race restrictions, 1900–1945

	1900–20	1921–29	1930–45
Columbus or County			
North	5	6	
Northeast	3	20	
East		6	
South		2	
West		2	
Northwest			
Worthington		1	3
Riverlea		1	
Bexley	3	3	
Whitehall		4	1
Marble Cliff		1	
Grandview Heights	1		1
Upper Arlington	8	5	11
Total restricted	20	51	16
Total platted	77	79	22

only single-family or residential (one-to-four family) structures on most or all of their lots. Developers realized the commercial potential of land bordering major streets or streetcar lines, however, and sometimes permitted commercial or apartment buildings on the major streets while reserving the interior lots for single-family homes. They did not require commercial or multifamily uses, though, and thus let individual lot purchasers decide what to build along the city's arterials.

For the most part, the smaller subdivisions platted in the 1920s were also those with few or no restrictions. Although professional developers sometimes assisted them, these plats' subdividers were not people who earned their livelihood at real estate development. More often these subdividers were small property holders who had inherited some portion of the family farm and saw in the rapid growth of the 1920s an opportunity to turn their land into cash. The medium-size and large subdivisions, with their quarter- to sixth-acre lots and white, middle income, residential use restrictions, on the other hand, were the creations of commercial land developers. These developers would either purchase a tract of land just outside the city limits (or act as trustee for someone who owned such a tract), plat the subdivision, then petition for annexation to the city in order to acquire municipal services. Annexation was most easily accomplished before the sale of lots to would-be home builders or contractors when one individual or corporation still held title to the entire subdivision. Had large numbers of lot sales preceded annexation, owners of one or more lots could have refused to join the annexation petition and created little "islands" of unincorporated territory within the city proper, making the city reluctant to extend services. Developers also found it easier to market lots that were served by water and sewer lines.

It was the professional real estate developers, who supported themselves by platting and selling residential lots and some of whom operated on a fairly large scale, who standardized the process of land development in city and suburban restricted residential subdivisions during the 1920s boom. Their activities during the depression and war years also left their mark on the city.

The Suburbs Grow: 1930–1945

Although the stock market crash of October 1929 was not mirrored by a similar crash in the real estate market, the depression did take its toll.[32] The number of subdivision plats recorded and building permits issued in Franklin County both dropped considerably. Then during the first half of the 1940s the nation directed its energies toward the Second World War.[33] Consequently, for fifteen years real estate developers reduced the scope and scale of their operations. However, they continued to serve a particular market — that of the upper middle income white suburbanite.

Only twenty-two subdivisions were recorded between 1930 and 1945 (10 percent of those discussed in this chapter). Just one was in the city of Columbus; all the others were suburban (Figure 2.6). Most development was in the north or northwest parts of the metropolitan area. On the east side, Bexley had all but filled its borders in the 1920s. Still farther east, Whitehall had begun to develop in the 1910s and 1920s, but its pace was very slow and residents of the area felt no need to incorporate into a municipality until 1947. Consequently there was little activity on the east side. Grandview and Upper Arlington thrived, however; indeed, half the subdivisions platted during the depression and war were in Upper

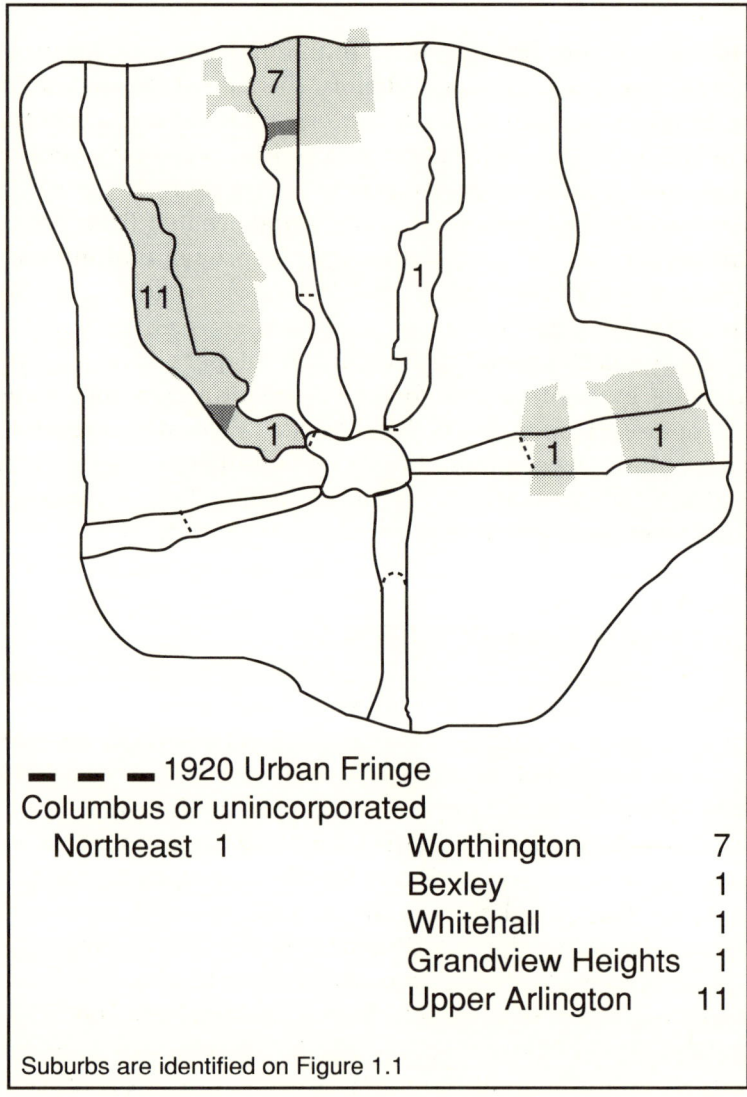

Figure 2.6 Number and location of subdivisions platted, 1930–1945

Arlington. The remaining activity took place in Worthington, ten miles north of Columbus.

The village of Worthington had been founded in 1803, before Columbus was established as Ohio's capital. Settled by people from Connecticut, it had been laid out like a New England village and changed very little over the next one hundred years. But it grew slightly in the early twentieth century, and by the 1930s a Columbus businessman with a real estate sideline realized residential development was approaching Worthington. The subdivisions Frank Medick platted in the 1930s and 1940s helped establish Worthington as a middle income community and paved the way for the town's large-scale suburbanization in the 1950s and 1960s.

Although it was not platted during the depression or war years, one final subdivision deserves attention here—the Village of Riverlea. In 1924 a commercial real estate company, Van de Boe-Hager, had platted a subdivision called Riverlea eight and one-half miles north of downtown Columbus and south of colonial Worthington, between High Street and the Olentangy River. Only a few lots had sold by 1932, however, when the rest of the subdivision was sold to the Riverlea Company for development. Van de Boe-Hager and the Riverlea Company placed identical restrictions in deeds for all the lots they sold, making the subdivision an upper middle income, white, residential area. Deeds stated that the restrictive covenants would remain in effect until January 1, 1940, or until the subdivision was covered by a municipal zoning ordinance.[34] But by 1938 neither Columbus nor Worthington had expanded its borders far enough to be contiguous to Riverlea, so it could not be annexed to either city or covered by either's zoning code. During the fall of 1938 and spring of 1939 residents of the subdivision of Riverlea simultaneously incorporated as a village and prepared a zoning ordinance, whose provisions were almost identical to the deed restrictions. Only the racial covenant in the deeds was not carried over to the zoning code. The residents thus made certain that controls would remain in effect even when the deed restrictions expired.

As the number of subdivisions platted during the depression and war was smaller, so too were their sizes. All the subdivisions platted then covered fewer than seventy-five acres, and 42.9 percent were smaller than ten (Figure 2.3). But having learned the preferences of the middle class during the 1920s, developers did not crowd the lots (Figure 2.4); almost 60 percent were platted at four or five lots per acre. A forty-foot building setback applied to lots in 40.9 percent of the subdivisions, while others ranged from twenty to fifty feet. Only three subdivisions (13.6 percent) had no setback line.

Seventeen of the twenty-two limited construction to residential or single-family use only, and three others were covered by a zoning code that permitted only residential use where they were located. Developers still preferred to use building cost rather than size minimums to reach middle and upper middle income buyers. Only one subdivision, in Grandview Heights, had a size limitation, but eighteen contained construction cost minimums. Half of those—most in Upper Arlington—required that dwellings cost between $5,001 and $6,000. Three more Upper Arlington subdivisions had minimums of $7,001–8,000, and two in Worthington specified $9,001–10,000 and $15,000–20,000. Only middle and upper middle income whites were likely to buy and build in the suburbs then. Should a black have possessed the financial resources to build in a new subdivision, his opportunities would have been quite limited, for seventeen subdivisions (77.3 percent) either explicitly prohibited blacks or permitted only Caucasians (thus excluding Jews and Asians as well as blacks).

Although the amount of real estate development was greatly reduced between 1930 and 1945, particularly compared to the 1920s, the nature and location of that development had lasting effects on the form of the city. Platting racially restricted, middle and upper middle income residential subdivisions in suburban locations, developers confirmed or established the character of those suburbs. Had they chosen to concentrate their efforts in other parts of town, those other parts would have become the desirable places to live.

The Developer-Salesman and the Community Builder

Two Columbus area developers had an especially notable impact on the city's structure between 1900 and 1945. They were partners in some ventures, but both operated independently on a very large scale. Both also used restrictive covenants very effectively. They developed so many restricted subdivisions that between them they were largely responsible for how and where Columbus grew.

In 1928, when the author of an extensive study on the use of deed restrictions was writing, she assumed that the land subdivider or real estate developer who applied them was not interested in selling lots so much as in establishing or laying the foundation for an entire community.[35] Certainly restrictive covenants served that purpose, but they were also effective marketing devices, as the career of Charles Johnson makes clear.

Charles F. Johnson was a large-scale developer and real estate salesman actively platting subdivisions and marketing lots through the first four decades of the twentieth century. He platted both land he owned and that for which he was a trustee. His activities were so dispersed throughout the metropolitan area, however, that it is difficult to characterize them as "laying the foundation for a community"—an exclusive neighborhood might better describe one of Johnson's subdivisions. His work is important because it occurred in the northwest suburbs, the north end, and the east side when these were the most actively growing sections of Columbus. Johnson either led growth to those areas or was in the midst of it.

Johnson began his real estate career in 1905, three years after he was admitted to the Ohio Bar. Between 1907 and 1923 he organized or had an active role in twenty-six separate land development or real estate companies, most of which he combined into Charles F. Johnson, Inc., in 1923. Johnson belonged to local, state, and national real estate organizations as well as many civic groups. During his most active years, his various corporations brought fifty-nine subdivisions to market.[36] He also assisted others in their land development projects and his name appears as a witness or notary on plats other individuals filed.

In platting his subdivisions Johnson effectively used restrictive covenants to set neighborhood character and market lots. In 1909 Johnson and his partners King and Ben Thompson platted two subdivisions on farmland on the east bank of the Olentangy River beyond the northern boundary of the city. The plat map filed for Kenworth Place showed lots fifty-feet wide with no building line setback. Deeds for the development, however, required that all structures be farther from the street than the setback—the distance of which was not stated. Except along High Street, where commercial structures were permitted, building was limited to residential construction. Their Webster Park was a bit more carefully developed. Its sixty-foot-wide lots were subject to a thirty-five-foot setback. Owners could build only single-family homes whose construction cost was between $2,000 and $3,500.

A year later Johnson platted three subdivisions on the east bank of the Scioto River, well northwest of downtown. All lots in Eastcleft-on-the-Scioto and Windermere-on-the-Scioto had forty-foot setbacks and permitted only single-family residential structures. The cost minimums of $1,200 to $2,500 were still middle income in effect though lower than Webster Park's—perhaps to compensate for the higher cost of somewhat larger lots. Adjacent to Windermere were the Windermere "parcels," twenty-four five-acre plots carrying the same restrictions. The size of the parcels was unusual for the time and it is not possible to determine Johnson's intent. He may have been trying to develop lots that would seem "manorial" to middle income purchasers but be too small to attract a farmer. Restrictions for all three subdivisions were to be a part of all future conveyances.

In 1911 Johnson platted Ardmore and Ardmore No. 2 just beyond Bexley's eastern edge. The Ardmore lots were narrower than those in his riverside developments, but they were no less select. All had a forty-foot setback except those on Broad Street, where, in keeping with the Bexley subdivisions they would soon join, the setback was seventy feet. Johnson restricted use to single-family homes with a minimum construction cost of $3,500, again except on Broad Street, where the minimum was $5,000.

These early subdivisions of Johnson's were essentially rectangular, with a rough gridiron street plan. Lots were thus also rectangular, and deeper than they were wide.[37] Johnson's riverside lots, with sixty-foot frontages, were unusually wide for that time. Even the narrower fifty-foot Ardmore lots were quite spacious, for most were three times as deep as they were wide and some were even deeper, making them, too, large for their era.

Johnson returned to the north end along the Olentangy River to plat irregular lots on curving streets around parkland that straddled a ravine in Beechwold. Here setbacks varied from twenty feet, where irregular lot shape or a sharp curve made a larger setback impractical, to fifty feet on the gentle curves or straight stretches of road. Lot owners could build only $5,000 single-family homes. Here, too, Johnson added a new limitation: no one of African descent could own, lease, or occupy the property.

Not all of Johnson's real estate endeavors were suburban. In 1924 with farmer George Wolfe he platted a small subdivision south of Kenworth Place, by then well within the city. This was essentially an "infill" development, as land surrounding it had since been developed. The only restriction Johnson imposed there was a building setback line, for the subdivision was subject to the city zoning code, which permitted only single-family homes or duplexes in that area. He was still interested in up-scale development, however, and that same year he platted Eastmoor two blocks east of Bexley, in which he included a fifteen-acre polo field. Johnson retained title to the polo field and platted lots on it, too, within two years. Like the nearby Ardmore subdivisions, Eastmoor had a grid plan and specified a much deeper setback on Broad Street than on interior lots. Its lots could contain only one single-family home and could not be purchased, leased, or occupied by non-Caucasians.

In 1926 Johnson concluded his land development activity in the areas of this study. As one of the trustees, he platted the Davis Estate Subdivision in the far north end between High Street and the Olentangy River. Restrictions there were less strict than usual for Johnson and the lots a bit smaller (though the streets gently curved). Moreover, the area was too far north to be seriously considered suburban to Columbus at that time. Consequently, lots were slow to sell and the neighborhood did not really develop until after World War II. However, Johnson's other 1926 subdivision stands as the epitome of his efforts. On an irregular tract of about three hundred acres bordering Big Walnut Creek and the Columbus Country Club on the far east side, Johnson and the club platted the Fairway and the Fairway No. 2. He set aside more than sixty acres as an undevelopable reserve and platted only 131 lots on winding roads on the rest. He instituted the usual single-family and race restrictions and set building lines that varied from fifty to seventy-five feet, depending on nearness to the club or creek. The construction cost minimum was the highest for any development in central Ohio of this period, ranging to a high of $25,000 for some lots. Johnson's own home was on a three-acre lot in the Fairway.

Johnson was not so much a community builder as a large-scale developer and salesman. He tailored restrictive covenants and physical layout to meet what he viewed as specific market demands. He platted wide lots on curving streets near the rivers and narrower lots on grid streets near Bexley, where the original plan was a large grid. Restrictive covenants allowed him to market residential exclusiveness along with a choice location. His impact on the growing city was considerable, for the subdivisions described here are only 22 percent of those he was involved with but they contained 2,775 platted lots and account for one-fifth the total subdivisions platted in their sections of the city through 1926.

If Johnson was a superb developer-salesman, his contemporary and sometime partner King Thompson was a true community builder, and equally influential. King Thompson and his brother Ben became aware of the real estate opportunities available near the university when both attended Ohio State. Having formed a partnership in 1907,[38] they then joined Johnson in the Columbus Lands Company and the Thompson-Johnson-and-Thompson Realty Company. They soon decided to concentrate their efforts, though, rather than disperse them as Johnson did his.

In the mid-1910s the Thompson brothers turned their attention to Grandview Heights, which was then ripe for extensive development as the Columbus area and its northwest side expanded. Their Northwest Boulevard Company platted 1,335 residential lots in five subdivisions between 1916 and 1922. When annexed to Grandview in 1921, these subdivisions comprised almost 40 percent of the little city's residential area. As Grandview was becoming a middle income rather than an exclusive suburb, the Thompsons scaled their efforts appropriately. The streets were curving but the lots modest in size and with a thirty-foot setback. Like Johnson, they made restrictive covenants a part of the property so the covenants would apply to all future conveyances. Though limited to residential use, buildings could house from one to four families. Still those families would be no less than middle income, for construction cost minimums specified $3,000 for single-family homes and $2,000 per unit for multiples. In the mid-1920s, the Thompsons raised these minimums to $4,000 and $3,000, respectively.

King Thompson had grander ideas than Grandview, however. While brother Ben generally handled the business details of their ventures, King provided the vision and the driving force behind their activities.[39] Through his professional real estate activities Thompson had come to know Kansas City's Jesse Clyde Nichols.

Much impressed with Nichols's Country Club District, he hoped to establish a similar development in Columbus.[40] When an 880-acre farm between the rivers north of Marble Cliff and Grandview became available for development, Thompson used it as the nucleus of his own "planned" community. Nichols's influence was evident in both the design and location of Thompson's development. Like the Kansas City community, King Thompson's residential suburb adjoined a country club and contained a "mall" or shopping arcade at its center. Thompson acknowledged his debt to Nichols by titling the prospectus for his community "The Country Club District." In 1918 the community incorporated as the Village of Upper Arlington.

Thompson platted the first lots in 1914 as trustee for farm owner James Miller. When Miller died, Thompson was one of his estate's executors. During the next thirty-six years, Thompson platted almost 4,100 lots on curving streets through several different real estate corporations. He would mark off lots in a group of blocks, file the plat, then annex the land to the city of Upper Arlington. He postponed platting a few strategically located blocks for many years so as to best be able to capitalize on the changing real estate market in the growing community. As an individual or through one of his corporations, King Thompson was responsible for platting almost every lot within the corporate limits of Upper Arlington from its inception through 1950.

Most lots were generous and Thompson used deed restrictions to set and maintain the character of the community. All lots except those across the street from the country club specified a forty-foot setback line. (The setback opposite the club was one hundred feet.) A race restriction, which Thompson had not used in Grandview, appeared in Upper Arlington deeds in the 1920s. After 1948, when such restrictions were no longer legally enforceable, Thompson accomplished the same purpose by mandating membership in a community or civic association as a condition of purchase.[41] Prospective members (i.e., potential lot purchasers) had to gain approval of those already in the association and the association retained first right of purchase on all lots offered for sale. Thus Thompson ensured that only the "right" people would buy into the area.

With two small exceptions the entire community was limited by deed to single-family residential construction. One exception was the area allotted to the shopping arcade (which Thompson buffered from the single-family homes by a few doubles and row houses). The other was a small group of blocks Thompson held off the market until 1949. On those lots deeds permitted apartments but only with the approval of the community association. The minimum construction cost in Upper Arlington was raised over the decades from $5,000 or $6,000 in the 1920s, to $8,000 or $10,000 on lots near the country club in the 1930s, to $15,000 for lots platted in the 1940s.

Like Charles Johnson, Thompson developed thousands of lots, and he applied restrictive covenants to property deeds to appeal to middle and upper income white suburbanites. Given the extraordinary scale of their operations, Johnson and Thompson between them played a large part in determining the form of the city. By deciding where to develop for the middle and upper classes, they also determined which areas would be left for others.

Thus, between 1900 and 1945, Columbus real estate developers, particularly professional developers, determined the spatial and social structure of the city. They experimented with different development densities, increasing lot size until they settled on the one-sixth- to one-quarter-acre size as the most marketable for middle and upper income neighborhoods. Then, pairing the appropriate lot size with use, price, and occupancy restrictions, they in effect decided who would live where in the growing metropolis.[42]

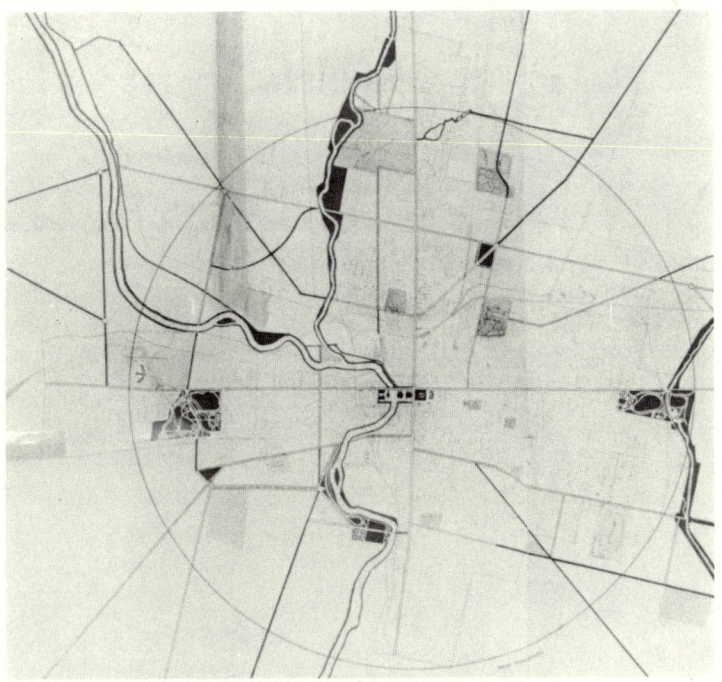

The 1908 *Plan of the City of Columbus* showed the Olentangy and Scioto Rivers joining and illustrated that little development extended much beyond three miles from the city center. (The circle on the map marks the three-mile radius.) Reprinted from *The Plan of the City of Columbus* (1908).

Columbus's Union Depot, with its colonnaded arcade of shops, was at the northern edge of downtown. Demolished in the 1970s, the rail depot had been designed by noted Chicago architect Daniel Hudson Burnham. Reprinted from *Architecture Columbus* with permission from the Columbus Architecture Foundation-AIA Columbus.

The 1908 *Plan* indicated that the rivers' confluence would be a good location for a playground. Reprinted from *The Plan of the City of Columbus* (1908).

The only explicit mention of housing in the 1908 *Plan* was to note that some would be removed. In the *Plan*, the caption for the above picture reads: "The proposed mall will wipe out this squalid neighborhood and in its place provide a park and some of the best building sites in the city." The caption for the picture below: "Present character of the neighborhood through which a wide approach to the capitol should be built." Reprinted from *The Plan of the City of Columbus* (1908).

The proposed civic center, with the state capitol at its center, stretched east from the Scioto River. Reprinted from *The Plan of the City of Columbus* (1908).

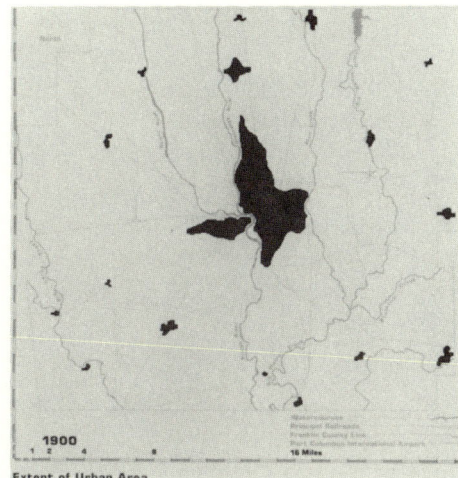

A.

A. through E. (Here and on the next page.) Although the developed area of Columbus gradually increased, there was consistently less development on the south and west sides. Reprinted from *Architecture Columbus* with permission from the Columbus Architecture Foundation-AIA Columbus.

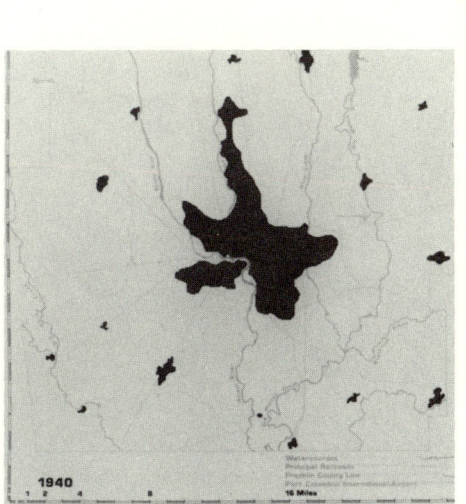

B.

C.

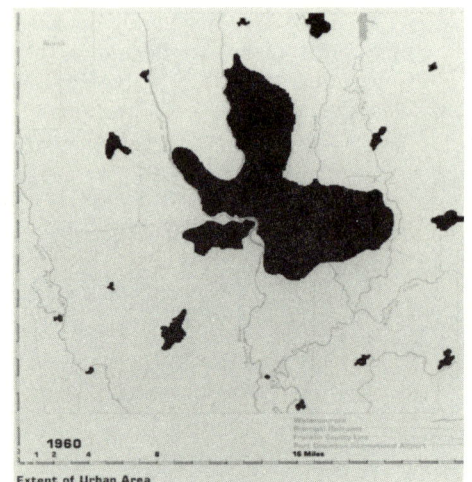

D.

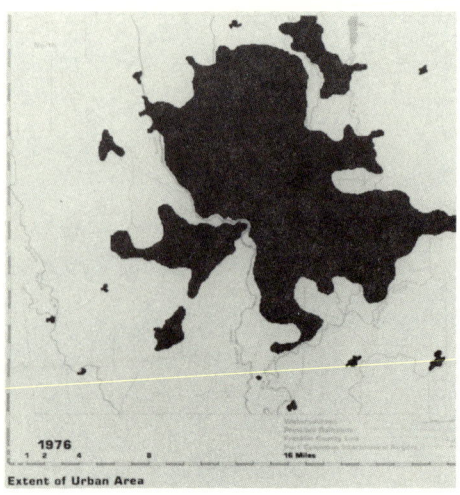

E.

The Ohio Asylum for the Education of Idiotic and Imbecile Youth on the west side's "Hilltop" was one reason that developers of upper income suburbs chose sites elsewhere. Reprinted from *Architecture Columbus* with permission from the Columbus Architecture Foundation-AIA Columbus.

The East Broad Street location preferred for their homes by such Columbus notables as the Firestones (above), Kelleys (top right), and Schumachers (bottom right) in the late nineteenth century fell into disfavor as the suburbs developed in the twentieth. These drawings were done by Columbus artist Bill Arter for a column titled "Columbus Vignettes" that appeared for several years in the local newspaper's *Sunday Magazine.* They are reprinted with permission from the Columbus (Ohio) *Dispatch.*

Other wealthy Columbusites preferred the near north side. Peter Sells, the circus impresario, chose that location for his home (below). Drawings by Bill Arter; reprinted with permission from the Columbus (Ohio) *Dispatch*.

Nineteenth-century German immigrants built homes just south of downtown (above and below). By the 1950s the area had deteriorated badly, lowering property values. In the 1960s the combination of good solid housing stock, relatively low price, and proximity to downtown made the area attractive to renovators. Drawings by Bill Arter; reprinted with permission from the Columbus (Ohio) *Dispatch*.

Columbus entrepreneurs and financiers Beaton (above), Huntington (below), and Jeffrey (top right) built expansive homes in Bexley. Reprinted from *Architecture Columbus* with permission from the Columbus Architecture Foundation-AIA Columbus.

Developer King Thompson built a spacious home in Upper Arlington, the suburb he planned. Drawing by Bill Arter; reprinted with permission from the Columbus (Ohio) *Dispatch*.

The cover (above) and plat plan (top right) of the prospectus for King Thompson's Country Club District (Upper Arlington) indicate his intention to target upper-middle and upper income purchasers. Reprinted from "The Country Club District," Special Collections, Ohio State University Engineering Library.

When a developer proposed building a luxury high-rise in Grandview Heights, the city's residents protested loudly, commenting particularly on the "transiency" of apartment dwellers. Despite residents' objections, however, the Summit Chase apartment tower was built in the 1960s. Reprinted from *Architecture Columbus* with permission from the Columbus Architecture Foundation-AIA Columbus.

Studies in the 1950s (above and right) showed considerable discrepancy between the amount of land zoned for multiple dwellings, commercial, and industrial uses and the amount actually used for those purposes. Reprinted from *A Report Upon Economic Base, Population, and General Land Uses* (1954), Harland Bartholomew and Associates.

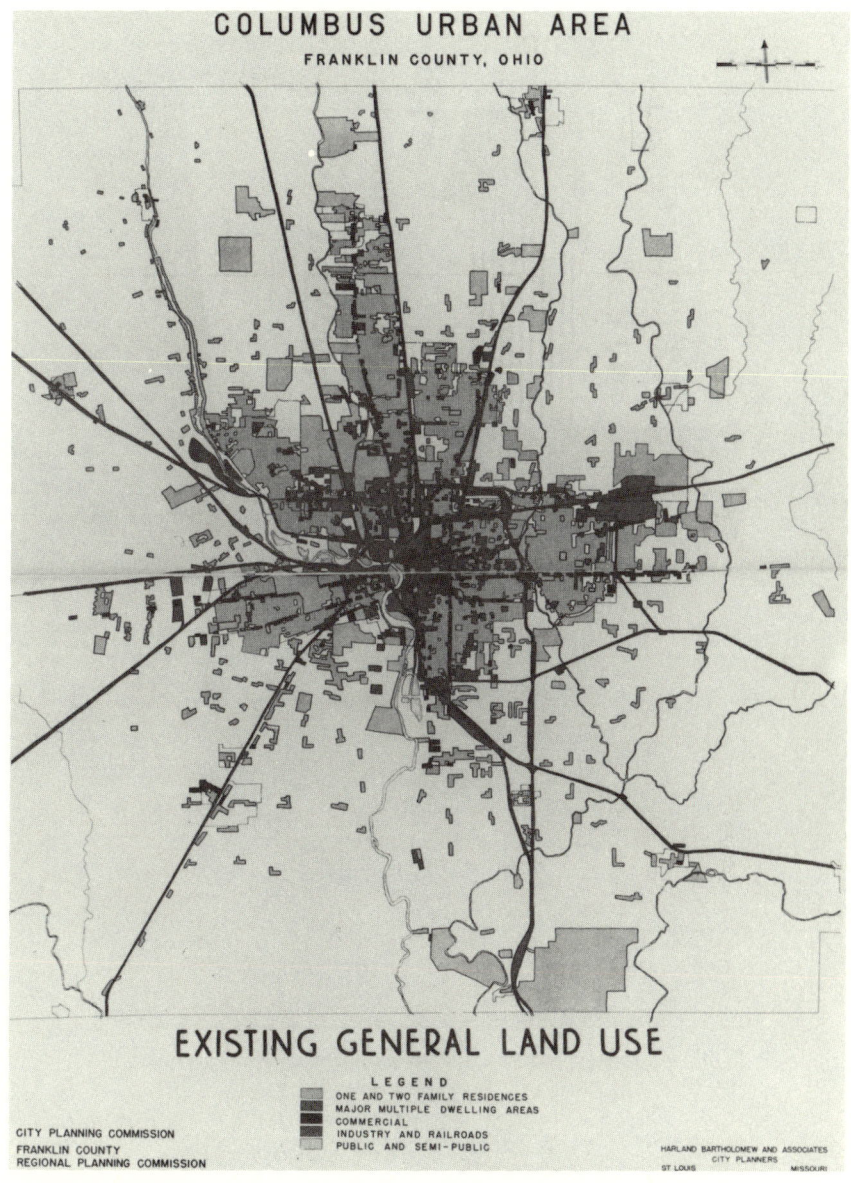

Reprinted from *A Summary Report: The Master Plan: Columbus Urban Area* (1957), Harland Bartholomew and Associates.

THREE

Planning and Zoning: In Theory and in Columbus

The incremental impact of private developers' and landowners' actions regarding land use was precisely what had concerned zoning advocates. By the twentieth century's second decade reformist city planners and lawyers were actively campaigning for municipal land use controls. They hailed New York's comprehensive zoning ordinance in 1916 and the 1926 Supreme Court decision in the *Euclid* case, and developed the concept of comprehensive planning as zoning's theoretical basis. Real estate and other property interests, whose support the reformers needed to advance the spread of zoning, accepted public controls on their land when they realized that protecting property also protected its value. This ambiguity of zoning's purpose—for reform and planning or for property value protection—was reflected in the application of zoning during its first thirty years in Columbus, Ohio, where property interests triumphed over planning. Such a result was apparently common, for during these same thirty years planners continually reiterated the theoretical planning-zoning connection and bewailed its absence in practice.

American City Planning Arrives at Zoning

American city planning had not yet formalized as a profession when New York City passed the nation's first comprehensive zoning code. Nevertheless, it existed in practice. Over a period of perhaps thirty years people concerned about overcrowded and deteriorated cities had been trying to improve them. They engaged in social, political, and economic reform activities, attempted to redesign the urban environment, and proposed idealistic alternative conceptions of the city itself. As the twentieth century's first decade ended, individuals from several disciplines and professions began to meet regularly to share ideas on and experiences with urban problems and planning. They learned of German land reform and saw in elements of it the potential to improve American cities. By the early 1910s they identified themselves as city planners and began to actively support the adoption of public land use controls. Finally, they organized the American City Planning Institute in 1917, one year after New York City adopted comprehensive zoning, an event they viewed with much promise.

Conditions in U.S. cities deteriorated in the latter nineteenth century due to increasing industrialization and immigration. Factories large and small belched smoke and poured sometimes hazardous effluent into rivers and lakes. Immigrants from rural areas and overseas met the factories' growing labor force needs. They also crowded the cities. Neither the housing supply nor public services could expand quickly enough to serve the burgeoning urban population. High rates of disease, death, and crime abounded in slum and tenement districts and competed with visual ugliness as a source of concern.[1] Such conditions gave rise to early efforts at city planning.

The modern planning profession emerged from the twin roots of reform and design in the late nineteenth century.[2] Reform efforts addressed various elements of the problems in overcrowded residential areas. Some focused on sanitary conditions (or their lack) and sought improved and expanded water and sewerage systems. Others focused on housing. Decrying tenements with windowless sleeping rooms and no indoor plumbing, they supported laws to regulate tenement construction. Still others focused on the social environment and educational opportunities for both children and adults. They worked in settlement houses and fought for provision of parks and playgrounds.[3] Living conditions grew worse when cheap industrial workers' housing sprang up around the factories, or factories and warehouses invaded areas of homes and apartments; and nothing prevented either occurrence.[4] Reformers sought to change that.

The sheer ugliness of late nineteenth-century cities prompted a parallel set of design efforts. Landscape designers like Frederick Law Olmsted believed large naturalistic landscaped parks—or better still, park systems—could provide both physical and visual breathing space. Members of municipal improvement societies and outdoor art organizations encouraged the beautification and adornment of public buildings and spaces. Architects, many of whom were trained in the Beaux Arts tradition, looked to London, Paris, and Vienna for inspiration when designing buildings in American cities. Art, architecture, and landscape design came together in the 1893 World's Columbian Exposition in Chicago. Built under the direction of Chicago architect Daniel Hudson Burnham, with a site plan and landscape design by Olmsted and buildings by the nation's foremost architects, the shimmering "White City" on the shore of Lake Michigan contrasted sharply with the dirty industrial city outside its gates and showed visitors what a city *could* look like. [5] Nor were the reform and aesthetic efforts unconnected. In both his writings and his designs, Olmsted developed the idea of the landscape artist as moral reformer.[6]

Burnham's work on the White City is credited with transforming him from an architect into a city planner.[7] And though the exposition may not have been the progenitor of contemporary planning's first real movement, it certainly shared characteristics with it.[8] The City Beautiful movement, of which Burnham was a foremost practitioner, emphasized landscape and building design on an often monumental scale as it sought to beautify American cities.[9]

While reformers and designers pushed for change in the urban United States, there was a current forming in England that would also affect American city planning. A minor British civil servant who had spent several years in the United States and was distressed by conditions in crowded industrial cities both here and in England conceived of an alternative urban form. Ebenezer Howard's Garden City concept proposed that self-sufficient cities, with a specified cap on population and surrounded by an undevelopable agricultural greenbelt to prevent excessive growth or sprawl, be built outside the industrial cities.[10] Drawing their residents from those cities, the garden cities would provide both housing and employment opportunities and a better quality of life for their own citizens and for those who remained in the now less crowded industrial cities. Howard first published his ideas in an 1898 book that was reissued four years later. Both the book and the two experimental garden cities built in England attracted a great deal of attention on both sides of the Atlantic.[11]

Implicit in the concerns and efforts of the reformers, the designers, and the garden city proponents were certain beliefs that would shape city planning theory and practice in decades to come. First, cities were too densely built. They needed more open space—preferably green—and for residential areas to be less crowded. Second, the mixing of industrial, commercial, and residential uses of land worked to the disadvantage of all three, aggravating the problems of congestion and deterioration. Hence, some separation of land uses would be desirable.

In 1909 a group of urban reformers, municipal officials, architects and landscape architects, and engineers met in Washington, D.C., at the first National Conference on City Planning (NCCP). Benjamin Marsh, executive secretary of New York's Committee on the Congestion of the Population, was instrumental in promoting this first meeting, and several days later he addressed the U.S. Senate Committee on the District of Columbia on housing conditions and planning in Washington. Congestion and deteriorated living conditions—and what might be done about them—were major topics at the first planning conference and at several that followed.[12]

Thereafter the group met annually, sharing ideas, experiences, and observations on planning both in the United States and in Europe. The reports of each meeting were published as a *Proceedings*. In 1917, after meeting in Kansas City, the group formalized its organization as the American City Planning Institute. Those present at that year's conference became members, and the group established criteria to determine who might join the organization in the future. Membership required a degree in a design or engineering field and two years' city planning experience. A separate membership category was reserved for lawyers.[13]

The planners also began publishing a journal to supplement their conference proceedings. Their first effort, *The City Plan*, began in 1915 and was short-lived. But in 1925 the American City Planning Institute began *City Planning* as its official publication.[14]

With means of regular communication in the conference and journal, the planning profession could grow and develop.

As early as the first conference city planners learned of zoning and its potential. The early planners believed zoning would provide orderly growth to existing cities. It would lessen land speculation and relieve population congestion by limiting density. Though business leaders would promote zoning because it benefited their financial interests, the "reformers viewed it in the broader perspective of the general social welfare; zoning would improve urban housing and living conditions by controlling population distribution."[15] Members of New York's Charity Organization Society and Committee on the Congestion of the Population, who led New York's fight for comprehensive zoning, spread reformers' views at the 1909 National Conference on City Planning. The reformist planners saw the speculative land developer as the creator of slums,[16] and believed that regulation would remove speculative pressure on land. No more would the speculator be able to strangle the development of the city, holding large parcels of land off the market to create scarcity and drive up prices. Such increases in land rents caused private dwellings to give way "to apartment houses, and homes to slums."[17] Although passage of the first comprehensive zoning ordinance required business support, the impetus for that ordinance came from the social reformist planners concerned with the housing conditions of the poor.[18]

A reformist approach to public land use controls had also been the basis of zoning in Germany, the country of its origin. Germany felt the full effect of nineteenth-century industrialization and rapid population growth, particularly in urban centers, and city governments responded to reform ideas concerning workers' living conditions.[19] German housing reformers did not believe that the free market could adequately house the working classes and called for municipally built housing to compete with that of speculative builders. Later, attributing rising land costs to developers' propensity to build at high density, they devised zoning to reduce that density.[20] Excessive population density caused high land prices, which in turn created the housing problems of the working class; zoning could reduce that density and thus break the cycle.

Zoning developed logically from municipal building regulations, which specified building lines, yard dimensions, building height, lot access, availability of light, street surfacing, and location of noxious industries, among other things.[21] In 1891 the Prussian government passed a zoning act. Modeled on legislation drafted by the municipal government in Frankfurt, it allowed local authorities to divide their cities into sections and subsections and control land use within each.[22] In the 1890s, then, several cities substituted regulatory uniformity by district or "zone," which would allow standards appropriate to the particular use of the property, for the existing practice of imposing uniformity for the entire city. Eleven years later the Prussian state government passed another law providing Frankfurt with additional power to control land use. The city was permitted to acquire parcels of privately owned land, then redistribute them for redevelopment in accordance with its plan, retaining up to 40 percent of the land for streets and parks if need be.[23] Coupled with the zoning act, this allowed the city to control the arrangement of residential, commercial, and industrial land uses while encouraging a rational plan for new development.

A further effort to control and direct development was the Increment Tax Act of 1903, also initially passed for Frankfurt. In Germany, as in the United States, rapidly rising land costs in growing urban areas prevented construction of inexpensive housing for industrial workers. To curb land speculation and the attendant price increases, the city was authorized to levy a tax on the gain with every transfer of ownership. So effective was the technique that other German municipalities quickly followed suit.[24]

In his presentation before the Senate Committee on the District of Columbia in 1909, Benjamin Marsh described German land regulations and discussed the potential they might have for those U.S. cities that shared Frankfurt's problems. Marsh's printed statement even included translated portions of the text of the Prussian acts. Frederick Law Olmsted Jr. had told those at the NCCP meeting much the same. Although some among both groups—senators and planning conference attendees—expressed reservations about the broad scope of the German laws and questioned the constitutionality of similar legislation for U.S. cities, others were favorably impressed. Here was a way to deal with deteriorated and overcrowded living conditions.[25]

The concept of restricting land use was not without precedent in the United States. Colonial Williamsburg specified the height of houses on the main street and how far back from the roadway they had to be.[26] California cities in the 1880s limited the location of commercial laundries, citing health and safety concerns, though San Francisco's ordinance indicated the real reason was to exclude the Chinese from residential areas. Boston led American cities in restricting building height in 1898 and 1904.[27] By the 1920s land developers and realtors continued to restrict land use through deed covenants in newly developed residential subdivisions as they had for several years, but they believed that citywide zoning would provide greater uniformity than individual deed restrictions.[28] These events determined how zoning developed in the United States.

The legal profession was well represented in early planning and zoning activities, and the efforts of attorneys Edward Bassett and Alfred Bettman were largely responsible for American zoning law. A member of the American City Planning Institute, Bassett had served on New York's Public Service Commission and he chaired the New York City Commission on Building Districts and Restrictions (formed in 1913) that prepared that first comprehensive zoning ordinance.[29] Later Bassett spread the idea of zoning by speaking to chambers of commerce and other civic groups throughout the United States, serving as legal counsel for the drafting of zoning ordinances in many towns and arguing test cases on the constitutionality of zoning.[30]

Bassett's efforts were complemented by those of Cincinnati lawyer Alfred Bettman. Though his early practice was largely in criminal law, Bettman is better known to planners for the amicus curiae brief he prepared in support of zoning when the U.S. Supreme Court heard *Village of Euclid* v. *Ambler Realty Co.*, the case that legitimated land use control by comprehensive zoning.

Although state courts had examined zoning, *Euclid* provided the first opportunity for the United States Supreme Court to decide on its legitimacy. The small city of Euclid, near Cleveland, Ohio, had in 1922 adopted a zoning ordinance dividing all land in the city into six use districts, three height districts, and four area districts. The first use classification, U-1, permitted only single-family homes. With each successive classification, U-2–U-6, additional uses were permitted from duplexes to apartments, then on to commercial and industrial activities. The city's building inspector was to enforce the ordinance under rules established by the Board of Appeals. Ambler Realty, which owned an undeveloped parcel in Euclid whose development the ordinance limited, challenged the zoning ordinance in its entirety under both the equal protection and due process clauses of the Fourteenth Amendment.

Writing for the majority in 1926, Justice Sutherland noted that building regulations that would once have been unreasonable or oppressive were now viewed as acceptable since they promised to relieve some of the problems caused by urban development and population growth. Moreover, courts had upheld legislation limiting the location of industries for reasons of public health and safety. Adding that the question at issue in *Euclid* v. *Ambler* involved setting aside some land in the city solely for residential uses, Sutherland referred to many reports that indicated the public benefits of separating industrial, commercial, and residential uses. Allowing apartments and other large buildings to overshadow homes would limit access to light and air, "depriving children of the privilege of quiet and open spaces for play." Although he noted that specific provisions of this or other similar ordinances might unfairly impose on a landowner, at issue here was the ordinance as a whole, and the Court believed it to be reasonable and a valid exercise of the police power to protect the public health, safety, morals, and welfare.[31] Bettman's brief in *Euclid* is credited with swaying the Court to support zoning.[32]

Active in the NCCP and other planning organizations, Bettman viewed land use zoning as the most direct means to guide private development and fulfill the objectives of comprehensive planning. He was insistent on the integration of zoning and comprehensive planning. In 1924 Bettman was appointed to Secretary of Commerce Herbert Hoover's Advisory Committee on Zoning. As a member of that committee, Bettman was largely responsible for drafting both the Standard Zoning Enabling Act and the Standard City Planning Enabling Act, which were then published by the U.S. Department of Commerce.[33]

Both acts were designed as model legislation for states to adopt that would provide their municipalities with the power to plan their development and to control land use through zoning. The Standard Zoning Enabling Act, which gave promoting the health, safety, and general welfare of the public as its purpose, called for a city's legislature to appoint a zoning commission. The zoning commission would study the city, hold public hearings, and prepare a report indicating the boundaries of districts for the various classes of land use, building height, and lot area and coverage. The model legislation also called for provision of a board of adjustment or appeals to allow exceptions to the adopted ordinance where needed to prevent hardship. Adding that a city plan commission, where such existed, could serve as the zoning commission, the act stated that the zoning regulations should be "in accordance with a comprehensive plan." The Standard City Planning Enabling Act called for cities to establish planning commissions of appointed citizens and public officials to "make and adopt a master plan for the physical development" of the city to guide and coordinate its growth and development. A zoning plan was to be one element of the master plan.[34]

The Department of Commerce's publication of these two model acts greatly encouraged the spread of zoning as many states passed legislation mirroring the model acts and their cities followed by adopting zoning ordinances. Planners and reformist lawyers were not alone in supporting zoning. Serving with them on Hoover's committee were also members of the real estate and land development professions, some of whom recognized benefits to their interests in planning and zoning and encouraged support for local public land use controls at annual meetings of the National Association of Real Estate Boards (NAREB).[35] The real estate interests' support of planning and zoning no doubt facilitated many states' passage of legislation based on the model acts, although their goals were very different from those of the reformist planners and lawyers.[36]

Bassett's seminal work, *Zoning*, gives one primary reason for the push for zoning in New York—to prevent overbuilding and congestion in certain parts of the city. Zoning was also to provide for adequate light and air and give no builder advantage over another.[37] A second purpose was to prevent the invasion of incompatible uses, which were thought to encourage blight and deterioration. Existing nonconforming uses might remain, but if destroyed or abandoned should not be resumed. Thus, initially zoning sought "to safeguard the future, in the expectation that time will take care of the mistakes of the past."[38]

American reformers, being concerned for the general social welfare, sought zoning to control population distribution and thereby improve housing and living conditions, but they also saw zoning as a means to provide for orderly growth in existing cities. Zoning would limit the fluctuation of property values and lessen land speculation. Reformers believed slum tenements existed because speculative builders built as densely and for as many people as possible. The resultant overcrowding created many urban ills. The land speculator worsened the situation as he "throttled and strangled the development of the city. He withdrew a large percentage of every city's total land area from circulation to create scarcity, and thus appreciate values. As rents increased on remaining improved land, private dwellings gave way to apartment houses, and homes to slums."[39] Since the municipal housing construction, land acquisition, and land transfer tax changes that German reformers suggested or their governments adopted were not politically acceptable in the United States, American reformers turned to land regulation by zoning to remove speculative pressure.[40] Early zoning proponents were essentially social reformers concerned about urban deterioration and overcrowding. They sought to improve housing conditions and saw in zoning a tool for reform since it would limit the size, type, and number of structures in an area and thus lessen population density. This in turn would lessen pressure on existing housing.[41]

Planners had even greater hopes for zoning in less developed areas. If smaller communities adopted zoning and regulated the development of land, they might prevent congestion from ever occurring. This would eliminate the need for the remedial measures necessary in the built-up, overcrowded urban areas that had first spurred the push for comprehensive zoning.[42]

From the first National Conference on City Planning in 1909 through the 1920s, planners and other reformers reiterated their concerns and looked to planning and zoning to improve things. At the 1909 NCCP John Nolen and Daniel Burnham, both better known as physical planners than social reformers, confirmed the reform goals of zoning and explicitly recognized the zoning/planning connection. Financier Henry Morganthau, who saw zoning as a constructive element of planning to combat the evils of overcrowding, echoed their comments. Charles Merriam illustrated the importance of separating uses, noting that conversion of structures to multi-family occupancy followed the arrival of a factory into a residential area to make the dwellings profitable when their value as single residences had diminished because of the nearby factory. The lowered rents encouraged landlords to try to house even more occupants and discouraged maintenance and repair, leading to further deterioration and producing a blighted neighborhood.[43] NCCP participants in 1921 reinforced the need for use separation. Industry was to be kept from residential areas and residences were not to be permitted in industrial areas, since any houses erected in such areas were "predestined to become slums," as industrial areas would lack the services and amenities appropriate for residential neighborhoods.[44]

Some planners recognized the less benign purposes zoning might be called upon to serve. At that same conference, Robert Whitten noted that zoning had been criticized as being antisocial because it could be used to maintain the exclusiveness of upper income neighborhoods while relegating working class housing to undesirable areas. He called that an important criticism, if true, for that was not zoning's intended purpose.

> The first function of zoning should be to protect those who cannot protect themselves, and the standards applied to the areas to be devoted to industrial housing should be the highest that it is practical to make without injury to the very class of people that we are attempting to serve. Industrial housing areas should be carefully protected against invasion by trade and industry; the provisions for side, rear and front yards should be liberal; and there should be a definite limitation on the number of families that may be housed on a given area of land.[45]

He added that one of the problems planning and zoning faced was how to have large numbers of people together in a city "without creating inefficiency and waste on the economic side or disease and degeneracy on the human side," how to have concentration without congestion. Although planning and zoning should deal with the physical structure of the city, the ultimate concern was the citizens and how to provide for them a better environment.[46]

Whitten came under fire a year later for his role in the design of Atlanta's zoning plan, which provided for designation of residential areas by race. He responded to his critics that racial segregation, like some socioeconomic segregation, tended to occur naturally in cities as people sought areas inhabited by others like themselves. Racial tensions and violence occurred as areas changed. Removing ambiguity by making black and white zones explicit was intended to relieve racial pressure, not encourage racial prejudice. Whitten believed that zoning could mitigate the worst results of people attempting to cluster by race and class in a time of rapid urban growth. Writing in *Survey*, he repeated the substance of his remarks from the 1921 NCCP meeting.[47] To a post-civil rights movement generation his comments seem specious, but in the context of 1920s racial attitudes and violence they might have been only naive.[48]

Three years later Alfred Bettman commented that unregulated development had led to blight, prompting the initial calls for controls and justifying zoning to promote the public health and welfare. Others felt restrictions would lessen speculative pressure on land value and prevent homes from becoming overcrowded tenements.

> If there are no private restrictions or zoning regulations to prevent the coming of the more intensive housing types, land values will mount with the growth of the city, being predicated on the estimated net returns from the housing of two, four, eight, or sixteen families on a lot originally intended for a single family dwelling. With the mounting taxes resulting from these increased land values it is easy to see that a man of moderate means will have difficulty in maintaining a private home. This increase in land value is largely speculative.[49]

Planners thus asked zoning to serve several different ends, but all their purposes were essentially reformist. And some recognized possible inconsistencies among their various goals. Limiting the number of families per acre or setting a minimum number of square feet per family was the easiest way to control for population density. But this type of restriction generally applied to single-family districts and neglected congestion in the least restricted zones (where many cities imposed no density controls), thus providing no solution to the overcrowding that initially spurred the push for zoning.[50] Moreover, while lessening population density and reducing speculative pressure, zoning also stabilized land value and essentially protected private property in the guise of regulating it. New York's pioneering ordinance, which seemed more concerned with preserving existing property values than guiding future growth, made this ambiguity apparent. The framers of New York's ordinance might have stirred more opposition to it and lessened the possibility of passage had they been bolder or more explicitly reformist in their efforts, and they noted that even a poor plan was preferable to none.[51] However, even when planners acknowledged that zoning might preserve property value, they continued to emphasize that convenience and prosperity were secondary results; zoning's primary purpose remained promotion of the community's health, safety, and welfare.[52] Thus, in the planners' view, zoning and planning were to serve the public welfare, improving the quality of urban life by lessening population congestion and its ill effects and preventing its future occurrence. Land use regulations would prevent or "correct the misdeeds of the private market."[53]

Zoning was very much a part of what might be viewed as the contemporary city planning profession's second movement: the City Efficient.[54] Burnham's 1909 *Plan of Chicago* is generally viewed as the epitome of City Beautiful planning,[55] and although City Beautiful-type plans continued to be drafted and implemented into the 1910s, the profession was clearly moving in other directions. As part of their efforts at professionalization, city planners had begun to emphasize the "science," rather than the "art," of city planning.[56] Motivated by many of the same social concerns as previously, they recognized in social science research the foundation for a more scientifically substantiable approach to improving cities. City Beautiful planning had been "comprehensive" in considering the city in its entirety, but only the physical city. City Efficient planning sought to be truly comprehensive by considering a city's social and economic elements as well, and by recognizing the relationship among the social, the economic, and the physical. John Nolen noted as much, and more, in his president's address to the nineteenth National Conference on City Planning in 1927, which like the first one was held in Washington, D.C.

Nolen used the occasion to review the previous two decades' progress on American city planning.[57] After commenting on how much cities had grown, and on the impact of both the skyscraper and the automobile, Nolen observed that earlier approaches to city planning were no longer appropriate. Moreover, planners had changed with the times. He appended his remarks with lists naming the cities that had prepared comprehensive plans (176 in number), adopted zoning ordinances (525), and created official city planning commissions (390). He also named the planned new towns or suburbs that had been built (35) and the colleges offering education in city planning (29). "The record is not spectacular," he concluded, "but . . . it is an honorable record. . . . and the results are creditable to all concerned."[58]

The Planning Theory of Zoning

Planners of the 1920s saw zoning as the greatest advance of city planning. Municipal control over private as well as public land, limiting owners' ability to use their property in ways injurious to others, was necessary to protect the general welfare.[59] Even the planners, however, knew that "zoning unaccompanied by comprehensive planning is at best most inadequate and at worst a positive menace to the future unity of the city."[60] Zoning and planning had to join together to avoid projecting past development errors into a city's future.[61] Planners also sought the extension of zoning and subdivision controls beyond municipal corporate limits to prevent "irreparable" damage should surrounding areas develop prior to annexation.[62]

Zoning and planning were tied together in the Standard Zoning Enabling Act, which required that zoning be "in accordance with a comprehensive plan." The planners and reformers expected a city to adopt a formal plan stating its goals for land use and development, then enact a zoning ordinance to implement that plan. However, in many cases the establishment of a planning commission and adoption of a plan followed zoning rather than preceding it—or never occurred at all. As Nolen noted in 1927, there were one-third more zoning ordinances than planning commissions, and almost three times as many zoning ordinances as comprehensive plans. And courts did not invalidate zoning ordinances solely because there was no comprehensive plan. The zoning of an entire community implied a plan, and since the plan itself had no force of law, its absence was not a hindrance.[63]

However, the planners who were zoning's earliest supporters saw comprehensive planning as the most important goal. Zoning was to be only a tool to direct private development so it would fulfill a larger plan for the community's betterment. Thus had Bettman insisted on connecting zoning and planning in the Standard City Planning Enabling Act.[64] Comprehensive planning would control population density by providing for a variety of housing types and income levels, noted Robert Whitten at the International City and Regional Planning Conference in 1925. A year later he advised an NCCP audience that cities needed to prepare broad general plans for their unbuilt areas, determining the best locations for industrial and commercial activities, the routes of major thoroughfares, and the standards and sites of different types of residential areas so as to foster community growth.[65]

Writing in *City Planning*, Alfred Bettman agreed. Zoning had to be "an organic part of the whole city plan" to be supported as a reasonable and not arbitrary use of power.[66] Zoning could be justified not to protect existing areas but to provide for future growth and development, as the city planned for a balance of uses appropriate to its needs. If the city made street widths and service provisions appropriate to the planned uses, the intrusion of inharmonious uses would not occur since heavy industries would not find desirable sites in residential zones and vice versa.[67]

As part of a comprehensive planning process, zoning would provide the right amount of land in the right places for various uses, and prevent the blight and deterioration resulting from unplanned successive changes of residence to other uses on a one-by-one basis: "Sweat shops and small factories established in abandoned homes prevent in many cases the sound business development which might have followed the residence period. The blighted areas, harboring unsanitary crowded living conditions and all sorts of miscellaneous manufacturing, become forsaken spots."[68] And the planning had to be comprehensive "since if the rights of one individual are to be limited, this limitation must be imposed for the *general* community benefit."[69] At the 1928 NCCP, planner Harland Bartholomew reinforced the connection between zoning and planning, stating that without a plan, zoning could be neither comprehensive nor effective. "If not so undertaken, the zoning ordinance becomes largely an instrument of expediency, subject to constant and often whimsical change."[70]

Though planners and the model enabling legislation joined planning and zoning, almost from the beginning the courts allowed them to separate, or allowed one to substitute for the other.

Some interpreted the "in accordance" provision as meaning only that a zoning ordinance had to be "comprehensive—that is to say, uniform and broad in scope and coverage."[71] Comprehensiveness involved the ordinance's scope as well as the dimensions of space and time (i.e., it took effect for all of the city at the same time). But early court decisions upheld ordinances that covered less than the entire city, although such zoning was not really comprehensive, feeling that it was important for rapidly growing industrial cities to be able to control at least some of their land while they completed the necessary studies to prepare a zoning plan for the entire city. Also, courts reasoned that if cities could interfere with property rights by zoning the entire city, they could certainly interfere to a lesser degree by zoning only part of it. This piecemeal approach to "comprehensive" zoning could produce a patchwork ordinance, lacking unity or internal consistency.[72]

Courts also allowed interim ordinances, quickly passed without an accompanying map and to preserve the status quo, though they, too, were not comprehensive. Early decisions recognized that cities could not create carefully planned, comprehensive zoning regulations overnight; and until such time as a city could complete all the preparations necessary for a fully comprehensive ordinance, it needed to prevent such misuses of land as might occur in the meantime. Courts had to guard against the stopgap interim ordinance, directed at individual uses rather than as a forerunner of a comprehensive code, but lack of comprehensiveness in time did not in itself invalidate the ordinance.[73] Comprehensiveness of scope referred to a zoning ordinance controlling all three factors of land utilization: area, height, and use. However, this aspect of comprehensiveness was rarely litigated.[74]

Spot zoning, where a single parcel was zoned for a different use than the surrounding area, was another matter altogether in the relationship of planning and zoning. Courts upheld such action if they saw it as a planned readjustment to altered circumstances; courts invalidated it as spot zoning if they felt the city had acted unreasonably and arbitrarily. How the court interpreted the action hinged on the action's conformity with some sort of plan, with the court asking if the action "may be defended as logically related to something broader than and beyond itself."[75] But the "plan" could be many different things. Sometimes it was the zoning ordinance itself, if that ordinance was comprehensive in time, area, and scope and internally consistent. Other times it was the community's general "policy" regarding land use and development, even if such a policy had not been stated in advance and in written form. Courts did not require that there be an actual physical document called a "Master Plan" or "Comprehensive Plan," adopted by ordinance, against which zoning actions could be measured. Some interpreted the concept of the plan so loosely as to mean only the general welfare of the community, and upheld zoning actions that benefited the city as a whole rather than an individual or group.[76]

The courts' unclear guidance resulted in part from the model legislation enabling planning and zoning. Though Bettman insisted that zoning be part of the comprehensive planning process, the legislation he drafted permitted a piecemeal adoption of the various plan elements. Consequently, zoning could be adopted as the first part of a comprehensive plan rather than subsequent to it.[77] Thus the "in accordance" provision was framed in such a way that it "allowed courts to assume that the zoning process alone could provide a rational and binding framework for local land use controls. Most courts took a restricted view of the statutory requirement and allowed a comprehensive and rationally developed zoning ordinance to substitute for an independently adopted comprehensive plan."[78]

So zoning and planning were disjoined, and the means became the end. Although city officials and planners continued to insist at their conferences and in their writings that zoning was part of the plan, in application they allowed the two to become separate.[79] Other interests took advantage of the separation.

Zoning and Property Value

Only the planners saw controlling and directing urban growth as zoning's primary use. Others saw in zoning a way to protect property values or prevent unpleasant intrusions into their neighborhoods. The planners' secondary by-product was the primary focus of their allies in the push for zoning's acceptance, as the real estate interests came to realize the negative impacts of congestion and inharmonious land uses on property values that zoning could mitigate.[80]

For the most part, local merchants, real estate boards, and utilities supported zoning efforts, though individuals or small groups—such as billboard interests or apartment builders—opposed specific aspects of zoning codes for their own short-term reasons.[81] Real estate interests discovered that once in place, zoning affected property values positively, stabilizing them or sometimes increasing them. This gained financial institutions' support for zoning, as stability and maintenance of property values made land attractive for investment and not just for speculation.[82]

As the business community had "discovered that indiscriminate land use affected their pocketbooks," real estate and financial interests were involved in zoning from its earliest days in the United States.[83] New York's Fifth Avenue merchants, seeing their exclusive area threatened by expansion of the garment district, allied with the reformers to encourage the passage of the zoning ordinance. Zoning was much more attractive than the reformers' other ideas, for it could increase the profitability of land.[84] New York's zoning ordinance consequently had only two general use restrictions. It prohibited business or industry in residential districts, and manufacturing, public stables, or garages in business districts.[85]

New York's experience was atypical, however. More interested in zoning than downtown business concerns were the real estate interests, who saw zoning's potential to control residential expansion on the urban fringe. Economic growth in the 1920s spurred a housing boom and a parallel interest in planning and zoning. Real estate interests realized zoning could control the ruinous competition of speculation. Regulations could guarantee their investment.[86] The realtors and land developers initially sought zoning to protect property values in upper income areas while limiting controls elsewhere so land speculation in those areas could continue.[87] Realtors who at one time opposed zoning soon saw it as the "ultimate promotional device, a form of government-subsidized free advertising." Property value hinged on zoning classification.[88]

Zoning served the realtors' and land developers' purposes the way deed restrictions did, by helping determine an area's character. Thus in Berkeley, San Francisco, and elsewhere, developers of new areas were among zoning's strongest supporters.[89] At the 1915

NCCP one realtor had challenged the planners to convince the real estate industry that planning made sense, that it would save money or make an investment more sound. The planners met the challenge. A year later Kansas City land developer Jesse Clyde Nichols called for zoning to prevent haphazard land development. Noting that "the value of the residence property that is offered in every city, is dependent upon what is across the street or in the next block," Nichols stated that the private developer needed the assistance of municipal controls.[90] The Arkansas Association of Real Estate Boards concluded, "If no higher motive existed, men in the business of real estate are the only group whose purely selfish interests demand the study of city planning and land planning. Realtors' experience has convinced them that sound planning is good business and that poor types of subdivision result in social and economic losses."[91] Hence realtors were instrumental in the passage of many cities' zoning ordinances.[92]

The spread of zoning was also related to increased suburbanization. Small cities and suburbs recognized zoning's exclusionary potential, though they framed its adoption in terms of promoting the general welfare.[93] Residents' property value interests were as strong as realtors' and land developers'. Expecting to recoup their expenses and make a profit when they sold their homes, residents reacted strongly to any zoning action that might lower their property values. A consumer of housing, the homeowner was also a producer in the "used" housing market, seeking stability and price appreciation for his neighborhood so he could move up to a more exclusive area with each change of residence.[94]

However, economic interests vied with the social concerns of suburban residents.[95] Zoning not only created a hierarchy of less-to-more valued land uses; it also created a hierarchy of land users and stated implicitly that categories of people should not be mixed because they would not get along.[96] Zoning advocate and lawyer Edward Bassett recognized this potential early and doubted its legitimacy. Observing that upper class suburbs tried to use zoning like restrictive covenants, sometimes even prohibiting schools and churches from the highest residential areas to maintain exclusivity, Bassett questioned that practice as a reasonable use of the police power. If the excluded uses were harmful to health and safety where lots were largest and density lowest, he reasoned they would be even more harmful in areas where they were not prohibited.[97] Bassett's reasoning did not prevail, however.

As zoning spread, the reform and planning motivations decreased in importance. Real estate interests were instrumental in its adoption, which the Standard City Planning Enabling Act and the Standard Zoning Enabling Act facilitated in the 1920s. Although reformist zoning lawyer Alfred Bettman partially drafted both acts, business-oriented individuals in the U.S. Department of Commerce promulgated them.[98]

Both planner-reformers and real estate interests recognized the apparent dichotomy of their purposes.[99] In 1927 the ten-year-old American City Planning Institute and the National Association of Real Estate Boards issued a joint statement that formed the basis of the Department of Commerce's Standard City Planning Enabling Act. Discussions producing that statement reflected the inherent disagreement between the two groups. Realtors were concerned that planning not be so "idealistic" as to "destroy real property value," while planners cared only that it not destroy "*all* real property value" (emphasis added).[100] At the 1927 NCCP planner Thomas Adams commented that the joint statement appeared to say that land should be developed to benefit first property values and then the community. Adams felt that the two should be reversed, as "land values should not be placed in front of the benefit of the community." Others echoed his comments, stating that the interests of home builders were less important than those of home buyers and occupants.[101]

Adams had previously established three main purposes for city planning: to stabilize economic conditions and control land use, to provide appropriate facilities for industrial development, and to assure wholesome housing conditions and promote homeownership. Zoning could be used to attain all three ends, but it was only one element of the comprehensive planning process. However, as business and real estate interests gained ascendancy in the zoning movement, zoning was divorced from comprehensive planning and, in many cases, substituted for it.[102] Clarence Stein, chairman of the American Institute of Architects' Committee on Community Planning, noted that the prevention of blight and of deterioration of housing had been the initial goal of zoning as a means to serve the common welfare. However, "zoning immediately passed beyond the matter of conserving that which would accrue to the advantage of the common welfare and proceeded to utilize the principle and the power to conserve, stabilize and enhance property values. And it is upon the efficacy of zoning as a measure which will stabilize or enhance property values that its popularity has come to hang."[103]

Early zoning ordinances thus seemed as concerned with preventing nuisances and preserving property values as with guiding future growth through zoning. However, had they been bolder, the planners who framed those ordinances might have stirred so much opposition as to prevent their passage.[104] Certainly there was initial opposition from those whose income came from land development. Then the realtors and land developers came to accept land use controls because it was clear that they could profit by stabilized values, and they joined the city planners in urging the adoption of zoning.

The planners' motives remained broader and less profit oriented than the land developers', however. Given the concerns they expressed and their motivations, planners essentially developed four broad goals for zoning. How effectively zoning met those goals would determine its impact on urban social and spatial structure. First, to be a part of the planning process, zoning had to be in accordance with a comprehensive plan—even if that plan were implied rather than explicit. Second, to meet a community's needs zoning had to provide appropriate amounts of industrial and commercial land in appropriate places and housing for all income levels. Third, to preserve residential areas, even for the poor, zoning was to prevent potentially harmful uses from locating near housing. Finally, to address the planners' underlying concerns for social equity, zoning actions were to serve all income groups equally. That meant protecting the neighborhoods of the poor as well as the rich, and perhaps providing for some low or moderate income multifamily housing in less dense outlying areas so that the poor were not confined to overcrowded, deteriorated slum tenements in the city while the rich lived in big new homes in the spacious suburbs.

Zoning in Columbus

The foregoing discussion presented reformist planners, working for a broadly defined public interest, variously allied with or arrayed against realtors and land developers, working for their own interests. The Columbus, Ohio, experience with zoning indicates that the lines were not so neatly drawn or the process so clear. It also reveals the gap between the planning theory and the practice of zoning.

What was the result for the city? Did zoning shape land use? By and large it did not, or did so only indirectly. Zoning protected single-family neighborhoods developed after 1920, but private development restrictions had already determined their character. When and if deed restrictions expired, the zoning code continued to provide protection. At the same time, older residential areas built before the widespread adoption of restrictive covenants had only the zoning code to protect them, and such protection was minimal. Responding to the requests of property owners, council and the zoning board allowed land use in these older areas to become increasingly dense and varied, thus permitting deterioration of residential areas primarily inhabited by renters.[105]

The First Columbus Zoning Code

In 1921 the Columbus City Council, as permitted by the 1914 charter, established a planning commission whose purpose was to make plans and maps for the systematic planning and development of the city. The *Plan* of 1908 had made no such provisions, and the original plan commission, being composed of consultants, ceased to exist once the *Plan* of 1908 was completed. Council also gave the new planning commission permission to frame a zoning ordinance "in the interest of the public health, safety, convenience, comfort, prosperity or general welfare."[106] This was the appropriate procedure under both the model Standard Zoning Enabling Act and the Standard City Planning Enabling Act, which were then in preparation.

As was common at that time, the municipal government structure of Columbus had no planning department or division staffed by city employees. It was generally believed that city planning commissions (and, later, boards of zoning appeals) should be composed of citizens. This would both allow for input or representation of the general public and insulate the planning and zoning processes from potentially corrupt local officials.[107]

The commission consulted with noted city planner and zoning expert Robert Whitten to assist in its task. After two years' work, the planning commission presented a zoning ordinance to City Council, which passed it August 6, 1923, with little public reaction.[108] The ordinance was comprehensive in design and the city did not adopt a master plan before passing it. In this respect the Columbus City Council acted as most of its contemporaries and successors elsewhere did. (In 1927 John Nolen had noted three times as many zoning ordinances as comprehensive plans; by 1941 there were ten times as many zoning ordinances as comprehensive plans for American cities.[109]) The newly adopted Columbus zoning code put all land in the city into one of five use districts. It also divided all land into four height districts and five lot-area districts. Thus for any piece of property, regulations specified the maximum height of all buildings, the lot size or density of development, and the permissible uses.

The code established a hierarchy of five uses. They were dwelling house (one- or two-family residences), apartment house (for three or more families), commercial, first industrial (less objectionable uses), and second industrial (heavy, more unpleasant industries). Some uses—such as petroleum refineries, cement manufacturers, or slaughterhouses—were prohibited altogether, and others (including amusement parks and stone quarries) were allowed only by special permit of the Board of Zoning Adjustment (BZA).

According to accepted planning theory and the concern of zoning proponents for protecting residential areas from harmful intrusions, the single-family home was the highest property use. It was followed in descending order by multifamily housing, commercial, and finally industrial uses. Those who owned and occupied single-family homes shared this perspective. The property owner as investor, however, had a very different perspective. As this individual sought to maximize the amount of income his or her property could generate, the investor's concept of "highest use" was that with the greatest earning potential. Hence single-family homes would be at the bottom of the list, with apartment and then commercial uses above them. Planning theory and real estate practice thus both created hierarchies of land uses but reversed the order of uses on each other's list.[110]

Under the Columbus zoning code, higher uses were permitted in lower use zones; thus single-family homes could be built in apartment house districts and any form of housing could exist in commercial or industrial zones to the limits of the height and area classifications. By codifying a hierarchy of land uses, the ordinance protected residential areas from commercial or industrial intrusions while not imposing on the property rights of those who might wish to build some type of housing (for personal occupancy or rent to others) in commercial or industrial areas.

The code permitted some occupations, such as doctors, dentists, or other "professional persons," in residential areas if carried out within the professional's own home. It also allowed restaurants and newsstands in apartment zones. The code allowed nonconforming uses (i.e., those uses in existence in August 1923 that would not be permitted by code for their location) to continue but not to expand; if discontinued, they could not be resumed.

To provide for adequate light and air, the code established four height districts. Each district specified a maximum height for all structures within its borders. The maximums were (1) 50 feet, (2) 75 feet, (3) 100 feet, and (4) 175 feet, with the lowest being in residential areas and the highest for some industrial and downtown commercial sites. Ornamental parapets and spires exceeding the height limit were permitted in each district, as were buildings higher than the maximum if those buildings were stepped back from the building line. This last provision, common in many cities, produced the tiered wedding cake form of many office buildings built in the 1920s and 1930s. In the 50- and 75-foot districts, the sides of a building had to be set back one foot from the required yard or lot lines for every two feet of additional height. In 100- and 175-foot districts, the set back was one foot for three.

The code established five area districts to control density of construction and to prevent overcrowding. These established minimums of (A) 4,800 square feet of lot per family, (B) 2,400 square feet of lot per family, (C) 1,200 square feet of lot per family, (D) 600 square feet of lot per family, and (E) unrestricted. The unrestricted designation was generally applied to those parts of commercial or industrial districts where residential uses did not exist or were unlikely to be built. Theoretically, however, one could erect an apartment building at much greater density than 600 square feet of lot per family if it was in an unrestricted commercial or industrial zone. Under those circumstances, the only limitation on population density would be the building height for that particular parcel.

The effect of the code was to determine the use, lot size, and building height for every piece of land in the city. Thus, in the A-1 dwelling house districts one could build only single-family homes less than fifty feet tall on 4,800-square-foot lots. In a C-3 apartment zone, one could build a structure one hundred feet tall on any parcel providing at least 1,200 square feet of lot for each apartment unit. The code permitted residential construction on lots smaller than the minimums for their district if the lot had been owned or the plat recorded before council passed the zoning ordinance. The ordinance determined the number of families on a given lot by the number of housekeeping units (defined as rooms with cooking facilities). In dwelling house districts with B area restrictions, one could also construct four-family row houses (four attached dwellings built as a single structure). In addition, the zoning code established building setback lines and side and rear lot lines.

The code contained a measure of flexibility as well. City Council could amend any provision of the ordinance. Under rules established by the Board of Zoning Adjustment, the building inspector was to enforce the code by granting building permits only for those structures that met its use, height, and lot-area specifications. (This was the same procedure outlined in the soon-to-be-legitimated Euclid, Ohio, ordinance.) Besides establishing rules, the five-member BZA could, at the request of a property owner, "vary the application of such provisions [of the ordinance] in harmony with the public interest" in cases of unnecessary hardship. The BZA could also allow certain other specified use exceptions if it determined such exceptions would serve the public interest and not injure neighboring property.

During the next thirty years council amended the ordinance to increase clarity, remove ambiguity, or deal with unforeseen circumstances. Council made the definitions of terms used in the ordinance increasingly explicit and repeatedly expanded the lists of uses permitted in the commercial and industrial categories. For example, it made clear that an establishment that killed and dressed poultry for wholesale was an industrial use while one that killed and dressed poultry for retail was a commercial use. Similarly, a large laundry (employing more than three persons) was an industrial use while a small laundry (with three or fewer employees) was a commercial use.

Amendments also clarified administrative procedures for council and the BZA to follow. Property owners requesting a rezoning (a change in use, height, or area classification affecting their property) first had to submit their request to the city's Planning Commission, which was required to make a recommendation to council for approval or denial. The commission's recommendation was only advisory, however; a simple majority vote of council was sufficient to grant the change regardless of the commission's recommendation.[111] Council had created the Planning Commission to draw up the original zoning plan for the city. The commission's only purpose after adoption was to make advisory recommendations on rezonings. The zoning board (or BZA), on the other hand, was created by the zoning ordinance itself to hear and decide requests for adjustment or variance from code provisions. The ordinance originally specified that a four-to-one vote was required for the zoning board to grant a variance. When it became clear that the board could do nothing if two members were absent, council amended the ordinance to allow granting of a variance by unanimous vote of three BZA members if only three were present.[112]

Although it became increasingly clear and specific, the zoning code's basic structure in terms of use, height, and area classification remained unchanged until 1948, when council divided the single broad commercial class into four distinct categories. The first category, A business uses, included banks, office buildings, and private schools. B business uses were such things as markets, drugstores, and delicatessens. C uses were less pleasant neighborhood commercial uses (e.g., gas stations, ice houses) or those generating congestion (e.g., theaters). D business uses were the most intense or least pleasant and included poultry dressing and sales, nightclubs, poolrooms, car lots, and stables. Like the use categories of the code itself, the business subcategories were hierarchical, with A uses permitted in all business districts and D uses allowed only in D districts. Also, the code still permitted residential and apartment structures in all business districts.[113]

Little more than a year later, council redefined and categorized the residential districts.[114] Three categories replaced the original dwelling house class. A-1-A permitted only single-family residences, with at least 1,500 square feet of floor area, on lots no smaller than 4,800 square feet. In A-1-B districts, where the same floor and lot sizes applied, land could also be used for parks, churches, and truck gardens. The B-1 district permitted several different residential forms, including doubles, duplexes, double-duplexes, and four-family row houses, as long as the site provided 2,400 square feet of lot per family and buildings were no taller than fifty feet. Council made no other substantive changes to the zoning ordinance until the entire code was rewritten in the mid-1950s. This slightly expanded code (outlined in Table 3.1) thus governed zoning activity in Columbus for over thirty years.

Land Use under the Code: Years of Adjustment, 1923–1930

The first years under the zoning ordinance were a time for both property owners and city officials to adjust to public land use controls. When property owners discovered that their lots were too small to construct new buildings or additions within the specified setback or area restrictions, they turned to the BZA for relief. Unwilling to impose undue hardship, the BZA generally granted property owners' variance requests. Meanwhile, use variances or rezonings by City Council allowed property owners to use their land more intensively than otherwise permitted by code, particularly in older parts of the city.

Although the city had not adopted a comprehensive plan prior to its zoning ordinance, the amount and location of land allotted to each use were fairly appropriate.[115] The use categories applied to the city's land in 1923 matched actual land uses to a considerable extent. The downtown core was zoned commercial, as were most major arterials extending out from the central business district. Thus the city determined that when outlying residential areas developed to the point of needing commercial services, those services would occur on the major streets where traffic was already heavier, rather than on interior lots, which would bring heavy commercial traffic into residential areas. The exception to commercial arterials was East Broad Street, whose frontage was zoned residential. Along East Broad some of the city's wealthiest

Table 3.1
Land use classifications of the Columbus zoning code, 1923–1954

1923	1948–49
Dwelling house	A-1-A
	A-1-B
	B-1
Apartment	Apartment
Commercial	A business
	B business
	C business
	D business
First industrial	First industrial
Second industrial	Second industrial

families had once built impressive homes; many still lived there in the early 1920s.

A C-shaped industrial zone of irregular width, broken by the East Broad Street residential strip, almost surrounded the central commercial core. Industrial areas had grown up on either side of the confluence of the Scioto and Olentangy rivers just west of downtown and along the Scioto south of the city center. A third industrial area had developed along the major rail line northeast of downtown. These early industrial areas had gradually expanded and the city's zoning code joined them into a single band, broken only by the commercial frontage of the major streets and, of course, the Broad Street mansions. In addition to existing and permitted industries, the industrial zone contained the state penitentiary and Fort Hayes army base, uses that might have detracted from nearby neighborhoods.

Except for a few isolated commercial or industrial spots, the rest of the city was zoned for some type of housing. Most of the outlying neighborhoods fell into the dwelling house district, with the newer ones in the A area zone, which permitted only single-family homes. Slightly older neighborhoods, somewhat closer to the city center, were B area dwelling house districts which permitted doubles and row houses (if the lots were large enough). The oldest residential areas, near or adjacent to the industrial or commercial districts, were zoned for apartments.

The apartment zone was the only one whose designation did not accurately reflect existing use. In addition to some apartment buildings, single-family homes, duplexes, and row houses covered the apartment districts, along with scattered neighborhood commercial and small-scale industrial uses. Although the apartments were a distinct minority use, they (along with the commercial and industrial structures) would have been nonconforming uses had these areas been given the dwelling house designation. Since singles and doubles were permitted in apartment zones, the city chose the designation that produced the fewest nonconforming uses for these mixed-use areas. The apartment districts, most of which were between one and one-half and three miles from the city center, were the scene of most zoning change requests during the next thirty years.[116]

From the adoption of the zoning ordinance to 1930, City Council and the Board of Zoning Adjustment issued 324 decisions on requests to alter some provision of the code.[117] Approvals outnumbered denials by 63.3 to 36.7 percent. BZA actions outnumbered council actions by an even greater margin (73.1 to 26.9 percent), indicating perhaps less dissatisfaction with use designation than with other code provisions. Table 3.2 shows the percentage each body granted.

Although property owners all over the city made requests, the requests were not evenly distributed.[118] Almost half the requests on the north side occurred within three miles of the city center, but others extended to as far away as seven miles, farther than in any other part of town. On the east and south sides almost all requests were within the three-mile zone, while they were much more dispersed on the northeast and west sides (Figure 3.1).

This was a period of adjustment to the imposition of public land use controls. City officials did not want to create hardships for property owners who had platted or purchased their lots or planned their buildings prior to the code's adoption. Consequently, the zoning board was fairly lenient in granting variances from the setback and lot size requirements. In older parts of the city, lots were too small and houses too large to allow residents to build garages within the designated setbacks, so the BZA often granted variances. The BZA also granted lot area variances, permitting greater density building than allowed by code. Persons wishing to alter the use of their property to something the code did not allow

Table 3.2
Requests granted by council and the BZA, 1923–1955

	1923–30	1931–35	1936–45	1946–55
Requests decided by council	87	23	89	153
Council approval rate	71.3%	69.6%	62.9%	67.3%
Requests decided by BZA	237	60	16	44
BZA approval rate	60.3%	51.7%	50.0%	75.0%
Total percentage granted	63.3%	56.6%	60.9%	69.0%
Total number of decisions	324	83	105	197

Note: Both approval rates and percentage granted are calculated as a proportion of known decisions made, not total changes requested.

met with less success, for only 37.5 percent of requests for a nonconforming use were granted. Existing nonconforming uses were generally permitted to expand, however. Table 3.3 illustrates the types of variances granted.

The use changes granted by either council rezoning or BZA use variance increased the intensity of land use. Council and the zoning board permitted sixty-four changes from apartment or row house to commercial use and eleven from row house to apartment. Only seven changes were granted, however, from single-family use to commercial or a denser residential use.[119] Most changes to commercial use occurred in older residential areas or apartment zones near the industrial or commercial districts (Table 3.4). Thus close-in, mixed-use parts of the city became denser. Spacious, owner-occupied, middle and upper income, single-family neighborhoods retained their residential character, while rental housing areas experienced incursions of nonresidential uses during the first years of the code.

The Depression Drop: 1931–1935

Although requests for some change in public land use controls dropped sharply after the initial period of adjustment, the decisions allowed further change in older residential areas.[120] Zoning board actions still outnumbered those of council,[121] as did affirmative decisions (Table 3.2). As before, most requests involved land fairly close to the city center, although on the west side several involved parcels just beyond the state hospital (Figure 3.2). The

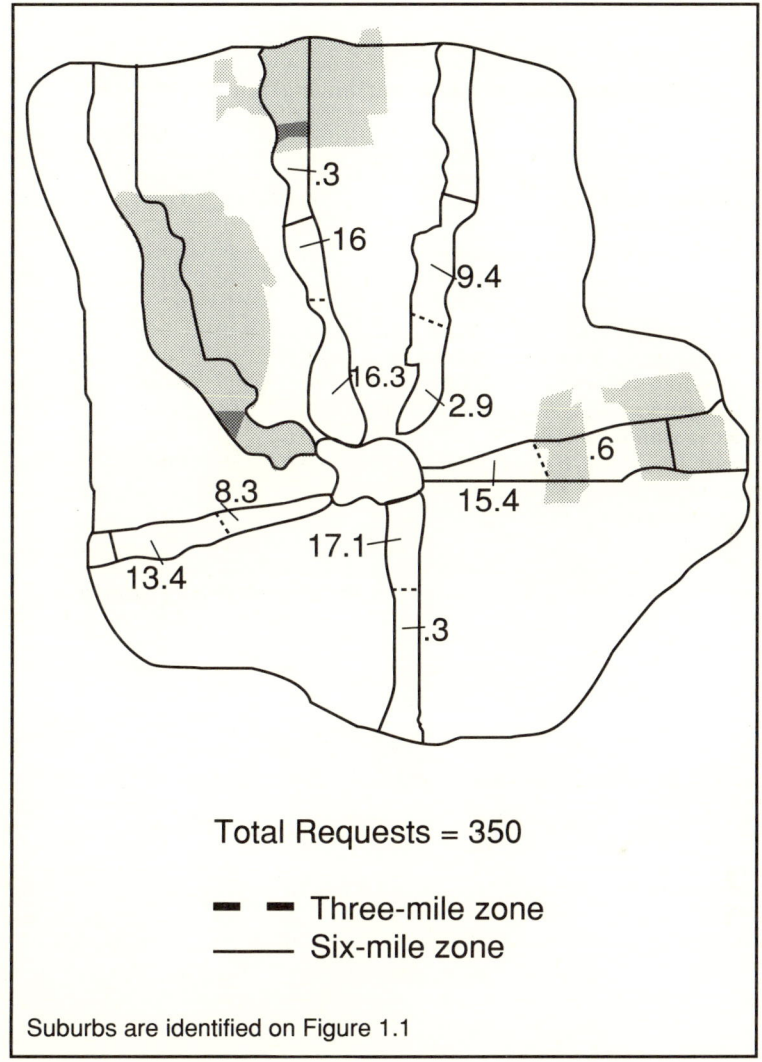

Figure 3.1 Percentage of requests for rezoning or variance by location, 1923–1930

BZA was still reluctant to impose a hardship on property owners and thus generally granted variances for setback and lot size. The board also permitted almost as many nonconforming uses as it denied (Table 3.3).

Perhaps the most striking feature about zoning decisions involving land use during this period is that only one type of use change

Table 3.3
Percentage of each type variance granted, 1923–1955

Action*	1923–30 %	(n)	1931–35 %	(n)	1936–45 %	(n)	1946–55 %	(n)
Setback for main building	70.0%	30	50.0%	4	66.7%	3	100.0%	1
Setback for addition	58.3	12	50.0	2		0	100.0	9
Setback for accessory	76.5	51	100.0	6	66.7	3	0.0	1
Height	77.8	9		0	50.0	2	100.0	3
Lot size or area	74.4	78	80.0	5	92.3	26	87.5	56
Floor area: main building	50.0	2		0		0		0
Floor area: accessory building	66.7	9	100.0	1	0.0	1		0
Begin nonconforming use	37.5	80	45.0	40	42.9	7	76.5	17
Expand nonconforming use	76.5	17	0.0	1	50.0	2	33.3	3
Alter nonconforming use	0		0.0	1	0.0	1	50.0	2
Special permit	62.5	16	100.0	4	0.0	1	100.0	4
Sign provisions		0		0		0		0
Parking requirements		0		0		0		0
Total requests		304		64		46		96

*(n) is the total of each type of action requested; the percentage is the proportion of each type of request granted.

Table 3.4
Changes to commercial use by distance from the city center, 1923–1955

Distance	1923–30 %	(n)	1931–35 %	(n)	1936–45 %	(n)	1946–55 %	(n)
Less than 3 miles	62.2%	43	81.8%	18	82.6%	19	69.2%	45
3 to 6 miles	33.8	22	18.2	4	17.4	4	30.8	20
More than 6 miles		0		0		0		0
Total	100.0%	65	100.0%	22	100.0%	23	100.0%	65

was granted—housing to commercial. Council or the BZA permitted twenty-two parcels zoned for row houses or apartments to change to commercial use. Most of those changes, like most of the nonconforming uses permitted by the BZA, were within three miles of the city center (Table 3.4). This further increased the variety and intensity of land use in an already varied area and detracted from the residential character of what had been designated a dwelling house or apartment zone.

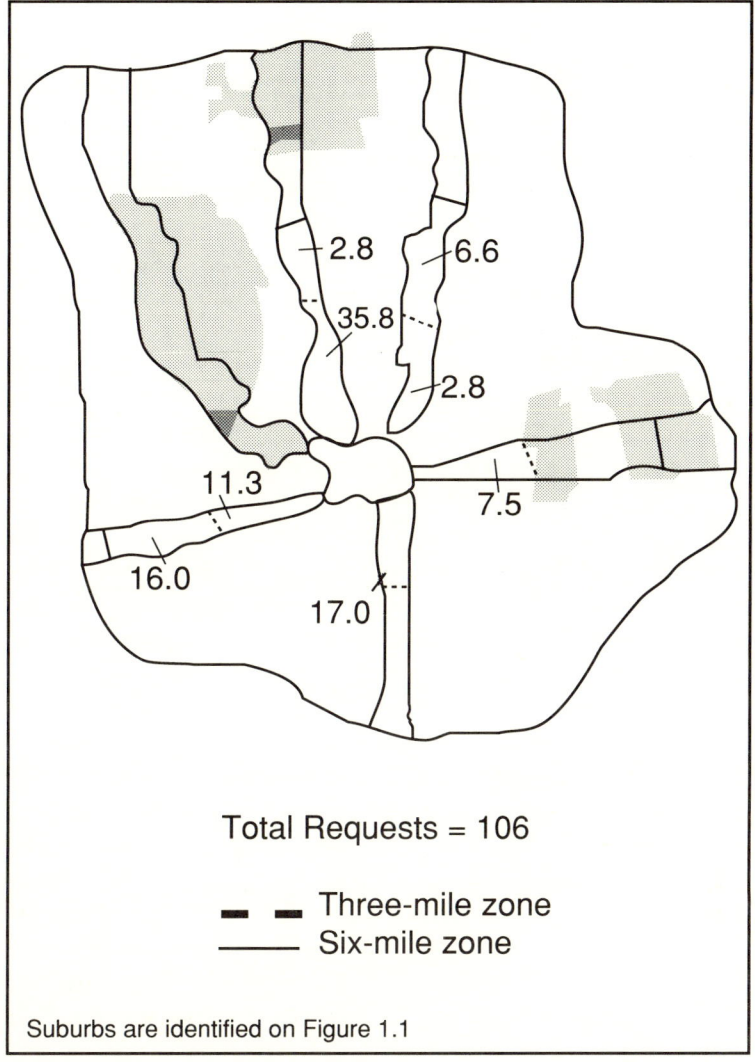

Figure 3.2 Percentage of requests for rezoning or variance by location, 1931–1935

Slow Times Continue: 1936–1945

Zoning actions through the remainder of the depression and war years continued the pattern previously set, but not without some changes. By the mid-1930s, property owners had apparently adjusted to zoning controls, for the number of requests made during the following ten years was only slightly greater than in the preceding five (106 from 1931 to 1935, 107 from 1936 to 1945). The nature of requests changed, however, as did the body responsible for making more decisions. Council made 84.8 percent of the decisions on zoning matters, indicating that property owners were more concerned about land use than lot or area specifications. Regardless of their concerns, they generally got what they asked for, which allowed additional change in older residential areas (Table 3.2 and Figure 3.3).

Property owners had learned to live within their building lines — only three requested setback variances. Twenty-six sought to increase their lot density, however, and overwhelmingly were allowed to do so (Table 3.3). If they wanted a use not permitted by code, they more often went to council for a rezoning than to the BZA for a use variance. As in earlier years, change to commercial use was the most desired and council or the BZA granted twenty-three such changes from row house or apartment use (Table 3.4). On the west side, however, four property owners bucked the trend and council rezoned their land from commercial to one-to-four-family residential.[122] Others sought to increase residential density and council rezoned seven parcels from row house to apartment use.

The changes that City Council and the Board of Zoning Adjustment granted increased both density and intensity of use, particularly in older areas of the city. The mixed areas became more mixed and the number of potential housing units increased. This latter occurred because of row house to apartment changes but also because lot area changes allowed property owners to build multifamily units for more households than their lots would otherwise have been permitted to hold. Thus the earlier trends continued despite the low level of zoning activity.

The Postwar Pick-up: 1946–1955

The ten years following the end of World War II saw an increase in zoning requests and an acceleration of existing patterns. Council again made the lion's share of decisions (77.7 percent), and property owners generally got what they asked for (Table 3.2). The affected properties extended farther from the city center than previously and they were not evenly distributed. The number of

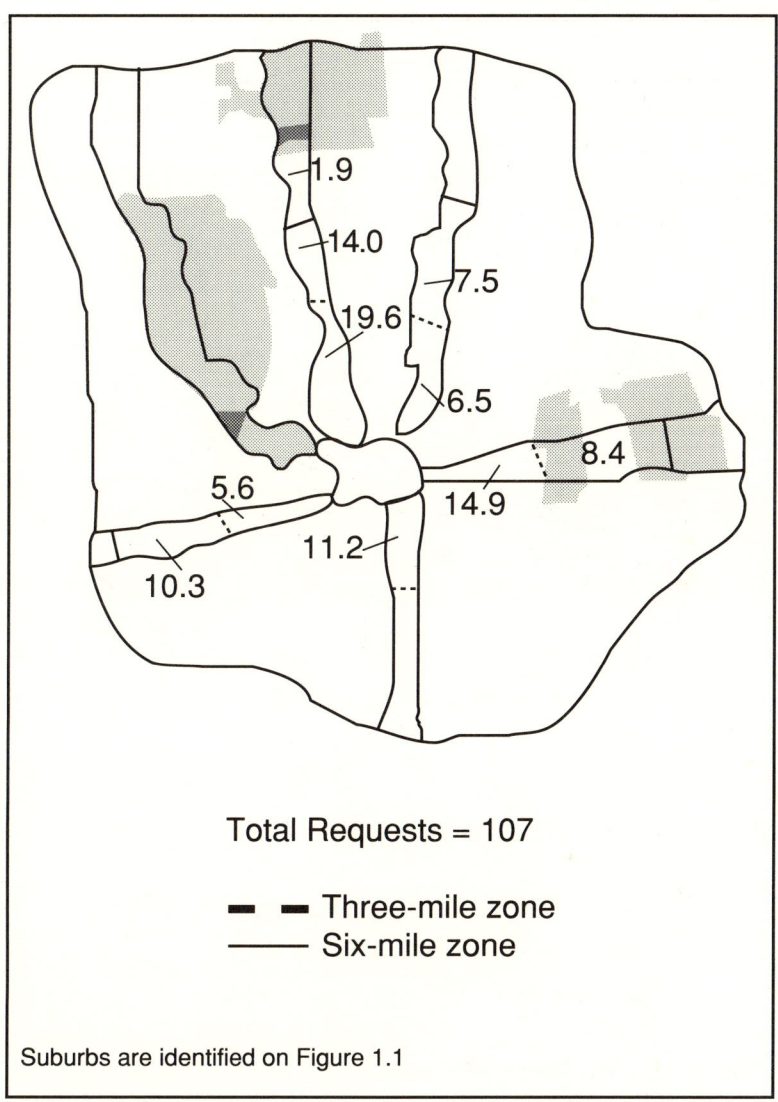

Figure 3.3 Percentage of requests for rezoning or variance by location, 1936–1945

requests ranged from a low of 19 on the south side to a high of 74 on the east. Reflecting its less developed state, all south side requests were within three miles of downtown, whereas north side requests extended to seven miles. Still, 60 percent of the requests on the north, east, and west sides were within the three-mile zone (Figure 3.4).

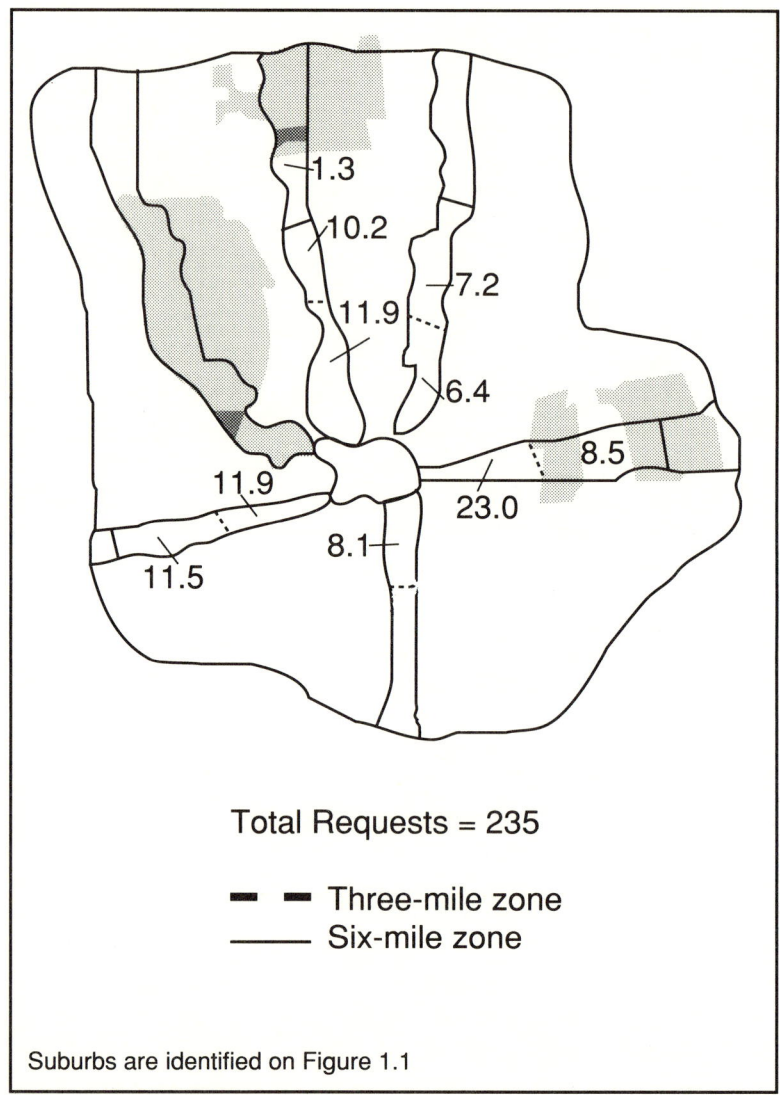

Figure 3.4 Percentage of requests for rezoning or variance by location, 1946–1955

The patterns established during the previous ten years continued for both council and BZA actions. The BZA permitted variances for a few setbacks or nonconforming uses. The board also granted some special permits for uses that were allowed in various districts only with the board's specific approval. As before, however, many more property owners were concerned about area restrictions: forty-nine, compared to eleven setback requests and twenty-two for nonconforming uses. Thus they requested and received lot size variances or rezonings of area classification to permit denser construction than the code allowed (Table 3.3).

Commercial requests outnumbered any other use change by a margin of sixteen to one. Council rezoned fifty-seven parcels from row house or apartment to commercial use and seven single-family lots to commercial use. Although the altered single-family lots were widely scattered, the newly commercial row house and apartment lots were often on the near north, east, and west sides. As before, a few property owners sought to increase residential density by rezoning from row house to apartment district and to change from commercial use. Council approved four of each request. Table 3.4 indicates the location of commercial use changes, showing that the patterns of earlier years continued. Land use in older residential areas became increasingly mixed, dense, and intense.

Protecting Columbus Property Values

For thirty-two years Columbus City Council and the Board of Zoning Adjustment changed the city's structure as it grew, though without the benefit of a comprehensive plan. Most of the city's growth by annexation occurred in the mid- and late 1920s. City Council promptly assigned use, height, and area classifications to the newly annexed territory. Except along the arterials, council zoned all the new land for the least dense dwelling house category, thus specifying that only single-family homes could be built there. Council zoned frontage along arterials for commercial use, with two exceptions. Some sections of High Street and Broad Street frontage on the north and east sides were given the low density, dwelling house designation of the subdivisions they bordered. This occurred mainly where preexisting deed restrictions permitted only single-family homes, which had already been built for middle or upper middle income persons. Since most land had been platted with developer-imposed deed restrictions prior to annexation to the city, the zoning code followed the land developers rather than directing their activity. Consequently, zoning designations usually matched land developers' use restrictions.

Where council or the zoning board granted changes primarily reflected where property owners requested them. It is not surprising that most requests involved land in the older, close-in residential areas, given the patterns of residential development. In areas developed after the 1910s, property owners found their land uses and building setbacks specified by deed restrictions that applied regardless of zoning provisions. A rezoning from residential to commercial might financially benefit one with a parcel in an unrestricted subdivision or in a subdivision whose restrictions had expired, but in newer areas such parcels were few and far between. The older residential neighborhoods, however, were well within the 1920 fringe of the city and thus not subject to extensive deed restrictions. Many of these areas had been platted in the 1870s and 1880s and the few restrictions imposed had expired before zoning's adoption. Consequently, zoning changes most often affected land in or near the three-mile zone.

The incremental impact of thirty years' changes was considerable, if unintended. Despite the apartment or row house zoning designation of most residential land in older areas, singles and doubles predominated there. The changes that council and the zoning board granted resulted in these areas becoming increasingly dense and the land use increasingly varied. The lot size variances or area changes allowed property owners to build more multifamily units than the code permitted on the basis of lot dimensions. This meant either building larger structures or subdividing existing single-family homes and doubles into multifamily units. Either way, population density increased.

The commercial rezonings increased the intensity of use, along with the potential for more traffic, noise, and congestion. They thus detracted from the residential character of these older neighborhoods. Altogether, over thirty-two years, 176 parcels in residential areas were rezoned for commercial use, most within three miles of the city center. Meanwhile, many lots along commercially zoned arterials remained vacant. Property owners wishing to initiate commercial uses, then, preferred to seek rezoning for land they already owned or for lower-priced residential lots rather than buy commercially zoned parcels elsewhere. Since these 176 changes occurred over thirty years, it is unlikely that council or the BZA deliberately set out to create commercial or mixed-use areas in the older neighborhoods. Certainly there was no adopted plan for that purpose, but the cumulative effect of their actions was to do just that.

Council and the BZA also served property interests through their actions. In newer residential areas, where middle and upper income people owned and occupied their own homes, zoning actions protected both residential character and property values. In older residential areas, where residents were more likely to be rental tenants, zoning protected only property values. Zoning increased the earning potential of income-producing properties by allowing more apartments or changes to commercial use. City Council and the Board of Zoning Adjustment did not use zoning to plan and direct growth and development for the benefit of the city as a whole during these thirty years. Rather, they reacted to the requests of individual property owners on a one-by-one basis to protect property value.

Planners, Planning, and Zoning over Time

There is no evidence that once the Columbus zoning code was in place those who administered it gave any thought to the larger purposes of zoning that early reformist planners had set for it. Unfortunately, the Columbus experience was common. During the same thirty years the amount of attention planners as a whole gave to zoning was not great. There was a spate of journal articles and conference papers dealing with zoning in the late 1920s but noticeably fewer in the 1930s and 1940s. Planners were caught up in the Great Depression and World War II and pondered the implications of those events for their profession. Zoning was sort of taken for granted; after all, the zoning battle had been fought and won years earlier.

During this time the planning profession continued to evolve, broadening its scope from cities to metropolitan areas and multistate regions. The profession also figured in the newly established relationship between the national and local governments that grew out of efforts to deal with the Great Depression. Moreover, the same issues that had prompted zoning—housing conditions, tenement and slum districts, and the overall quality of urban life—continued to concern planners.

Even while the U.S. Department of Commerce's model acts encouraged and facilitated cities to adopt zoning, planners recognized that cities were changing, and they expanded their focus. During the 1920s the Russell Sage Foundation funded the *Regional Plan for New York and Its Environs*. A staff of planners prepared volumes of analysis and recommendations for the three-state metropolitan region surrounding the city of New York under the direction of Thomas Adams.[123] The *Regional Plan for New York and Its Environs* was a detailed, specific, and pragmatic approach for dealing with a city whose growth seemed unstoppable.

It was, however, much too practical for the era's other major proponent of a regional vision, Lewis Mumford, about whom had gathered a loosely defined group of housing reformers and planning-oriented architects known as the Regional Planning Association of America (RPAA). Believing that urban growth was neither necessarily good nor inevitable, they preferred deconcentration of the urban population. They were also the garden city movement's strongest advocates in the United States and the moving force behind Sunnyside Gardens and Radburn.[124] The RPAA felt that the formless sprawling of metropolitan areas destroyed a sense of community; members believed that residential areas, coordinating physical and social planning as outlined by Clarence Perry's Neighborhood Unit concept, could counteract existing trends. Community planning could both preserve the integrity of small towns and make big cities more livable. Although Mumford condemned the *Regional Plan of New York* as a "failure of imagination," he praised its acceptance of Perry's Neighborhood Unit. Still, he and other RPAA members urged a more active government role.[125]

That more active government role, especially for the federal government, arrived with the New Deal.[126] Local governments could not cope with the exigencies of the Great Depression and the federal government's response involved planners in a number of ways.[127] They supervised the housing and planning components of the Tennessee Valley Authority, designing the new towns to be created.[128] They also planned the "greenbelt" towns, which reflected some garden city principles and were built by the U.S.D.A.'s Resettlement Administration under Rexford Tugwell.[129] Housing reformers, including RPAA member Catherine Bauer, helped shape the landmark 1937 U.S. Housing Act, which authorized public construction of rental housing for low income persons.[130] Finally, they served on the National Resources Planning Board (NRPB), created to survey the state of the nation's physical and human resources and to encourage planning that would promote their wise and efficient use. The NRPB's Urbanism Committee produced the first comprehensive study of urban America, a three-part report entitled *Our Cities: Their Role in the National Economy*.[131]

As depression merged into war the NRPB continued its activities until its disbanding in 1943. Still, many plans and projects begun at the board's instigation provided a legacy.[132] Meanwhile both in their own cities and at their national meetings planners recognized the need to prepare cities for the postwar world.[133] Concerns about the quality and quantity of housing continued, for although New Deal programs and defense industry needs had produced some new dwellings, much present and anticipated need remained unmet. Overcrowded and inadequate dwellings still filled city slums. Adjacent to them were blighted areas of vacant or outmoded industrial and commercial structures, spawning interest in redeveloping central cities. The Housing Act of 1949 and its 1954 successor, which reflected some planning profession input, joined housing and revitalization efforts funded in part by the federal government.[134]

City planning, both as a profession and as an activity, had changed considerably by the mid-1950s. So had the environment in which it functioned. At the time New York adopted the nation's first zoning ordinance, city planning was in transition from the City Beautiful to the City Efficient. Private consultants, generally trained in a design field, drafted the plans of individual cities, which were often paid for by business leaders. By the 1950s planning, though still largely physical, was less oriented toward aesthetics, planners were often public employees, cities were part of complex multijurisdictional metropolitan regions, and the federal government as well as local governments actively promoted planning.

It is not surprising, then, that planners gave zoning much less conscious attention than previously. Other aspects of the profession were actively developing and changing. Zoning, on the other hand, had developed and been legitimated in the 1920s; once in place, the zoning process was expected to function as planning theory said it should. Zoning had become a normal part of everyday planning life, largely unexamined and unquestioned.

Nevertheless, some were uneasy. When they did discuss zoning, planners reiterated their goal of promoting the public health, safety, and welfare.[135] And only a decade after New York's pioneering effort, some planners found zoning so affected by the commercialism of American society or by property concerns that its practice served neither the needs of the community nor of all its residents equally well. "I have always wondered," commented one, "why a smaller front, side, and rear yard is needed to promote the health, safety, and general welfare of the inhabitants of a two-family house than the inhabitants of a one-family house."[136]

Zoning was not to be "a sanctification of the status quo"; it was to be a blueprint for future growth. Planners warned small-town officials in frequent contact with citizens and business owners not to do the politically expedient thing when zoning or responding to requests for zoning changes. Such an approach would produce inconsistency and render the zoning code useless.[137] Planners J. Talmadge Woodruff and Harland Bartholomew agreed, repeating earlier dictums of Bassett and Bettman and reminding others that zoning had to be part of the comprehensive plan.[138]

Planners pointed out the ramifications of zoning without planning in 1935. The amount of land zoned for various uses did not match communities' needs, and zoning boards granted too many special favors—all because zoning was not following a comprehensive plan. Five years later planner Hugh Pomeroy noted that zoning could encourage adequate housing for all income levels and rehabilitate blighted areas, but only if it followed a comprehensive plan. The point was made again in 1941. Zoning had become separated from or substituted for comprehensive planning, and unless it became part of planning again it would continue merely to maintain the status quo.[139] One planner even wondered whether the public interest had become the status quo. Noting that Stamford, Connecticut, placed 80 percent of its territory in a residence zone with lot size and frontage minimums of one acre and one hundred feet, respectively, Flavel Shurtleff pondered whether the Connecticut court would find that action an "unreasonable and arbitrary control of private land, ... or ... that the regulations make for the public welfare in its broadest sense," since they made the town a "more convenient and attractive place."[140] Others repeated the same concerns when the 1953 national planning conference held a clinic entitled "Modernizing Our Zoning." There were too many and inappropriate nonconforming uses and variances, said one. We need comprehensive master plans so zoning can do more than preserve an outdated status quo, said another.[141]

By the 1950s zoning authorities Richard Babcock and Charles Haar thought the planners had lost sight of zoning's purpose as well as their own. At a national planning conference, Babcock told the planners they had abdicated their place in formulating zoning's role. He was concerned, as they did not appear to be, about the conflict between property protection and social equity. Haar added that the "safety valves" of the zoning process—the variances, amendments, and exceptions—had become the system. Zoning was "non-planning," as too many planners and public officials responded to concerns about property rights and values.[142]

These concerns were only periodically expressed, however. Zoning had taken on a life of its own in practice as planners became preoccupied with its technical aspects. They were so busy looking at trees that they did not see the forest. Planners often discussed the design of zoning ordinances, details of their administration (how and by whom it should be done), and the standards that should be followed—all without reference to the larger purpose to be served.[143] By the 1950s zoning ordinances had become increasingly complex, with proliferating categories and subcategories of use and varying standards and specifications for each. And the zoning board of appeals, that instrument to provide flexibility and prevent undue hardship, had become part of the problem rather than the solution.

Between the 1910s and the 1950s, reformist city planners and lawyers devised the idea of zoning to control land use and improve the urban environment. They developed the concept of comprehensive planning to be zoning's theoretical basis, and for more than thirty years consistently (if infrequently) paid lip service to zoning as part of comprehensive planning for the public interest. In application, however, as the Columbus experience made clear, zoning often operated without planning and consequently exacerbated the very conditions it had been created to cure.

FOUR

Standardizing the Process: Residential Development, 1946–1970

For forty-five years after the turn of the century, real estate developers had experimented with different aspects of the development process, varying the size and density of their developments and the restrictions they put on land use and occupancy. They retained and refined those processes and standards that proved profitable or effective and altered or discarded those that did not. In doing so, they established patterns in both development activity and the form of the city, seemingly without reference to local zoning codes (where they existed). During the twenty-five years that followed World War II, the real estate industry essentially institutionalized the process it had previously developed. Local government also affected what private developers did. Still, responding to the housing needs and wants—both real and perceived—of different groups, the development industry followed the spatial and social patterns previously set.

The Postwar Development Process

Subdivisions platted after the war exhibited less physical variety than those developed earlier. Consequently, many outlying areas tended to resemble one another more than they resembled their predecessors, and more than their predecessors had resembled one another. In those older areas of the city platted after 1900, developers had experimented with various lot sizes and subdivision layouts and with development restrictions. But little unplatted land remained in those older areas by 1946, although in some sections of the city many platted lots remained unbuilt. And except for a few small parcels, the older suburbs, too, were fully developed. Consequently land development after the war occurred in the outlying suburbs and beyond. The city of Columbus leapfrogged its suburbs on both the northwest and east sides.

In the 1950s local government joined the land development game. Water and sewer service was its entrée. Early in the twentieth century the Franklin County Department of Sanitary Engineering began building sewers for developments on unincorporated land but then arranged with the City of Columbus for discharge into the city's treatment system. The suburbs of Bexley, Marble Cliff, Grandview Heights, and Upper Arlington all initially had their own systems, but in the 1920s and 1930s they, too, joined the city's system. Moreover, the city had generally been liberal with extensions; trunk lines extended to Worthington and Riverlea in the north and to Whitehall on the east, though capacity was not adequate for the population.[1]

By 1950 there were problems. The city's water came from two reservoirs on the Scioto River. Facing a shortage Columbus put a freeze on extensions and then added a new reservoir on Big Walnut Creek, well north of the city's far east side. City officials also realized their system was fiscally precarious. Although the city provided water and sewer service to outlying areas, it received no property tax revenues from them, and current city residents bore the full cost of the suburban extensions. Moreover, little undeveloped land lay within the city proper, while the suburbs were growing rapidly. To gain the tax revenues from new development, then, Columbus initiated a policy of extending water and sewer service only to land within its corporate limit. If a real estate developer or landowner wanted utilities, he would have to annex his land to the city. The only alternative was to annex to one of the suburbs that had a service contract with the city.[2] But since Columbus had the treatment facilities the suburbs needed, Columbus determined how large and in which direction those suburban service areas could grow. Columbus drew the service areas so that the suburbs could expand some, but at the same time the city itself would never be totally surrounded by other municipalities.

Although the city did not technically initiate the annexations that followed, it certainly encouraged them. The Columbus City Planning Commission's Community Relations Office performed studies and made information illustrating the benefits of annexation readily available to property owners and land developers. City staff worked with petitioners to facilitate the annexation process.[3] The city indicated no preference for one area of the county over any other in accepting annexations and extending water and sewer lines. The only geographical restriction on an annexation was the state requirement that it be contiguous to the city it was joining. Under this policy both the city and some suburbs greatly expanded in the 1950s. The annexation requirement added another step to the land development process, but there is no indication developers felt themselves constrained by it. They continued to plat subdivisions much as they had before.

Postwar developers used deed restrictions with increasing sophistication. Earlier, many developers using restrictions had tried to attract only the upper end of the market. Consequently, they kept the level of standards in deed restrictions high enough to assure upper middle income occupancy—regardless of subdivision location. After World War II, however, developers varied the standards of their restrictions depending on the location of their development. Those areas that by 1945 were considered desirable or exclusive had more stringent restrictions than those intended for people with modest incomes. Previously moderate income or working class homeowners had not purchased new houses but had acquired the used dwellings vacated by wealthier people moving to exclusive suburbs.[4] In the 1950s, however, builders like Levitt and Sons and their counterparts in Columbus began to target that group explicitly for new, albeit modest, homes in suburban locations.[5]

Real estate developers' use of restrictions also indicates that they now considered applicable zoning codes. Much platting still occurred prior to annexation, but with utility extensions contingent upon joining Columbus or a suburban water and sewer service district, developers had to consider the public land use controls of the jurisdiction they would join. If the zoning code's development standards in the adjacent part of the city or suburb were appropriate for the market segment the developer was trying to reach, his deed restrictions often mirrored city code provisions. Where code provisions were loose or standards fairly low and the developer was targeting moderate income home buyers, the standards of his deed restrictions were equally low. But if real estate developers felt that city standards would not provide sufficient protection for their intended market, they would impose much stiffer restrictions. A city council might change the zoning code; it could not change a deed covenant.

Land developers also changed the procedure by which they applied restrictive covenants. Through the mid-1940s they generally inserted the covenants on a deed-by-deed basis as each lot was sold. After 1945 the developer often recorded his plat, then transferred ownership of the entire subdivision, including all the numbered lots in one deed, to another corporate entity he controlled. This second corporation then effected another deed transfer, again of the entire subdivision but this time specifying all restrictive covenants, back to the developer or to a third corporation, which would market the lots. Thus developers accomplished in two deed transfers processed the same day what had previously required dozens or hundreds of deed transfers and many years.

Other prewar trends and patterns were unchanged. The development level of the south and west sides of Columbus remained low. The tendency toward lower density also continued, especially in the middle and upper income suburbs. Meanwhile in the city, or in areas likely to be annexed to it, the code minimum of six lots per acre became the norm. The size of individual, platted subdivisions remained fairly small, although an entire development itself might be large. Rather than platting a whole tract of one or two hundred acres at one time, a developer might plat only ten, twenty, or thirty acres of it. When lot sales on the first parcel reached a point where his initial development expenses were covered, he platted the next ten- or twenty-acre parcel. Thus there came to be three Kilbourne Village subdivisions (each with a different number) and four Worthingway subdivisions in Worthington, three Orchard Views and five called Shelbourne Heights in Upper Arlington, and more than a dozen named Oak Park in the northeast part of Columbus. Columbus was not atypical in this respect. This was common practice nationwide for such large-scale developer-builders as Eichler, Levitt, Ryan, and Ryland—regardless of where in the country they operated or what segment of the market they built for — because they could rarely obtain loans sufficient to finance development of large tracts of vacant land all at once.[6] Consequently, proceeds for one part of a neighborhood financed the next.

The Suburban Boom: 1946–1960

The words *explosive growth* most vividly describe what happened in the Columbus metropolitan area in the fifteen years following World War II. After the spate of annexations during the 1920s, the city's borders had remained virtually unchanged for fifteen years. Then, between 1946 and 1960, Columbus annexed 11,609 acres encompassing much of the north, northeast, east, south, and west sides. Particularly in the northeast, and to a lesser extent on the north side, some isolated pockets of unincorporated township land remained where residents chose not to become part of the city; but they were few. The city, of course, encouraged annexation by its 1954 policy of withholding water and sewer service from developments that did not annex to it or one of the suburban service areas.

Like Columbus, those suburbs with room to grow benefited from this policy. The older suburbs of Bexley, Marble Cliff, and Grandview Heights found themselves unable to expand, but both Worthington and Upper Arlington grew. Aware of increasing land development pressure, the Village of Worthington annexed several hundred acres of adjacent farmland before developers purchased and platted it. This allowed Worthington to ensure that the development standards of its zoning code would apply to all new subdivisions. It also allowed Worthington to determine which areas it wished to reserve for future commercial or industrial use. King Thompson's planned suburb also greatly increased as Upper Arlington annexed hundreds of acres — much to the dismay of some residents. Besides vacant farmland, the annexations included some small subdivisions that had been platted in the 1910s by landowners and developers other than Thompson. Those areas contained smaller lots and more modest homes, and many of the residents of the original village vigorously protested their annexation and circulated petitions opposing it. After much public discussion, pro-growth forces won the day, the "substandard" areas joined the city, and their residents received the benefits of the Upper Arlington services and schools they had desired. Both Worthington and Upper Arlington attained the legal status of "city" (rather than "village") during the 1950s as their populations passed the necessary threshold of five thousand persons.

The postwar years also saw the incorporation of the last of the suburbs under study here. Late in 1947 residents of the subdivisions that had been platted on and adjacent to White Hall Farm on the far east side filed for incorporation. Though the village of Whitehall was not densely settled and contained some small farms and truck gardens, it was growing rapidly. Five years later the village extended its borders east to Big Walnut Creek and the Columbus Country Club, bringing in Charles Johnson's exclusive Fairway subdivisions. With both farms and Fairway, land use in Whitehall was thus quite varied. Whitehall also grew enough in population to become a city in the 1950s.

Real estate developers were as growth oriented as the municipalities and platted seventy-five subdivisions in the fifteen years after World War II (Table 2.1). Favoring those parts of the city where they had succeeded before, they extended the northwest, north, northeast, and east sides and all but ignored the south and west. Except in the northeast, where no incorporated suburbs existed, they also tended to favor suburban communities. They platted a few small infill parcels (unplatted acreage surrounded by platted or developed subdivisions) in the older suburbs but were most active in the newer, outlying areas. Figure 4.3 illustrates the location of subdivisions by municipality and section of the city.

Land developers minimized their financial risk for the most part by keeping the scale of operations small (Figure 4.1). Twenty subdivisions contained fewer than 10 acres, twenty-six were between 11 and 25 acres, and fourteen between 26 and 50. The only subdivision larger than 100 acres was platted on a 230-acre tract in Worthington. Density of development continued the trend begun before the war, with half the subdivisions platted at three or fewer lots per acre (Figure 4.2). Lots in the suburbs were generally larger than those on unincorporated land or land to be annexed to Columbus.

Although the use of restrictive covenants in deeds had become standard practice by the postwar years, there were some differences in their application from previous eras (Tables 4.1–4.5).

Figure 4.1 Comparison of subdivision size, 1945–1970

Table 4.1
Subdivisions platted with setback restrictions, 1946–1970

	1946–60	1961–70
Columbus or County		
North		
Northeast	9	7
East	1	4
South	3	
West	1	
Northwest	4	1
Worthington	9	6
Riverlea		
Bexley	1	
Whitehall	12	3
Marble Cliff		1
Grandview Heights	3	
Upper Arlington	22	15
Total restricted	65	37
Total platted	75	40

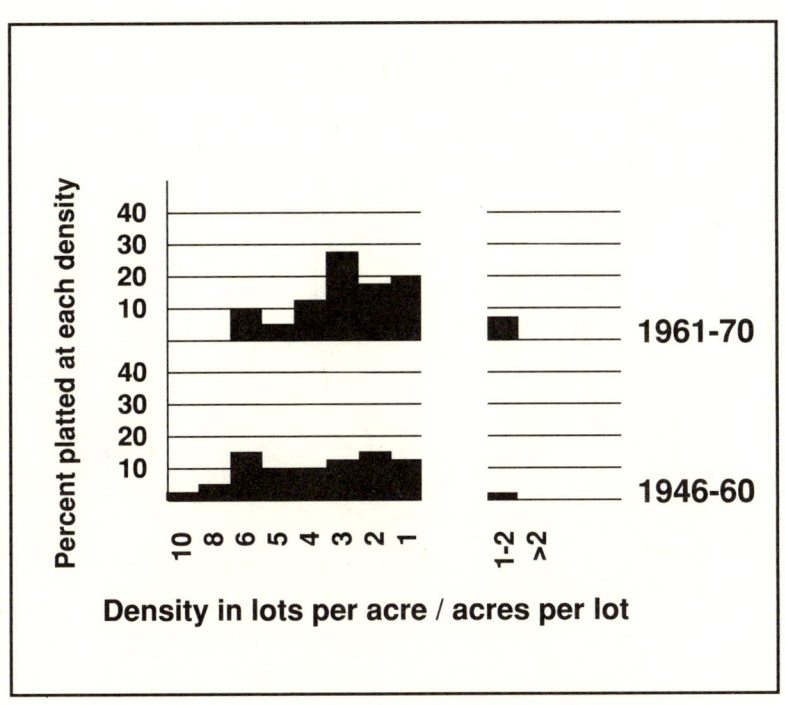

Figure 4.2 Comparison of subdivision density, 1946–1970

Table 4.2
Subdivisions platted with use restrictions, 1946–1970

	1946–60	1961–70
Columbus or County		
North		
Northeast	5	6
East	1	4
South	2	
West		
Northwest	4	
Worthington	8	6
Riverlea		
Bexley		
Whitehall	8	2
Marble Cliff		
Grandview Heights		
Upper Arlington	22	13
Total restricted	50	31
Total platted	75	40

109

110 • Standardizing the Process

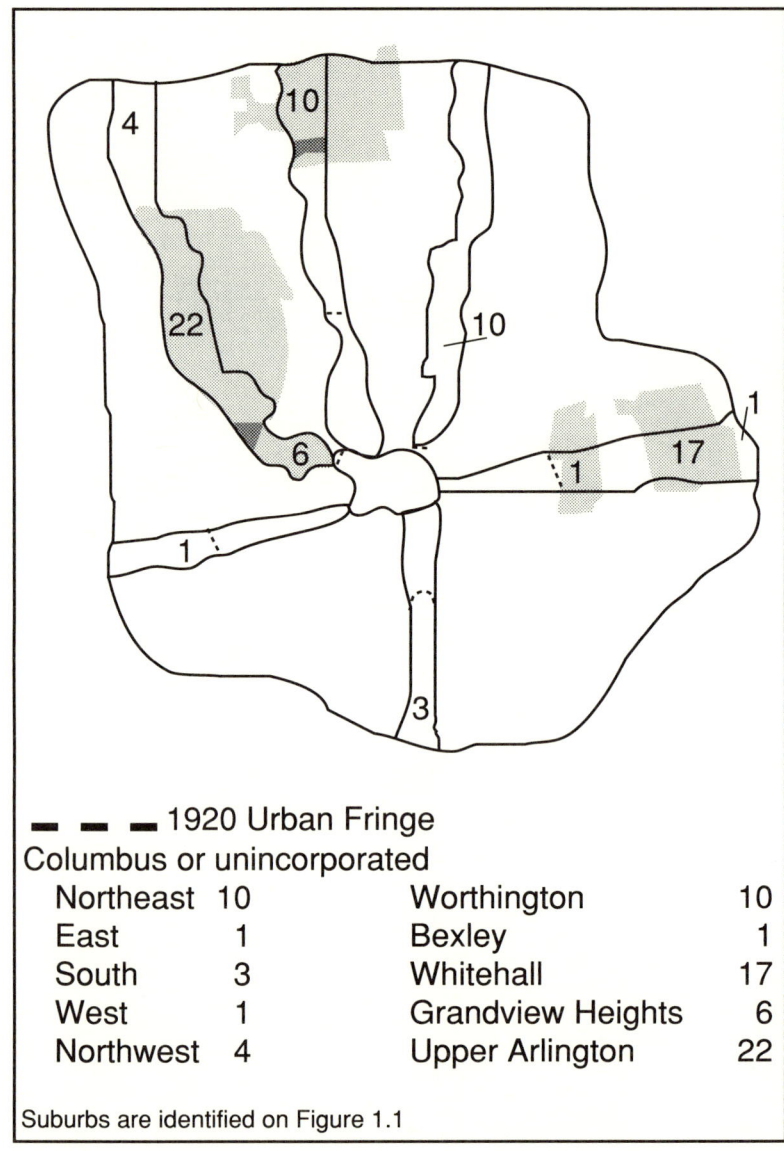

Figure 4.3 Number and location of subdivisions platted, 1946–1960

Table 4.3
Subdivisions platted with price restrictions,
1946–1970

	1946–60	1961–70
Columbus or County		
North		
Northeast	5	3
East		
South	1	
West		
Northwest		
Worthington	4	
Riverlea		
Bexley		
Whitehall	7	
Marble Cliff		
Grandview Heights		
Upper Arlington	14	2
Total restricted	31	5
Total platted	75	40

Table 4.4
Subdivisions platted with size restrictions,
1946–1970

	1946–60	1961–70
Columbus or County		
North		
Northeast	7	6
East	1	4
South	2	
West		
Northwest	4	
Worthington	5	4
Riverlea		
Bexley		
Whitehall	6	1
Marble Cliff		
Grandview Heights		
Upper Arlington	4	3
Total restricted	29	18
Total platted	75	40

Table 4.5
Subdivisions platted with race restrictions,
1946–1970

	1946–60	1961–70
Columbus or County		
North		
Northeast		
East		
South		
West		
Northwest		
Worthington	3	
Riverlea		
Bexley		
Whitehall	1	
Marble Cliff		
Grandview Heights		
Upper Arlington	8	2
Total restricted	12	2
Total platted	75	40

Twelve percent specified no building setback line, a proportion comparable to those with no setback platted in the 1930–1945 period and much greater than the proportion without setbacks in the 1920s. Some of these were subject to municipal zoning codes at the time of platting, and real estate developers may have felt the cities' setback standards sufficient. Those with specified setbacks often reflected conformity with the building lines the various municipal codes established, for most Upper Arlington deeds or plats mandated the forty-foot setback that the city had adopted to match its earliest development. Other plats specified the twenty-five or thirty-foot building lines more common in other municipalities.

Reflecting the 1948 U.S. Supreme Court decision *Shelley* v. *Kraemer*, the use of race restrictions dropped sharply, but it did not disappear altogether. Developers of twelve subdivisions sought to limit ownership or occupancy. Deeds in eight subdivisions stated that only whites or nonblacks could own or occupy the premises although it was not a legally enforceable provision. One cannot determine whether the developers themselves knew the restriction could not be enforced or whether they perhaps thought that lot purchasers would assume it was a valid restriction since it appeared in the deed, a legal instrument. The four subdivisions King Thompson's company platted in Upper Arlington in the 1950s tried a different approach to exclusion. They made membership in a community association a condition of purchase, with existing association members voting on whom they would or would not accept for membership.

With respect to the racial issue, the Federal Housing Administration (FHA) made the land developers' job easier. The FHA examined the character and stability of the surrounding neighborhood, among other things, to determine mortgage insurability of a home whose mortgage it considered insuring. Applying criteria initially developed by the Home Owners Loan Corporation, its predecessor agency, the FHA decided that the government should not insure mortgages in racially mixed or minority neighborhoods because property values there would decline. Land developers thus did not have to prohibit minority ownership by deed since builders and realtors in moderate income developments whose customers would want or need FHA mortgages would not sell to blacks.[7] Not surprisingly, after *Shelley* v. *Kraemer* race restrictions appeared in those areas targeted at upper income people, who were not likely to apply for FHA mortgages.

If land developers did not directly control by race who used the land, they could and did attempt to control by socioeconomic status who used it, as well as how it would be used. Fully two-thirds of the platted subdivisions limited construction to single-family homes or residential use only. Those zoned by local government for residential use that also required it by deed thus ensured a residential future regardless of subsequent municipal action. A few subdivisions applied both size and cost minimums, but most tended to have one or the other, with thirty-two imposing size restrictions and thirty-three setting a minimum construction cost. The greatly increased use of size restrictions compared to prior eras illustrates that real estate developers had come to realize one of the weaknesses of a minimum cost restriction: its inability to keep pace with the changing value of the dollar. Many lots had been platted in the late 1920s with construction cost minimums that would have provided for middle or upper middle income occupancy. When residential construction dropped off during the depression and war, some of those lots remained unbuilt. Then, when homes were actually constructed on these lots in the 1950s, costs had risen such that the minimums specified produced much more modest homes than they would have thirty years earlier. Thus developers who wanted to ensure a certain standard of development, regardless of when construction actually occurred, began to apply size restrictions more often after the war.

Developers tailored the provisions of their size or cost restrictions to the particular segment of the market they hoped to attract. Those subdivisions aimed at an upper middle income clientele required 1,400–1,800 square feet of floor area (exclusive of basements, garages, porches, and attics) per home or specified construction costs of $15,000, $20,000, or $25,000. More modest areas required only 500–1,000 square feet of floor area or a construction cost of $4,000 to $6,000. This was in line with similar developments elsewhere in the United States. At this time the Levittown, Long Island, Cape Cod homes with a ground floor area of about 750 square feet and an unfinished upper story sold for $7,990.[8] Equally interesting is which level of development appeared where in the metropolitan area. Conventional wisdom has it that the suburbs are for the upper and upper middle classes, so one would expect the higher size and cost restrictions to appear more often in the suburbs. The Upper Arlington and Worthington subdivisions confirm that view. Suburban Whitehall, however, defies the generalization, for several of its subdivisions specified less than 800 square feet of floor area or $5,000 construction cost minimums. Clearly some Whitehall developers were seeking a broad market rather than an exclusive one.

Postwar developers in Columbus knew their customers' attitudes about lot size, density, and neighborhood location and character. A 1959 study confirmed this with findings from research in six newly developed subdivisions: the three lowest in income were in Columbus, while the three highest were in Worthington.[9] Lot size was clearly important, for 14 percent of the residents wanted as large a lot as they could possibly acquire. Half the residents of the Columbus subdivisions looked forward to moving, either anticipating a job transfer or so they could have a larger lot. Somewhat fewer Worthington residents (37 percent) expected to move, and almost invariably because of an employment change rather than to acquire a bigger yard. The greatest amount of residential dissatisfaction was in the lowest income Columbus subdivision, where residents felt there were too many houses too close together. Two-thirds of the Columbus households intended to move as soon as they could afford to.[10]

Residents of all areas overwhelmingly gave one of two reasons for their choice of neighborhood. They cited access to the husband's employment and presence of a good school system equally often and much more so than any other reason. All but two households (a widow and a retired individual) owned cars and they expected to commute to work by car. As one-fourth of the households had two cars, few expected to use public transportation (which they felt was limited). Expecting to commute by car and judging employment access important, residents felt that being near a limited-access freeway would raise the values of their homes. Residents of both Columbus and Worthington neighborhoods believed the Worthington School District to be superior, and more than half the Worthington households had chosen their neighborhood on that basis.[11]

Although residents did not mention or seem to recognize the importance of formal planning controls, they expressed a decided preference for "strictly residential" neighborhoods. Worthington residents in particular commented on the lack of "good residential areas" in other sections of the city. At the same time, they were not quite comfortable with the idea of zoning; they sensed that it segregated people by income and they did not like to feel "snobbish." Being perceived as neighborly was very important. Many said they would prefer to fence their yards but relatively few had, fearing public opinion would consider that an unneighborly act.[12]

Whether they lived in Columbus or Worthington, the new suburbanites almost universally assumed they would be able to resell their houses at a profit sometime in the future. Consequently, they did not consider easy marketability a factor when judging the merits of various neighborhoods. All expected to sell high and move up the ladder.[13]

Developers gave the home buyers what they wanted. For upper middle and upper income people they provided for comfortably large homes on spacious lots in implicitly "good" residential areas in suburbs with "superior" schools. Those who could not afford the suburbs could live in equally new but scaled down versions of suburban subdivisions in fringe areas of the city while they anticipated moving up and out to bigger and better things.

Completing the Process: The 1960s

If the fifteen years after the Second World War was an era of explosive growth, the decade that followed was a time to consolidate the gains made. No land was annexed to the City of Columbus (in the areas under study) during the 1960s. In most directions previous annexations had taken the city's borders almost to Interstate 270, the planned beltway that would encircle the city and its suburbs. Only a few tracts remained unincorporated or to be annexed after 1970. In 1920 Columbus contained 23.891 square miles; by 1970 it covered 134.580 square miles.

Real estate developers continued to be active, although the city and suburban annexations of the 1950s meant that many more subdivisions than before were platted within municipal boundaries. Despite the fact that many of their subdivisions were thus subject to zoning codes that specified land use, lot size, and square footage for various types of buildings, developers continued to apply restrictive covenants in their deeds. A city council's legislative action or a zoning board's variance or special exception could change zoning ordinance provisions. Deed restrictions theoretically were permanent. Columbus developers used a technique Jesse Clyde Nichols designed decades earlier to ensure that restrictions would last. Deeds stated that the restrictions would remain in effect for a specified period—usually twenty-five or thirty-five years—and then be automatically renewable without change for successive periods of ten years unless voted on otherwise by owners of all or a majority of the lots so covered. Altering the restrictions thus required a concerted effort on the part of property owners.

Location of development in the 1960s exhibited a familiar trend (Table 2.1). None of the forty subdivisions platted was on the south or west side. The suburbs no longer marked the metropolitan area's outer limits, though, for east of Whitehall and north of Upper Arlington developers platted land that was or would become part of the City of Columbus. Figure 4.4 illustrates the location and distribution of platted subdivisions.

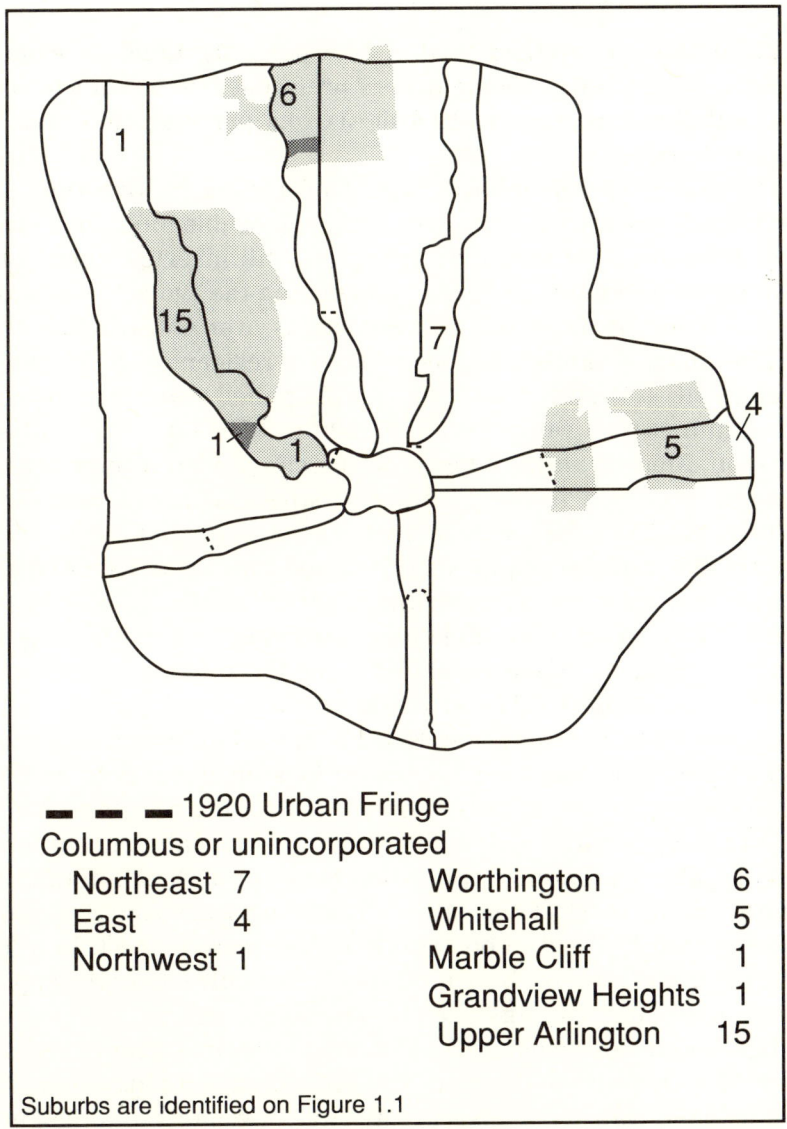

Figure 4.4 Number and location of subdivisions platted, 1961–1970

In the 1960s small plat size triumphed. No subdivisions were larger than fifty acres and almost half were in the eleven to twenty-five acre range (Figure 4.2). Density continued to be low (Figure 4.3). Three lots per acre was the most common density (eleven subdivisions for 27.5 percent), with one or two per acre also popular (for a combined total of 37.5 percent). Land developers clearly recognized the homeowners' preference for larger lots; only four subdivisions were platted at six lots per acre and none at higher densities.

Developers specified building setbacks of twenty-five, thirty, or forty feet following the standards of the applicable municipal code. Two holdouts, both in Upper Arlington, still inserted unenforceable racial covenants in deeds. Also during the 1960s the balance tipped firmly in favor of size restrictions over construction cost minimums to establish the income level of residential development (Tables 4.1–4.5). Fewer than one-fourth applied a construction cost minimum, which ranged from $5,000 to $20,000, depending on location. More than half, however, specified a minimum square footage. Six were in the Levittown Cape Cod range, but eight required 1,251–1,500 square feet, three required 1,500–1,750 square feet, and one required 1,751–2,000. Others varied by type of house (one or more stories) and location of the lot within the subdivision. With Whitehall again proving the exception, the higher standards appeared in or beyond the suburbs.

The lone Marble Cliff subdivision was to be developed as condominiums and the Grandview Heights one as an apartment complex. Developers imposed no restrictions on these two, as both were subject to very stringent municipal zoning regulations governing multifamily construction. Both also initially encountered considerable community opposition because of their multifamily character. In most of the other subdivisions developers limited construction by deed to one single-family home per lot. In a few they permitted one-to-four-family units, but only where the appropriate municipal zoning code allowed such construction.

Real estate developers in the 1960s thus continued the processes they had institutionalized in the preceding fifteen years. The double deed transfer to insert restrictive covenants and the automatic renewal clause became standard devices. Deed restrictions provided for a particular income level of the neighborhood, and developers varied the standard by location to attract specific market segments.

Land developers in Columbus at this time acted much like their counterparts elsewhere.[14] In order to target specific segments of the market, developers had to determine the value of land in various parts of the metropolitan area. A parcel's location value depended on its relative position in the spatial pattern of the entire area, the transportation network, and social values. Because the location itself was fixed, changes in the metropolitan context determined changes in value, making one place rather than another the "right" neighborhood.[15] A developer's use of deed restrictions could help shape those contextual social values and thus affect land value.

Developers generally followed one of two approaches when developing residential land. They sometimes took a marketing approach, where having determined a specific price range of housing demand in the city or suburbs, they searched for a tract of land that they could profitably develop to meet that demand. Otherwise, they followed a contract approach. Upon learning that a particular tract of land was or would be available for development, the developer assessed the tract for its "highest and best" (i.e., most profitable) use given the locational context, then determined whether there was sufficient demand for housing of that type and price range. Developers preferred the marketing approach because it afforded greater control over the scale and nature of their activities. When following it, they often tried to bracket the market, providing housing at both the top and bottom of the particular market segment they sought.[16] Consequently, some subdivision deed restrictions specified a range—though generally a small one—of construction cost or size minimums. Then the developer could not only appeal to all potential purchasers within that market segment but might also appeal to persons on the edges of the adjacent segments. In this way developers responded to market demand. At the same time, they could also help shape it through the use of deed restrictions.

Though real estate developers, rather than builders, pioneered the concept, in the years after World War II large developer-builders like Levitt and Sons also began to apply private control through restrictive covenants. And in cities without zoning, such as Houston, covenants were the principal means of land use control.[17] Lacking a municipal zoning ordinance to perpetuate the property value protections they might establish, Houston's developers used "a barrier of restrictive covenants, generally much tighter than zoning would be," for upper income residential neighborhoods. In less exclusive areas, they developed the interior spaces for modest housing and saved the arterial street frontage until its price rose as the interior lots sold and were occupied. The developers then sold the street frontage for commercial use of an often inappropriate type, thus causing the modest residences nearby to be less desirable. The big investor—or the well-heeled resident in an exclusive area—gained considerably by this practice; the small residential property holders suffered.[18] Houston land developers, like those elsewhere, claimed to be merely giving the public what it obviously wanted, since the covenants designated land use on the basis of present or anticipated markets. After all, developers did not insert provisions that might slow lot sales. They viewed restrictive covenants as a "device of the market to maximize the value of homes. Most American homeowners prefer to live in a homogeneous single-family environment.... Restrictive covenants come close to achieving this."[19] But the system served primarily upper middle and upper income homeowners. Those buying more moderately priced homes in Houston lacked the property value protection provided by extensive restrictions on the surrounding area that upper income persons enjoyed; they also lacked the protection that zoning theoretically afforded those in other cities. As the Houston and Columbus experiences show, the private land use control device of the restrictive covenant could protect property value in different ways under different circumstances.

Shaping Columbus

From the turn of the century through 1970, real estate developers gave the Columbus metropolitan area its spatial and social structure. Initially through their choice of location to develop, then through the restrictive covenants they placed in property deeds, they decided who would—and would not—live in what kinds of neighborhoods where. Local government assisted, rather than hindered, their efforts.

Like Boston, Chicago, and many other cities, Columbus grew first along major transportation routes, and early suburban communities benefited from the access they provided.[20] The old National Road became U.S. Route 40 and crossed Columbus from east to west, while U.S. Route 23, stretching from Lake Erie to the Ohio River and beyond, bisected the city from north to south. The "Maltese cross" noted by the authors of the *Plan of the City of Columbus* of 1908 was centered on these two arteries. When interurban railroads and street railways replaced travel by horse, their routes followed these same arteries, providing access for new communities. Later, the automobile replaced the streetcar and streetcar lines became major traffic arterials; a second generation of suburbs appeared beyond the first, rather than in the interstices between.

As in other cities utility extensions were also a factor in real estate development,[21] which would have been sparse and slow without water and, especially, sewer lines. But the City of Columbus largely followed the developers' lead in this respect. The city did not limit or direct land development to one area or another based on its own capacity. Instead the city extended water and sewer lines when and where developers requested them. It tied extensions to municipal annexation in the 1950s for fiscal reasons but imposed no locational constraint other than contiguity.

Still, development was not evenly dispersed throughout the city. Table 2.1 shows the distribution of subdivision activity beyond the urban fringe from before 1900 to 1970. Only 6.6 percent of that development occurred on the south and west sides. Certain features of the city itself combined with the deliberate actions of developers to produce this phenomenon.

The south and west sides of the old walking city both ended where major railroad lines crossed the arterials. Early suburban developers would have had to go well beyond the rail lines to create pleasant neighborhoods on the south and west sides. The walking city's east side ended at Alum Creek and its northern edge was very indistinct. The first suburban communities in Columbus, as in other cities, were developed for upper and upper middle income persons, for only they could afford to live beyond the walking city. Turn-of-the-century land developers could anticipate greater success with this income group if their neighborhoods were in picturesque areas with natural amenities. Thus Bexley, home to some of Columbus's most successful business leaders, grew up on the east bank of Alum Creek. The first homes in Marble Cliff and Grandview Heights were built on a bluff above the Scioto River.[22]

Real estate developers also knew that location was important for maintaining the quality of the residential environment they created. Desirable sites were on high ground, upstream; in Columbus this led the north side along the Olentangy River to grow first and farthest. Desirable sites were also upwind of industrial districts. Prevailing winds in Columbus came from the northwest, making the high ground between the Olentangy and Scioto rivers thus doubly attractive. Early industrial development in Columbus occurred at or below the rivers' confluence, causing winds to carry polluted air south of Bexley. In the first prospectus for his Upper Arlington development, King Thompson noted the importance of wind and water currents.[23]

Wind and water worked in favor of the northwest, north, and east sides. Other factors worked against the south and west. As previously noted, two large State of Ohio facilities were located on the west side. Early maps label them the "Hospital for the Insane" and the "Institution for the Feeble-Minded"—not what upper income suburbanites would choose as neighbors. Over several decades the south side became home to the sewage treatment plant, the landfill, and the women's workhouse—again, not the sort of land uses developers of upper income neighborhoods would want nearby.

Early in the century, developers of Columbus's first suburban communities wisely chose the best locations. Bexley was accessible to the city but separated from it by Alum Creek as visibly as by a moat. With their high riverside vistas, Grandview Heights and Marble Cliff were as ideally sited as their names imply. Indeed, local legend has it that the former acquired its name when a developer's wife exclaimed over the "grand view" from the bluff above the Scioto.

Those subdividing land in the 1910s and 1920s followed suit. Charles Johnson platted neighborhoods along both the Scioto and Olentangy rivers, adjacent to Big Walnut Creek and the Columbus Country Club, and next to Bexley. King Thompson gave location careful consideration when planning Upper Arlington. His prospectus for what he termed "The Country Club District" said he wanted to give residents "all the charm of country living and yet not deprive them of city conveniences." The south and west sides he "at once eliminated as being undesirable locations for development of this type." Land east of Bexley lacked the knolls, ravines, and trees he thought desirable, and though he found the high land north of the city attractive, he could not acquire a large enough tract close enough to downtown. However, the Miller farm, which he finally chose, covered close to one thousand acres, was on high land with hills, dales, ravines, and knolls, only three and one-half miles from the city's business center, and served by streetcars so residents would "have very little difficulty in obtaining desirable servants."[24] Thus land development in Columbus covered a fan-shaped area from northwest to east, and the south and west sides by 1970 were still less well developed and contained no exclusive neighborhoods.

The location of the first suburban communities set Columbus's development patterns. Developers' use of restrictive covenants, particularly in the 1910s and 1920s when close to 40 percent of the subdivisions were platted, continued those patterns. Activities in the postwar years cemented them in place. When one examines all the subdivisions platted through 1970 together as a group, the importance of the restrictions becomes clear. Seventy-five percent established a building setback line to limit crowding and to provide a more uniform street appearance. One hundred sixty subdivisions (47.7 percent) permitted only single-family homes or one-to-four-family units on all lots. Thirty others specified a particular land use that varied with the lot's location: generally single family on interior lots and multifamily or commercial along major streets. One hundred seventy-two subdivisions (51.3 percent) specified a minimum construction cost for all structures, and 21.2 percent set a minimum size. Developers applied some sort of race restriction to 30.5 percent of their subdivisions. Many subdivisions, of course, had more than one type of restriction. Altogether, only fifty-three subdivisions (15.8 percent) had no restrictions at all imposed by their developers, while only twenty subdivisions (6.0 percent) had a building setback line as their sole development restriction.

As early as the 1910s, and continuing through the 1960s, developers of the most desirable or exclusive areas imposed both more, and more stringent, deed covenants. Thompson actively used them as a selling point for Upper Arlington, claiming that he gave no other question "more thought and consideration" than the self-perpetuating restrictions. Homeowners would benefit by "protective restrictions on land, adopted with a view to preserving the residential character of the neighborhood and to safeguarding the owner in the use and enjoyment of his property."[25] In later years developers gave similar protection—though at a much lower level—to moderate income households buying modest new houses in outlying areas.

If real estate developers directly determined land use in the suburbs, they indirectly affected it elsewhere. Long after early suburban communities, such as those developed by Charles Johnson that did not become separately incorporated suburbs, joined the city and ceased to be "suburban" in location, their land use remained fixed. If they had been platted in or after the 1910s, restrictive covenants in the deeds determined their future as well as their present. Older areas of the city, however, where once-fine homes for the wealthy had been built on lots platted in the 1870s or 1880s, were not so protected. In later years, if the city's zoning code or variances to it permitted, property owners could convert spacious Victorian homes to commercial use or subdivide them into flats or rooming houses, thus changing the character of the neighborhoods. The result for the city's spatial structure was a wide band of homogeneous, largely single-family, neighborhoods surrounding a dense, highly varied area around the business district.

Although the neighborhoods within that outer band were internally fairly homogeneous, there was wide variation among them—again reflecting developers' restrictions. In the northwest suburbs, the north side, and the east side (except Whitehall) were middle to upper income neighborhoods. On the south, west, and northeast sides—and in Whitehall—much more moderate income families lived. In those areas land developers had either imposed fewer restrictions or explicitly targeted low-to-moderate income home buyers.

Developers also affected the racial distribution of Columbus. The city's initial African-American population was concentrated on the near east side. Areas developed in the 1910s, and especially the 1920s, had covenants prohibiting black entry. Thus, the minority population could expand into unrestricted areas only as it grew through immigration and natural increase. After *Shelley* v. *Kraemer*, income-based covenants and FHA mortgage policies kept African-Americans out of new developments. Consequently, stopped by

Alum Creek and exclusive Bexley from expanding due east, the minority area first expanded straight north into the oldest part of the northeast side. Later, it expanded south as well, and then jumped downtown to settle in the west side's bottoms. Restrictive development or lending policies prevented movement elsewhere.

A Matter of Taste

Real estate developers used restrictive covenants most often for business purposes, but they sometimes used them for more personal reasons as well, expressing their own idiosyncracies. Through deed restrictions some developers defined or protected their own residential environments. Although a general provision requiring landscaping of the lots was not uncommon, deeds for some northeast Columbus subdivisions specifically prohibited the planting of catalpa trees.[26] In the postwar era of Levittown-style mass building and FHA financing, some soon-to-be Upper Arlington subdivisions forbade one-story homes or "bungalows." George Urlin's Urlin Terrace subdivision in Grandview allowed no one to build a home closer to the street than Urlin's. Thus, some developers imposed their own preferences on the subdivisions they platted.

Worthington's Frank Medick epitomized the use of deed restrictions to define the developer's personal environment. Medick was a Columbus businessman whose company manufactured and sold photography mounts.[27] In the late 1910s and 1920s, he developed a side interest in real estate and began actively buying and selling both single lots and blocks of lots in several developing subdivisions in Columbus and its suburbs. Late in the 1920s, while living on Columbus's north side, Medick purchased about ninety acres of farmland between the Village of Worthington and the Olentangy River. He then built a stone hunting lodge as a weekend retreat near the center of this tract on the highest level place. Ten years later he turned his retreat into a proper home with an impressive two-and-a-half-story stone addition. On its hill above a creek, the house resembled a moat-surrounded castle from which its owner could survey his domain.

Shrewd businessman that he was, Medick knew suburban growth would come to Worthington. He platted two upper income subdivisions in the village just before World War II. In the 1940s he had his riverside land surveyed and marked off in irregular lots of one-half to one acre. He dedicated his entrance drive as a public right-of-way and then transferred title of the entire tract to Medick Estates Incorporated, which would also be the subdivision's name. Medick was determined to maintain his splendid surroundings as the lots were sold between 1952 and the mid-1960s, however. He established building setback lines that protected his unobstructed view of the river. Deed restrictions required that a representative of Medick Estates Incorporated approve the architectural style of all homes. Moreover, no home could be taller than Frank Medick's. Construction cost minimums increased over the period from $25,000 in the 1950s to $40,000 in the mid-1960s, except on the lots closest to Medick's home, where $50,000 was the minimum. Covenants prohibited nonwhites except as servants. They also prohibited all animals other than domestic dogs and cats as pets and forbade kennels for housing or raising dogs as well. Although the restrictions may have made his lots more marketable, this was not Medick's major concern; real estate was neither his principal interest nor major source of income.[28] What the restrictions primarily did was protect Medick's own environment and impose his preferences on his neighbors.

The Northeast Anomaly

Whether for business or personal reasons, to a considerable extent land developers shaped the growing city. The locations and corresponding restrictions of their subdivisions determined in part who would live where. On one occasion, however, factors beyond the developers' control limited the effectiveness of their efforts. Part of the northeast side, which stands in contrast to many of the general patterns noted, attests to this.

A three-mile strip in the northeast, containing twenty-nine subdivisions platted between the late 1890s and 1960, exhibits the pattern of land development discussed in chapter 2 and this chapter. Twenty of the subdivisions were outside municipal boundaries when platted and thus not subject to public controls. Six of those within the city at the time of platting were recorded after World

War II and came under the jurisdiction of the Columbus zoning code's subdivision standards.

Examination of the platting activity through the 1920s reveals both an increasing level of development and increasing use of restrictive covenants. Given that more than three-quarters of the lots (78.7 percent) in this section of the northeast were platted before 1930, the restrictions on those lots could have set the tone and character of the entire area, as they did in other parts of Columbus or the suburbs. As they did elsewhere in the city, developers used restrictions to limit ownership or occupancy to white Americans. Construction cost minimums, which ranged from $3,500 to $7,500, were middle or upper middle income in intent. Single-family homes were generally specified, except along Cleveland Avenue, the major arterial. Thus up to 1930 developers in this part of the city attempted to create a white, upper middle income residential area.

Between the stock market crash and the end of World War II, however, real estate development ceased in this section of the city. (It continued, though at a reduced level, in those suburbs that had already established themselves.) The ten subdivisions platted after the war contained only 21.3 percent of the total lots in this section of the northeast. Deeds for only five imposed construction cost minimums, some as low as $4,000 or $6,000. This much more modest level of development would have seemed very out of place had the land developers of the pre-1930 subdivisions actually realized their aims. But factors they could not control had limited their effectiveness.

In the 1910s and 1920s, when developers discussed the use of deed restrictions, they also urged adoption of municipal zoning codes. They suggested that their colleagues annex their subdivisions to the city in order to gain protection of the city zoning ordinance, for they knew the impact of restrictions would be lessened if a restricted subdivision were surrounded by or adjacent to unrestricted ones.[29] The theory was that municipal zoning codes would apply on a public basis the same level of development standards that deed restrictions applied on a private basis, but zoning would cover a much larger area. Applying to several contiguous subdivisions, public controls would provide greater protection.

In many parts of Columbus and its suburbs the theory worked as expected. Subdivisions were annexed to a city, then zoned to match the deed restrictions. Indeed, Upper Arlington's first zoning ordinance essentially codified into law what King Thompson had written into the deeds. On the northeast side of Columbus, however, several subdivisions, containing almost 30 percent of the lots platted, never annexed to the city. As those subdivisions never came under municipal controls, public planning did not take over where private planning ended.[30] Developers' inability to effect annexation and subsequent coverage by municipal zoning codes meant that they could not perpetuate their standards. When the deed restrictions expired, lot owners could build whatever they liked.

The second factor that developers could not control or prepare for was the drop in building activity that accompanied the Great Depression.[31] In Columbus, the valuation for building permits issued had steadily increased through 1925, then it leveled off.[32] In 1930, the first full year after the stock market crash, total permit valuation was 19.3 percent of the pre-crash amount. At the depths of the depression in 1933, it was 2.85 percent of the pre-crash figure. Rather than capitalizing on the 1920s' boom, developers in this stretch of the northeast platted their subdivisions just in time for the bust. Examination of the entire metropolitan area indicates that Columbus grew first to the east and the north. By the time the area between was ripe for development, the depression had hit, halting the process.

The result was that much land lay platted — some with restrictions — but without buildings. Not until after the Second World War were many of these lots, platted twenty to forty years earlier, actually developed. And they were developed under the restrictions that had been applied at their platting — if such restrictions had not yet expired. Standards that would have been comfortably middle income or higher in the 1920s allowed much more modest homes in the 1950s. Hence, the lower middle income provisions of the subdivisions platted in the 1950s proved to be in keeping with the level at which those platted much earlier actually developed.

Up though the 1920s, developers on the northeast side, like those elsewhere in Columbus, had attempted to create an upper middle income community through the use of deed restrictions. Inability to control annexation or the actual timing of construction partially negated their efforts by 1960. This area stands as an exception, however—a victim of poor timing. For the most part, developers were much more successful in determining where and when the city grew and who lived where.

For over seventy years, then, Columbus area real estate developers played a major part in shaping the city. They did not operate in a vacuum, of course. Both the city and its suburbs adopted zoning codes. How those codes were designed and administered, especially after World War II, also affected the metropolitan area's spatial and social structure. Still, though the private developers were not the only participants in the land use game, they had largely created the playing field. As the next two chapters show, municipal officials defended some areas of the field differently than others.

FIVE

Planning and Property Values: Zoning in Columbus, 1955–1970

Under the city's first zoning code, the Columbus City Council and the Board of Zoning Adjustment had increased both the density and intensity of land use in the city, particularly in the older residential areas within three miles of the city center. In 1954 Columbus adopted a more complex code, which became effective the following year. Still, the older patterns persisted, although details varied.

The city's aggressive annexation policy from the 1950s onward meant that much more land was subject to zoning prior to development than in earlier years. However, City Council usually zoned newly annexed land for low density single-family housing, with no indication of where in the future other needed uses ought to be. Rather than deciding on the basis of some plan for the general well-being of the entire city where various types of apartments or businesses should locate, council abdicated its role of determining land use and instead waited for developers' proposals. The apartments and shopping centers were built where the developers asked to build them. Meanwhile, residential quality in older parts of the city continued to deteriorate, as parking lots now appeared among the dense and varied land uses.

Guidance in planning and zoning was available, had the city sought to use it, for several planning studies completed in the 1950s spoke to issues of land use and zoning. Moreover, the focus of city planning itself had broadened since zoning's early years to take on a regional dimension. But Columbus adopted only the form, not the substance, of such planning—a condition mirrored by other cities.

The Move to Regional Planning

As noted earlier, the profession of city planning had begun to broaden its scope, both substantively and geographically, as early as the 1920s, and continued to do so in the 1930s and 1940s. Reports of the National Resources Planning Board, and even the board's very existence, indicated a growing awareness of the importance of planning.[1] After World War II the federal government aided that process.

Realizing that years of depression and war had put American cities at risk, Congress passed the Housing Act of 1949. The Housing Act of 1949 addressed two major issues: the shortage of available, affordable housing, and the redevelopment of blighted urban areas. Under the act, the federal government would provide some funding to city housing or redevelopment agencies to address these issues.[2] Cities proposed redevelopment projects and applied to the federal government for funding. Redevelopment projects had to conform to a general plan for the locality as a whole to gain approval. Thus the federal government explicitly mandated planning. However, the act defined neither locality nor general plan precisely. Nor did it require that such a plan be adopted by ordinance and carry the force of law. The act gave its administrators responsibility for determining if and when the planning provisions were met.[3] As had been the case twenty years earlier with the Department of Commerce's model Standard City Planning Enabling Act and Standard Zoning Enabling Act, planning was part of the process but it did not necessarily have to produce a legally adopted, enforceable plan.

Five years later Congress upped the ante with the Housing Act of 1954. The 1954 act addressed the same two issues as its predecessor: housing provision and redevelopment. It also included neighborhood conservation and rehabilitation as possible approaches to redevelopment. And under guidelines set by the Housing and Home Finance Agency, it required a "long-range, general plan and such means of carrying it out as a program of public improvements, a zoning ordinance, and subdivision regulations."[4] Moreover, the federal government would provide some funds to assist with the planning itself under Section 701 of the act. Neither the 1949 nor the 1954 act explicitly defined the geographical area to be included in the plan. However, the congressional subcommittee report on which the 1954 legislation was based conditioned receipt of federal funds on continuing efforts toward regional cooperation at the state or metropolitan level. Section 701 funds to help pay for technical planning assistance for cities and towns would be available to states or to "metropolitan area governmental planning agencies." Thus, cities were expected to look beyond their own borders and coordinate their efforts with other jurisdictions in their area.[5]

In Ohio, Franklin County was ready. In 1943 the elected Board of Commissioners of Franklin County created the Franklin County Planning Commission, a countywide planning agency. The Board of Commissioners remembered the housing shortages and other problems that had followed the First World War and hoped a countywide planning commission could ease the adjustment to a peacetime society the second time around. But state law limited the jurisdiction of such a planning commission to unincorporated territory within the county. It had no role in the various municipalities. Recognizing this weakness, in May 1950 the Franklin County Planning Commission disbanded and was replaced by the Franklin County *Regional* Planning Commission (FCRPC). The FCRPC included as members representatives from the county, the townships, the City of Columbus, and the smaller cities and villages as well.[6]

The reconstituted commission was primarily concerned with issues of regional importance that might cross jurisdictional boundaries, such as water and sewer service, storm-water management, and transportation. But it also dealt with matters involving land use. It served the county as the official agency for enforcing subdivision regulations in unincorporated areas. Moreover, it prepared a countywide zoning plan designating land use and density of development outside the county's municipalities. The importance of zoning the unincorporated territory in metropolitan areas had been noted as early as the late 1920s, but cities lacked the authority to control land use beyond their borders.[7] However, a county-level regional planning agency could prepare a zoning plan that covered all the unincorporated land. Thus, the FCRPC prepared a zoning plan for all territory not covered by an existing municipal zoning code. Residents of each township in the county had to vote individually to accept the zoning plan for their own territory, but once it was adopted, the FCRPC would administer the plan, as it did subdivision regulations. Lack of local township-level administration, as well as resistance in rural areas to the very idea of land use controls, caused many townships to vote against adopting the county zoning plan. Consequently, it was not in force in much of the county's unincorporated territory. Still, the plan existed on paper and could provide guidance for those officials wishing to use it. Finally, in addition to its official county functions, the regional planning commission was available on a contract basis to perform planning services for the various municipalities in the county.[8]

As an organization, the regional planning commission was a voluntary agency. City, village, and township officials could choose not to participate. And except for those functions it performed as administrator for the county, the FCRPC's actions carried no force of law. Its plans and proposals were recommendations only.[9] Nevertheless, it provided a vehicle for communication among jurisdictions and a structure for planning on a metropolitan basis. Moreover, it would meet the requirements of the 1954 Housing Act, which it preceded by four years.

Planning in the city itself was also reenergized in the 1950s. City Council had created the first City Planning Commission in the 1920s as authorized—but not required—by the state. Council had charged it with drafting the zoning ordinance, which it did. The City Charter adopted in 1914, however, contained no provision for a planning commission and thus did not spell out its other duties and responsibilities; and later charter amendments did not rectify the situation. Consequently, the commission's powers were the limited ones council had granted it under the state's municipal code. In ensuing years it had effectively ceased to function, since creation of the zoning code had been its major purpose. In 1953 City Council reestablished the City Planning Commission by ordinance and broadened the scope of its activities to those permitted by the Revised Code of Ohio. Not only was it to review, and possibly revise, the zoning code, in the future it could also review subdivision plats for conformance with regulations and prepare capital improvements programs to provide for such municipal needs as highways, water and sewer service, fire stations, and parks. The appointed commission could also appoint or employ the staff necessary to perform its duties. This it did and those staff members became city employees. Thus two different, though related, entities performed different elements of the planning process. The nonprofessional, citizen-volunteer, appointed Planning Commission established policy and made recommendations to City Council on specific planning-related issues. The city's paid professional staff of city planners provided technical assistance to the City Planning Commission, City Council, and the Board of Zoning Adjustment and collected information to assist those bodies in their deliberations. The professional staff also handled the day-to-day administrative tasks. This was the norm in other cities as well.[10] Then, on those irregular occasions when a major planning effort was required—such as producing a new or revised master plan, or rewriting land use regulations—cities would often contract with a consultant for the project.[11]

Regional planning could now begin in metropolitan Columbus, as the structure was in place at both the city and county levels. With the FCRPC as the formal applicant, the city and county planning commissions applied for, and received, one of the first federal grants in Ohio for planning under Section 701 of the Housing Act of 1954.[12] The city and county jointly supported studies and reports on water and sewer needs and storm-water management. And they commissioned the planning consulting firm Harland Bartholomew and Associates of St. Louis to conduct studies for the preparation of a master plan for the entire metropolitan area.

Representatives from the Bartholomew firm set up shop in FCRPC offices and went to work. Between May 1954 and January 1956 they produced seven reports.[13] Examining economic base, demographics, land use, transportation, schools, parks, housing, and the central business district, the reports collectively described the present state of the metropolitan area, made projections about its future, and offered recommendations. The consultants pulled all their work together in February 1957 in *A Summary Report: The Master Plan: Columbus Urban Area*.[14] The studies and concluding *Summary Report* effectively satisfied housing act requirements for a general plan for the locality and enabled the city to request federal funds for housing and renewal projects. And although the city and county did not formally adopt a master plan, the studies and reports were there to assist officials of both the county and the various municipalities in matters of land use or other concerns.

Harland Bartholomew, founder and principal of the consulting firm, was a nationally recognized authority on land use and zoning. In 1932 he had published a major study on land use to guide municipal officials throughout the United States in conducting zoning matters. *Urban Land Uses* presented the results of extensive research in twenty-two cities of different types, ranging in population from 1,500 to 300,000.[15] The study indicated how much land was actually being used for such purposes as single-family homes, apartments, commercial structures, industries, public buildings, and streets. Bartholomew hoped that city officials would use his study to determine the appropriate amount of land for their city size and type to allot to different zoning categories, for he realized some cities had greatly over- or underzoned certain land uses.[16]

The conclusion of *Urban Land Uses* noted that the first necessity for the preparation of a zoning ordinance, or the revision of an existing ordinance, was an accurate survey of land uses.[17] In line with this, he conducted such a survey as part of his 1954 studies in Franklin County. The *Report Upon Economic Base, Population, and General Land Uses* examined actual land uses in Columbus and compared them with the existing zoning provisions. In Columbus, Bartholomew and Associates found some problems, observing: "It is evident from the present arrangement of population and land uses in the Columbus urban area that the city has not grown entirely satisfactorily in the past, even though it compares favorably with most other American communities of similar size."[18] The city's zoning ordinance was essentially unchanged from its original. The amount of land zoned for both commercial and industrial uses was too large, given the economic structure of the city and its population. There was too much commercially zoned street frontage for it all to be developed profitably. The problem of strip commercial zoning along the major streets was aggravated by having a large commercial district south of the central business district and numerous spot commercial zones. The report could find no reasonable justification for the total amount of commercial zoning. Nor was there justification, in any planning sense, for the industrial zoning of a large area southeast of downtown that was almost entirely residential in actual use.[19]

The consultants recognized that other incorporated municipalities in the greater urban area—such as Bexley, Upper Arlington, and Whitehall—had their own zoning ordinances and the City of Columbus could do little to determine land use outside its own borders. Still they felt a major revision of Columbus's zoning code was in order: "In addition to being poorly related to a comprehensive land use plan, the city ordinance is inadequate and largely obsolete. While revision of the text has been under consideration for some time, this would be ineffectual without a complete realignment of [zoning] districts and district boundaries."[20]

A revised ordinance would also have to be administered carefully. If properly drawn to meet the city's needs, in the future it would require few changes or amendments. This was important, for the report noted that public confidence in both planning and zoning would be greatly undermined by "haphazard, ineffective or discriminatory zoning administration."[21]

Variety under the New Code: 1956–1965

Simultaneous with the Bartholomew report, in the mid-1950s the Columbus City Council replaced the zoning code with a new code whose provisions, though more complex and explicit, were in many respects much like the original ordinance's. City Council had recodified all the city's ordinances in 1952, making the zoning ordinance of 1923 and all its subsequent amendments part of the Code of the City of Columbus. Then in 1954 council supplemented the Code of 1952 by enacting Chapter 47, "Zoning,"[22] which replaced the amended ordinance of 1923.

The new code was more complex and less ambiguous than its predecessor. It provided four classes of residential use: three for single-family homes and the fourth for one-to-four-family units. The R-1 and R-2 single-family districts both specified lot and floor area minimums and lot frontage minimums, while the R-3 district specified lot area and frontage limits but no floor area. The R-4 zone (one-to-four families) also specified a minimum lot frontage and area per family unit. These revised designations made more explicit what had been provided in the original ordinance's five area districts. Similar lot area and frontage provisions affected the apartment zones. Where one general apartment use designation previously had employed different area or height classes to determine density, the new ordinance had three separate and distinct apartment zones, each with its own height and area specifications.

The new ordinance had four commercial categories, corresponding to the previously amended type A, B, C, and D commercial zones, as well as a separate Central Business District (CB) zone and a Civic Center (CC) designation. Two manufacturing districts, light (LM) and heavy (HM), corresponded to the original first and second industrial districts. In addition, council provided a new category, parking, with different classes for private and public parking of automobiles. The original ordinance had contained no provision for parking lots, nor had it required developers to provide parking for a proposed building's occupants.

The new code had a larger range of both area and height restrictions. Council replaced the previous five area districts with six, ranging from unrestricted to 7,200 square feet per family. Each area district corresponded to one or more residential or apartment categories. Since only the residential and apartment zones specified height limits by definition, the new ordinance retained four height categories for other uses but changed the maximums to 35, 60, 110, and 200 feet. The new ordinance's greater range of lot minimums and height maximums allowed the city greater specificity.

The zoning ordinance of 1923 had created a hierarchy of land uses, with single-family homes at the top and heavy industry at the bottom. Higher uses had been permitted in lower classifications but not the reverse. Thus single-family homes could exist anywhere but industrial uses could occur only where specifically designated; apartments could be built in apartment, commercial, or industrial districts but not in single-family districts. This was very common in the 1920s, when zoning was in its infancy, for it minimized the number of nonconforming uses when applying zoning to areas that were already built up. It also was believed to provide sufficient protection to residential areas while minimizing interference with property rights. Single-family neighborhoods were protected from all intrusions and apartments from nearby commercial or industrial uses but the property owner wishing to put a house or apartment in a commercial or industrial district could do so.

The revised code of 1954 changed this, as use categories were no longer totally hierarchical. The four residence classes and three apartment classes were each hierarchical within their categories, but the categories themselves were exclusive. Thus, single-family homes could be in one-to-four-family residence districts but neither single-family nor one-to-four-family residences were permitted in apartment zones. Both residence and apartment uses were allowed in commercial districts, however, and apartments could be built in the CB zone, subject to height and lot area requirements. Also, the code allowed commercial uses in the manufacturing zones but not residences and apartments. Columbus and other cities had initially specified hierarchical land use categories on the theory that lower use districts (such as commercial or industrial areas) could not be harmed by nearby residences. But the reverse proved not to be so. The residential environment of such homes in lower use districts—generally occupied by a city's poorest—was doomed to decay. Moreover, infrastructure was not always appropriate. Such problems were apparent by the 1940s and 1950s. Thus, as cities revised their codes, they more often specified exclusive use categories. Columbus only partially followed the trend.

The new ordinance contained an extensive list of definitions to ensure clarity about the meaning of such terms as lot, dwelling, and floor area. It also included an alphabetical list of more than 1,700 different specific uses, indicating in which zone each was permitted. As under the old zoning code, some uses—such as amusement parks, dog pounds, and swimming pools—council allowed only by special permit. Others—including glue manufacture, animal slaughtering, and trailer courts—council prohibited altogether.

All in all, the new ordinance provided much greater clarity and specificity than its predecessor, thus meeting some of the concerns of Bartholomew's report. However, the new ordinance did not deal with one major criticism, as zoning districts were not redrawn to accompany the revised code. Instead, the new ordinance contained a conversion table, indicating which new designation corresponded to which old one. Thus the former A-1-A residence district became the new R-1. The former C-1, C-2, and C-3 height and area apartment zones were all included in the new AR-1 designation. All other categories were similarly relabeled.

Although council amended the revised ordinance to deal with unforeseen circumstances or administrative procedures during the next fifteen years, the basic structure of the ordinance remained unchanged except for the addition of some new use classes. After only a year, council found it necessary to add three additional residential districts: suburban residential, rural residential, and restricted rural residential. These provided for minimum lot sizes of up to 20,000 square feet. Council also added another apartment district and an apartment-office (AO) zone (an entirely new, mixed-use category). A few months later, in April 1956, council added still another residential district, this one with minimum lots of one acre. In 1967 council added a low-density apartment district, with a larger minimum lot area per household than existed at the time. One final new category—a Planned Community District, providing for multiple uses within a single area—was added in 1970.

The zoning code in force in 1970 contained many more categories and classes than its predecessor and the categories were more explicitly defined, but in effect the two were similar. Council had revised the text of the ordinance but had not realigned the districts or their boundaries. Consequently any inconsistencies in 1923 between actual land uses and their mapped code designations remained in 1970. Table 5.1 shows the increase in categories of land use under the new zoning code.

Although the city to which the zoning ordinance of 1954 applied was much larger than that covered by the first code, the pattern of allowing increased variety and intensity of land use in older areas continued. Not surprisingly, City Council and zoning board members found themselves facing more than three times as many requests for a zoning change as in the previous ten years. In the first decade of the revised code, council and the BZA issued 632 decisions.[23] But although the code had changed somewhat, its administration did not; three times as many requests were granted as denied. Property owners made almost twice as many requests of the zoning board (65.7 percent), however, than of City

Table 5.1
Land use classifications of the Columbus zoning code, 1923–1970

1923	1948–49	1954–56	1966–70
Dwelling house	A-1-A	LRR	LRR
	A-1-B	RRR	RRR
	B-1	RR	RR
		SR	SR
		R-1	R-1
		R-2	R-2
		R-3	R-3
		R-4	R-4
Apartment	Apartment	AR-1	AR-1
		AR-2	AR-2
		AR-3	AR-3
		AR-4	AR-4
		AR-0	AR-0
			LD-AR
Commercial	A business	C-1	C-1
	B business	C-2	C-2
	C business	C-3	C-3
	D business	C-4	C-4
		CB	CB
		CC	CC
First industrial	First industrial	LM	LM
Second industrial	Second industrial	HM	HM
		P-1	P-1
		P-2	P-2
			PCD

Council (34.3 percent). This mirrored the situation of the original ordinance's first decade rather than the immediately preceding twenty years (Table 5.2).

As before, requests were not geographically balanced throughout the city (Figure 5.1). The northeast section of the city contained the fewest, which was not surprising since the city surrounded several small unannexed parcels of land in the northeast. But despite the presence of two separately incorporated suburban municipalities on the east side, that side contained more requests for some type of zoning change than any other. Also as before, over half the total requests involved land within three miles of the city center—despite the city's greatly expanded borders.

Property owners continued to request variances from building setback lines to erect or alter their buildings, and the BZA contin-

Table 5.2
Requests granted by council and the BZA, 1956–1970

	1956–65	1966–70
Requests decided by council	217	172
Council approved rate	70.0%	80.2%
Requests decided by BZA	415	224
BZA approval rate	74.9%	87.5%
Total percentage granted	73.3%	84.3%
Total number of decisions	632	396

Note: Both approval rates and percentage granted are calculated as a proportion of known decisions made, not total changes requested.

ued to grant them. The zoning board also granted lot area variances, although less often than setback requests. Two new types of variance request appeared because of revisions in the code, as property owners found provisions affecting signs and parking burdensome. The new code exempted existing buildings from the parking requirements, but individuals building new commercial structures had to provide off-street parking for both employees and customers as did those building houses and apartments for residents. Those building new structures as well as those converting existing buildings to different uses often requested permission to provide fewer parking spaces than the code required, especially in older parts of the city. Property owners also wanted to change the way they used their land. Thus they asked for, and generally received, permission to initiate or expand nonconforming uses (Table 5.3).

By the type and location of use changes they permitted, council and the BZA continued their practices of the previous thirty years. They allowed increasing density and variety of use in the older residential areas. In the late 1950s, hospitals on the near north and west sides sought to expand their facilities. Both were located in apartment or row house districts, and granting their requests meant making fourteen changes from a use providing housing to a semipublic or institutional use, thus lessening the residential nature of an already mixed area. At the same time, within three miles of downtown on the north and east sides, council or the BZA granted fifteen requests to change apartments to rooming houses,

142 • Planning and Property Values

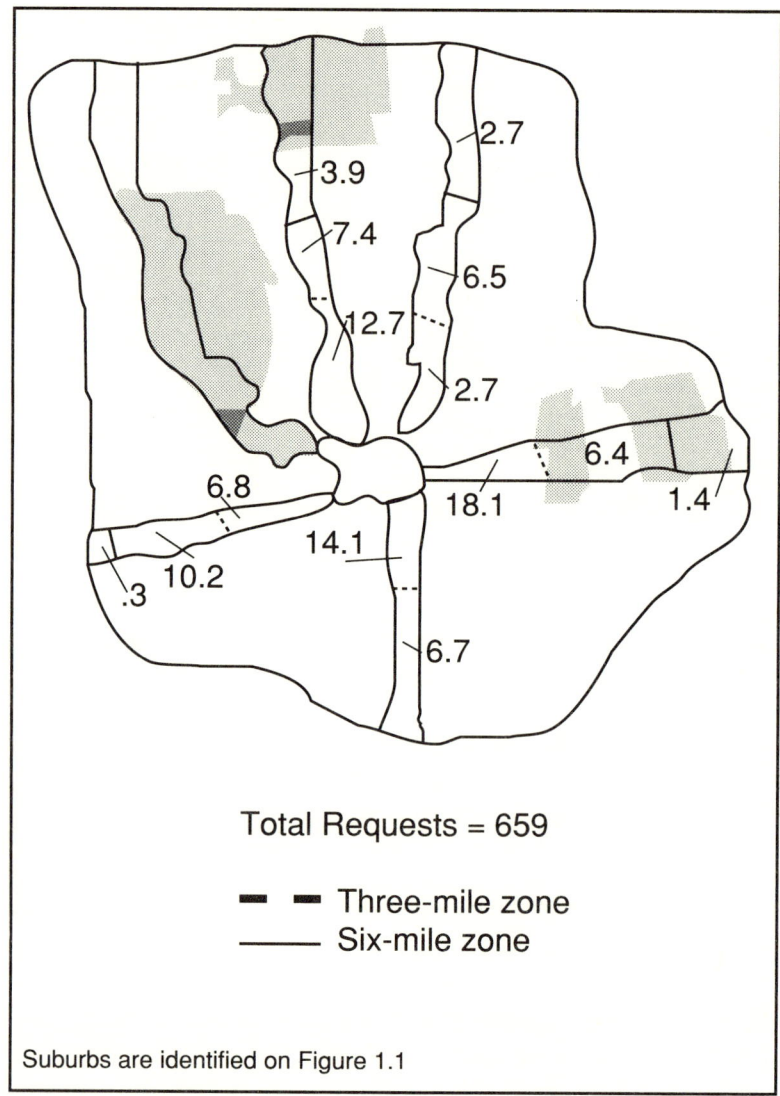

Figure 5.1 Percentage of requests for rezoning or variance by location, 1956–1965

Table 5.3
Percentage of each type variance granted, 1956–1970

Action	1956–65 %	1956–65 (n)	1966–70 %	1966–70 (n)
Setback for main building	71.9	64	92.5	80
Setback for addition	90.0	40	94.1	17
Setback for accessory	100.0	16	100.0	12
Height	86.4	22	100.0	27
Lot size or area	63.1	84	81.4	43
Floor area: main building	25.0	4		0
Floor area: accessory building		0		0
Begin nonconforming use	73.7	167	72.7	11
Expand nonconforming use	85.7	42	95.5	22
Alter nonconforming use	100.0	7	93.1	29
Special permit	100.0	21	100.0	11
Sign provisions	66.7	12	88.9	9
Parking requirements	75.0	12	83.3	42
Total requests		491		303

Note: (n) is the total of each type of action requested; the percentage is the proportion of each type of request granted.

the code provision for which allowed greater population density per building lot.

Although there was a net increase in commercially zoned land, at least some property owners felt their land could be better used otherwise. Consequently, council or the zoning board permitted thirty-three such commercially zoned parcels to be rezoned for apartments. On the other hand, still more land became potentially commercial, as council or the board granted fifty-three changes from apartment or row house to commercial use and another nineteen from single-family to commercial. As before, more commercial changes occurred within the three-mile zone than outside it (Table 5.4).

Taken as a whole, the number and type of changes permitted during the first ten years of the revised zoning ordinance continued the patterns established under the old one. Single-family neighborhoods remained single-family although the major streets adjacent to them experienced some land use changes. However, the older, once-residential areas closer to the city center, which had become increasingly mixed and dense under the first code, became even more so. At the same time, decisions by council and the zoning board increased the profit-making potential of lots in those areas.

Table 5.4
Changes to commercial use by distance from the city center, 1956–1970

Distance	1956–65		1966–70	
	%	(n)	%	(n)
Less than 3 miles	48.0	36	63.0	34
3 to 6 miles	33.3	25	18.5	10
More than 6 miles	18.7	14	18.5	10
Total	100.0	75	100.0	54

The Patchwork Is Completed: 1966–1970

The final five years continued patterns already established despite one noticeable change from prior eras. Property owners generally obtained their requests, requests that were designed to increase their property values. Those requests also increased the density and variety of land use in older parts of the city. The notable exception was a sharp increase in requests affecting undeveloped land on the far northeast side. Here, too, zoning actions increased profitability, although they did not alter the character of an established area.

Council and the zoning board made a total of 396 decisions between 1966 and 1970.[24] The Board of Zoning Adjustment again accounted for more zoning actions than City Council, and as before, regardless of which body made the decision, the answer was overwhelmingly affirmative (Table 5.2). The distribution of requests changed from earlier periods, however. Although the north side regained preeminence, there was also an increase in requests on the south side, where property owners requested one-third again as many changes as on the northeast, east, or west sides. Almost half the requests concerned property within three miles of the city center, except on the northeast side. On the northeast, requests were much more widely dispersed and the greatest number occurred at or near major intersections. Figure 5.2 illustrates the location of requests for some type of zoning action.

The pace of change in older areas continued unabated, though its nature changed a bit. By the late 1960s, some structures in the older parts of the city had been demolished. Property owners found

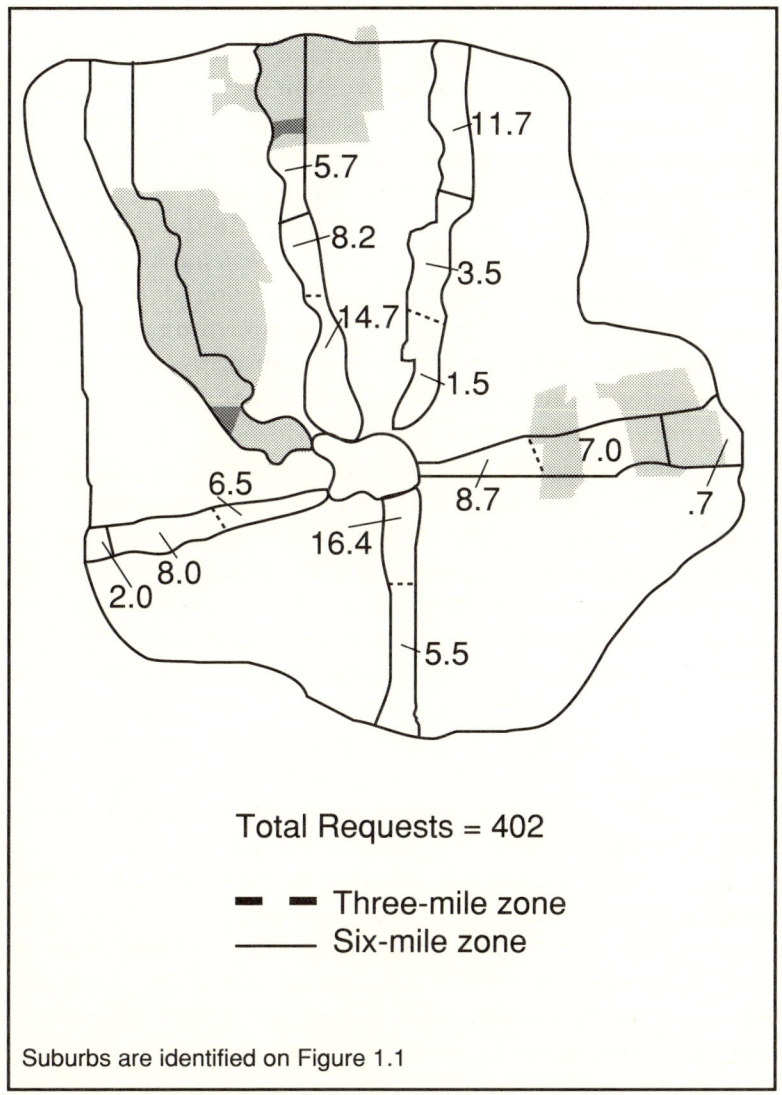

Figure 5.2 Percentage of requests for rezoning or variance by location, 1966–1970

their vacant lots too small, however, to build as densely as they would have liked. Thus they requested variances from building setback lines and from lot area provisions—variances they almost always received. The impact of the automobile was apparent as well. As noted, council had put off-street parking provisions into the revised zoning ordinance, indicating some concern with potential traffic congestion and the problem of having too many cars parked on the streets. These provisions required a given number of parking spaces for apartment and commercial buildings of various sizes,. but council's efforts were undercut by the zoning board, which generally granted exceptions to the parking provisions when asked. Rather than initiate new nonconforming uses, property owners more often wanted to expand the ones they already had or to change from one nonconforming use to another, and council and the board acceded to their desires (Table 5.3).

The greatest number of setback variances, lot area variances, parking exceptions, and nonconforming uses occurred in the older dense, mixed-use areas that had once been residential. Except in the northeast part of the city, use changes also tended to be in these areas. It had been the city's practice to zone newly annexed land, on the northeast side or elsewhere, for one of the low density single-family residence categories, with no indication of where neighborhood or community facilities should be built when needed. By the late 1960s, development had reached the farthest three miles of the northeast side. Having zoned this land for single-family use, City Council waited for property owners or developers to propose an alternative use, rather than deciding in advance which use should go where. Subsequently, council rezoned five single-family tracts for apartments and eight for commercial use in the far northeast part of the city in response to developers' proposals. Still in older areas it was business as usual as council or the zoning board permitted forty parcels zoned for apartments to be used commercially (Table 5.4). Apparently making some effort to provide parking space for the commercial spots, council enacted twenty-one apartment to parking rezonings. Many of the newly created parking lots, however, were on the north side, just south of the Ohio State University and near Batelle Memorial Institute, a large research facility.[25]

The general impact of the last five years of zoning actions was further deterioration of the residential environment of older areas. Commercial structures and parking lots joined the nonresidential uses permitted during the preceding decades. At the same time, setback and lot area variances permitted construction of larger multifamily structures than the code allowed. Instead of serving the residents of the older areas, council and the zoning board served the property owners by allowing them the most profitable use of their land.

Land use patterns in Columbus in 1970 exhibited similarities to those in the unzoned city of 1923 although there were some major differences. Downtown remained a center of retail and office commercial activity. But empty buildings and warehouses joined a smaller number of manufactories in the industrial districts as both industrial technology and the city's economic base changed. Single-family and duplex residential areas developed after the 1910s maintained their character, but the single-family homes on the arterials adjoining them had in many cases been converted to or replaced by commercial structures or apartments. Also, before 1955 those apartment residents and business employees or customers driving cars parked them on the street near their destinations. Thus the major streets were bordered by parked cars, flanked by storefronts; the residential areas behind were visible only at the intersections. Commercial and apartment buildings built under the code of 1954, however, had off-street parking lots in front of, beside, or behind the buildings, thus lessening overall building density.

All major arterial frontage was zoned for commercial use, but, as the Bartholomew report had noted, not all of it could be so developed profitably. This accounted for some of the apartments along the major streets, as well as some vacant lots and storefronts. The arterial strip commercial situation was further complicated by large shopping centers planned or built in the 1950s adjacent to major streets several miles from downtown on the north, northeast, east, south, and west sides. By 1970 there were even larger regional malls still farther out on the north, east, and west sides as well. Land use along arterials was thus quite mixed.

Meanwhile, the older residential areas closer to the city center, most of which had been zoned for row houses or apartments, also became increasingly jumbled. Some of the original nonconforming industrial or commercial uses remained, joined by many more as well as by parking lots. Consequently, by 1970 land use downtown and in outlying neighborhoods was much as it had been fifty years earlier, but in the areas and on the arterials between, land use patterns had changed considerably.

Planning or Protecting?

One can make three generalizations about how zoning functioned in Columbus, Ohio, through 1970. The effect of that functioning was to detract from the residential character of older areas of rental housing not far from the city center. First, zoning was reactive rather than proactive, responding to requests of property owners and developers rather than directing their activities. Second, zoning actions increased lot density and intensity of use in apartment and duplex districts. Third, zoning served primarily to protect the value of private property. The result was that older residential areas where renters lived deteriorated, while single-family neighborhoods where middle income households owned and occupied their own homes remained stable. Incompatible uses proved a disincentive to the maintenance of the single-family homes that had once filled older neighborhoods near the city center. Consequently, the owners of those homes either subdivided their dwellings into apartments or sold them to apartment or commercial developers, while they themselves moved out to newer areas where their residential environment would be protected.

Zoning was reactive in that it confirmed actions already taken by developers or responded to their requests for change. Most of the physical growth of Columbus occurred during two bursts of annexation activity during the 1920s and the 1950s. When land was annexed to Columbus, City Council promptly assigned use, height, and area classifications to the new territory. In the 1920s, except along the arterials, council zoned all the new land for the least dense dwelling house category, thus specifying that only single-family homes could be built there. With two exceptions, frontage along the arterials was generally zoned for commercial use. Some sections of High Street and Broad Street frontage on the north and east sides were given the low density dwelling house designation of the subdivisions they bordered. This occurred mainly where pre-existing deed restrictions permitted only single-family homes, which had already been built to serve middle or upper middle income people. Since most land had been platted with developer-imposed deed restrictions prior to annexation to the city, the zoning code followed the developers instead of directing them. Consequently, zoning designations usually matched developers' use restrictions. By the 1950s, the practice was to zone a newly annexed tract in its entirety for very low density residential use, even along arterials. When a developer found a parcel he felt was suitable for an apartment complex or shopping center, he requested—and usually received—a rezoning for the desired use.[26]

In addition, City Council took few actions affecting specific parcels of land on its own initiative. Only twenty-five actions (1.3 percent) involved undeveloped land that council reclassified without having been asked to do so by the property owner. The zoning board, by definition a board of "adjustment," could not act on its own initiative; its purpose was to examine and respond to requests of property owners who felt that the zoning ordinance imposed a hardship on them.

The location of changes granted by council or the BZA also reflects the reactive nature of the process, for both bodies made changes where property owners requested them. During the forty-eight years examined here, 55.9 percent of the zoning decisions dealt with land within three miles of the city center. Another 36.4 percent affected land between three and six miles out. Fewer than 8 percent of the actions concerned land more than six miles from the city center (Table 5.5). Thus most rezonings and variances affected land that was already developed for one use or another.

Though most residential land in the older areas was zoned for apartments or row houses, singles and doubles actually predominated. However, variances allowed property owners to provide more multifamily units than lot dimensions allowed. This meant either building larger structures or subdividing existing single-family homes and doubles into multifamily units, increasing lot density.

At the same time, commercial rezonings detracted from the residential character of these older neighborhoods, increasing intensity of use as well as traffic, noise, and congestion. Altogether, over forty-eight years, owners of 667 parcels requested rezoning for a commercial use, most within three miles of the city center. This could lead one to conclude that the city lacked enough commercial land to meet its needs, but Bartholomew's 1954 land use survey had found much commercially zoned land either undeveloped or serving other purposes. Moreover, almost three-quarters of these requests (73.6 percent) occurred after 1954. Zoning

Table 5.5
Number of changes requested by distance from the city center

Distance	1923–30	1931–35	1936–45	1946–55	1956–65	1966–70
Less than 3 miles	210	79	62	144	359	192
More than 3 miles	140	27	45	91	300	210
Total	350	106	107	235	659	402

actions thus served commercial interests rather than the city's needs while lessening residential quality for some citizens.

Zoning actions also continued to protect property values. In newer residential areas, where middle and upper income people owned and occupied their own homes, few changes occurred. Thus, the spacious, single-family character was retained and both property values and residential quality were protected. The nature of changes granted elsewhere protected property value by increasing profitability. Of the changes granted, 12.5 percent reclassified single-family residential parcels to row house, apartment, or commercial use. Changes from row house or apartment use accounted for 26.4 and 29.0 percent, respectively. There were only 17.1 percent changes from the profitable commercial category, however. The other half of the picture is revealed when one considers the uses requested and granted, as the row house category accounted for 13.3 percent, apartments for 17.3 percent, and commercial for 35.9 percent. Moreover, these changes did not take place in outlying areas where new development and population growth were greatest.

Although changes occurred within the three-mile zone in disproportionate numbers (Table 5.5), they were not evenly distributed among sections of the city either overall or by time (Table 5.6). Particularly noticeable are the north side overall, and the east side after World War II. The preponderance of requests on the north side is understandable, given that more land was subject to zoning for a longer period of time on the north side than on any other. The east side presents a very different case. It contains less city-zoned land than the others because it includes both Bexley and Whitehall. Yet for twenty years after the Second World War the near east side led all others in requests for change. Patterns of new residential development may partially account for this. At the turn of the

Table 5.6
Changes requested by area

Corridor	1923–30 %	(n)	1931–35 %	(n)	1936–45 %	(n)	1946–55 %	(n)
North	32.6	114	38.7	41	35.5	38	23.4	55
Northeast	12.3	43	9.4	10	14.0	15	13.6	32
East	16.0	56	7.5	8	23.4	25	31.5	74
South	17.4	61	17.0	18	11.2	12	8.1	19
West	21.7	76	27.4	29	15.9	17	23.4	55
Total	100.0	350	100.0	106	100.0	107	100.0	235

Corridor	1956–65 %	(n)	1966–70 %	(n)	Corridor total %	(n)
North	24.1	159	28.6	115	28.1	522
Northeast	12.0	79	16.7	67	13.2	246
East	25.8	170	16.4	66	21.5	399
South	20.8	137	21.9	88	18.0	335
West	17.3	114	16.4	66	19.2	357
Total	100.0	659	100.0	402	100.0	1859

century, the near east side was home to some of the wealthiest families in Columbus. By the 1920s, however, such upper income residential suburbs as Bexley and Upper Arlington were attracting the wealthy. At the same time, the zoning code of 1923 classified much of the east side south of Broad Street as an apartment zone, making it less desirable to its original inhabitants. By the 1950s and 1960s owners of once-grand homes that they had subdivided into apartments requested permission to convert their properties again to rooming houses or commercial use.[27]

Over almost fifty years public land use controls affected the form of Columbus. Private developers established middle and upper middle income neighborhoods at or beyond the urban fringe, and as the city grew the zoning code protected and maintained these areas. It also preserved, and refined the borders of, the downtown business district and the industrial areas. At the same time, in its application the code allowed older neighborhoods to lose some of their residential character. They lost population as well, though that was never an established goal of the city. As single-family homes were converted to apartments, and variances allowed apartment buildings to house more families than the code allowed, lot density increased. There was no incentive to own and occupy a private home in an increasingly dense area when that same home could house four or five families and earn rental income as well. Meanwhile, the intrusion of more and more commercial uses detracted from the residential nature of these older areas, providing further incentive for single-family owner-occupants to leave. Then, in the 1960s, parking lots for commercial and apartment buildings replaced some dwellings. Population overall within the three-mile zone dropped as those who could afford to quit the area did so, leaving behind those with no other housing options.[28] The high population density of overcrowded slum districts had concerned early zoning proponents, and they and other planners supported deconcentration of the urban population. Zoning actions in Columbus produced this effect, but they did so while increasing housing density per lot and allowing incompatible uses that lowered residential quality. Thus zoning had its most negative impact on low income persons living near the city center.

Zoning disproportionately affected blacks as well. But there is little indication that either council or the zoning board intended to use zoning in a racially discriminatory manner.[29] Rather, blacks sometimes felt the greatest impact when city officials acceded to property owners' requests. Over fifty years as the city's African-American population increased, the area it occupied gradually expanded. By 1970 the first three miles of the east side and the first four miles of the northeast, as well as the area between them, were 50 to 100 percent black.[30] Since more requests in the postwar years affected the near east side than anywhere else, largely black areas suffered the sharpest change. But private property owners, not city officials, determined through their requests where the various changes occurred and who was most affected. The city could have defended or protected from change areas where blacks lived, just as it could have protected areas where the poor lived. Nevertheless, though city zoning officials did not protect these areas, they also did not initiate the changes that occurred. Their crime was complicity in acceding to private property owners' wishes.

Although the public at large had not reacted strongly when Columbus passed its first zoning ordinance, residents of various neighborhoods increasingly objected to council rezonings in later years.[31] In the 1920s zoning actions prompted only 2 percent of the episodes of neighborhood activism. The proportion of zoning-related incidents then increased until by the 1960s zoning actions prompted a total of 62 percent, with 36 percent involving downzoning from a higher to a lower residential class and 26 percent involving a change from residential to nonresidential use.[32] Downward rezoning, whether residential or commercial, was often controversial. Individuals and groups sought to exclude certain uses or people from their neighborhoods, with the specific target of objection most often being high density, multifamily housing.[33] In Columbus, homeownership and the presence of school-age children correlated strongly with incidents of activism. It is not surprising, then, that the increase in objections to rezonings corresponded to an increase in homeownership—from 40.9 percent in 1920 to 62.0 percent by 1970.[34] Opposition notwithstanding, however, council continued to grant rezoning requests. And as had been the case for fifty years, where zoning was concerned planning took a back seat to profitability.

Evolution and Tension in the Planning Profession

While planning and zoning officials in the City of Columbus continued to act much as they always had, the profession of city planning continued to evolve. Once the professional city planner would generally have been a private consultant like John Nolen or Harland Bartholomew, but by the 1950s he—or occasionally she—was as likely to be a municipal employee. The growing and changing postwar metropolitan environment meant that cities and suburbs needed some professional planning staff to advise elected and appointed local officials in their efforts. Moreover, the planning requirements—implied or explicit—associated with various federal programs encouraged cities to maintain a permanent professional staff. But planners were not always of a single mind.

Urban blight and the postwar housing shortage—the two conditions that had prompted passage of the housing acts of 1949 and 1954—were the focus of much planning attention. This, of course, was nothing new; similar conditions at the turn of the century had sparked the design and reform efforts that became city planning. By the 1950s and 1960s cities began to actively attack these problems—with assistance from the federal government. In cities across the country redevelopment authorities assembled tracts of blighted land, prepared revitalization plans and projects, and used local and federal funds to leverage private developers' involvement. Believing they could stop the spread of blight by planting spores of new development in deteriorated areas, local officials sought to improve the economic health of central cities. Professional city planners were involved in all stages of the redevelopment process.[35]

They also worked with housing reformers such as Catherine Bauer Wurster to provide housing for low income households. But there was no unanimous vision on housing issues, for no single approach could serve all purposes. One goal was to wipe out slums, for planners and housers agreed that no one should have to live in dangerous dilapidated housing. The difficulty was in siting the new housing. Land costs were lower in outlying areas but there were drawbacks. Such areas lacked infrastructure, building there would not replace existing slums, and appropriate land was often in another jurisdiction. On the other hand, tearing down tenements and other slum dwellings and building new homes for low income people in the same location saved on infrastructure (since streets and water and sewer lines were already there), but land assembly costs were much higher. The issue was further complicated in cities where low income housing was paired with redevelopment efforts.[36] Depending on the specific city or project, planners sometimes found themselves on the side of the low income housing debate supporting fringe area sites and sometimes on the side trying to replace central city slums with new low income housing.

Planners were active in suburbs, too. Changes in the home building process pioneered by the Levitt Corporation and increased mortgage availability through the Veterans Administration and the FHA greatly facilitated the spread of moderately priced suburban subdivisions. At the same time, highways—largely paid for by the federal government under the 1956 Interstate Highway Act—put vast tracts of outlying land within reasonable commuting distance of central cities.[37] Struggling to keep pace and impose some control on the process, suburbs followed the lead of big cities and hired their own professional staffs or commissioned consultants to prepare master plans.[38]

Expanding professional opportunities for trained city planners prompted a similar expansion in planning education. More colleges and universities offered coursework or degrees in city or regional planning than ever before. Also the professional literature of the field began to change. Prior to the 1950s the professional literature had addressed various elements of the practice of city planning. In the 1950s, and even more so in the 1960s, it attempted to develop a theory of city planning.[39]

Efforts in this direction revealed friction and tension within the field. The most obvious split was between academic theorists and planning practitioners. Based in universities and trained as often in the social sciences as in design or engineering, the academics could observe, analyze, and evaluate planning practice impartially from a distance. Practitioners, caught up in the day-to-day political and economic concerns of the real world, often had little time for reflection; there was too much to do. Within each group was dissension, too. Noting that the poor and minorities had borne the greatest burden of renewal projects and inner-city highways, some questioned how a profession premised on serving the "public interest" could justify such a result. Others believed that such matters as equity and values were outside the purview of city planning. Planners were technical experts, apolitical and value neutral; the political process, not city planners, should decide political questions. As the decade of the 1960s drew to a close, planning practitioners and academics could agree that city planning involved questions of urban growth, development, and land use, but they could agree on little else.[40]

What did the evolution of the planning profession and tension within it portend for zoning? Planners in the 1950s and 1960s daily faced issues involving land use regardless of whether they worked in big cities, small cities, or suburbs. And they had long viewed zoning as the principal means of addressing such issues. The formal professional discourse, however, revealed the same lack of uniformity for zoning as for the profession as a whole. Some of the city planners and land use attorneys attending the annual national planning conferences and writing in the profession's premier journal viewed zoning largely in technical terms, whereas others reiterated the importance of the planning/zoning connection or questioned its impact on social equity. Still others questioned the validity of zoning itself.

Through the 1950s technical discussions addressed the appropriate level of standards for different zoning categories as well as how and by whom various aspects of zoning ought to be handled. Planners were also coached on serving as expert witnesses in zoning disputes. Their purpose, they were reminded, was to serve the public interest in its largest sense. A planner had to make that point clear to the attorney who hired his or her testimony, especially if the public interest conflicted with that of the attorney's client.[41]

The larger purposes planners were to serve also played a part in discussions about zoning and the comprehensive plan. Planner Walter Blucher blamed his colleagues' unwillingness to set accurate and adequate standards for the excessive amount of ad hoc spot zoning and special permits he had observed. (What happened in Columbus, it seems, was not an aberration.) In an exchange between planner Hugh Pomeroy and attorney David Craig about what members of each other's profession did not know about zoning, Pomeroy emphasized that zoning was to effect the comprehensive plan; it was not primarily a restriction to prevent a nuisance or to protect private property value. Craig responded that the planners' kind of zoning was "virtually a myth."[42] Others reminded planners that to zone effectively, they had to plan comprehensively first. Unfortunately, noted one, "Zoning is not a tool of planning... planning has become a tool of zoning." The zoning ordinance was "all too frequently better served in the breach than in the observance."[43]

Others wondered how planners defined the public interest, lamenting that zoning had ceased to serve its initial goals. What had happened to concerns about low income housing or protecting working class neighborhoods from deterioration? Frank Horack remarked that planning and zoning had lost their early focus and instead emphasized the "preservation of economic values of land"— either its income-producing potential or the upper income single-family neighborhood. Attorney Craig scolded planners who did not realize that the "zoning tool has been snatched from them and distorted into just one more legal device for the protection of narrow private property interests." Planners needed to reaffirm their role.[44] And what of social equity? Early zoning proponents had expected its greatest potential to be in newly developing areas outside overcrowded cities, where problems could be prevented rather than cured. Ironically, their prediction came true—though not as some would have hoped—as upper income suburbs effectively used zoning to exclude low and moderate income residents.[45]

Then came questions about the very concept of zoning. A presentation at the 1963 national conference stated that urban conditions had so changed that "the traditional concepts of land use controls have become less and less relevant."[46] Four assumptions about urban areas underlay comprehensive zoning as expressed in New York's 1916 ordinance: that suburban development could be either absorbed into the city proper or addressed by a cooperative, responsible suburban government; that the American "melting pot" would erase ethnic and economic differences; that federal or state intervention in municipal activities was unnecessary; and that "metropolitan areas were distinct and separate"—megalopolis was as yet unconceived. By the 1960s, however, urban areas consisted of dozens or hundreds of local governments using zoning to play one-upmanship against one another, friction between races and income groups was clearly evident, the state and national governments actively participated in local affairs, and metropolitan areas crossed state lines and merged with one another indistinctly. Traditional land use controls were not only inadequate for the new urban reality, they probably aggravated its worst problems.[47]

Then in 1964, planner and planning educator John Reps issued a "requiem" for zoning. "Zoning is seriously ill and its physicians—the planners—are mainly to blame." They had preserved "a lusty infant not only past the retirement age but well into senility."[48] Planners vigorously supported zoning as it had been conceived of and justified in the 1910s and 1920s. But the gap between early zoning theory and current zoning practice was wide. Small units of local government adopted rigid zoning codes that were not based on any community plan and that often contradicted—or at the very least did not coordinate with—other local codes and regulations. Based as it was on the police power to protect the public health, safety, and welfare, zoning could be only proscriptive, not prescriptive. Reps proposed replacing the existing system with a more flexible one based on a state-mandated legally adopted plan, relying on deeded covenants and administered on a metropolitan basis (if not by a newly created regional government). Then, three years after Reps's requiem, public officials from the largest unzoned municipality in the United States presented "Alternatives to Zoning: The Houston Story" and treated their audience to a discussion of "how we do it [i.e., control land use] without zoning."[49]

Was zoning a technical device to implement a comprehensive plan, a means of achieving social equity, or an outmoded concept? Planners and land use lawyers gave mixed signals. Even assuming they heard the debate, it is not surprising that city councils and zoning boards—in Columbus, Ohio, or elsewhere—continued to administer zoning as they always had. If they were not doing the right thing, no one could tell them unequivocally what the right thing was.

Abdication

For almost fifty years, from 1923 to 1970, Columbus officials essentially abdicated their role of planning land use and directing growth and development through zoning. They need not have done so. The original zoning ordinance adopted in 1923 was comprehensive in scope and could have served as a guide to land use and growth had it been adhered to rigorously. Later, Bartholomew's 1954 report and other planning studies gave the city the opportunity to mend its ways. But Columbus adopted only the form, not the substance, of planning.

Over that fifty years differences existed as to whether council or the zoning board was responsible for more zoning actions, about the specific type of change requested, and about which part of the city was involved; but a pattern affecting the city's spatial and social structure clearly emerged. Officials consistently granted property owners' requests for zoning changes involving land within three miles of the city center. Local government followed where the developers led, as "land developers who benefit[ed] from rezoning [did] not wait patiently for plums to fall into their open mouths but vigorously [shook] the tree."[50] City officials thus allowed private developers and property owners to determine the city's form. Residential developers had established the character of many neighborhoods after 1910 through deed restrictions, and homeowners in those areas sought few changes. Meanwhile, residential neighborhoods in older parts of the city, unprotected by deed restrictions and where low or moderate income residents were more likely to rent than own, were allowed to decline as property owners sought more profitable uses for their land.[51]

Like many other cities, Columbus did not effectively use zoning as a planning device to control land use and direct growth and development. Was the problem a fault of zoning itself, as Reps and others had come to believe? Or were there conditions in the Columbus metropolitan area that hampered the city's efforts? Clearly the city could not control land use or direct development patterns on land in other jurisdictions. The experience of zoning in the suburbs may thus provide a useful perspective from which to evaluate both zoning and its impact on the City of Columbus.

SIX

Zoning in the Suburbs: A Success Story?

The experience of zoning in suburban municipalities was quite different from that in Columbus; in the suburbs zoning was effective in directing land use patterns. Even the suburbs, however, were not equally successful. Three conditions made success more likely. First, the community needed a clearly understood, if not explicitly stated, vision of its desired future. Second, officials had to draft a zoning ordinance that was both appropriate to that vision and comprehensive enough to provide guidance if they did not formally adopt a comprehensive plan. Finally, officials had to administer the zoning code carefully in a manner consistent with the understood goals. However, even where zoning was most effective, it perpetuated or expanded land use patterns developers had previously set.

Zoning perpetuated those land use patterns because those patterns, by and large, served the suburban public interest. As discussed in chapter 3, the reformist planners and lawyers who promoted zoning and developed its theory based its legitimacy on the ability to serve the public interest. They defined this interest as promoting the health, safety, and general welfare, which they believed zoning would do by providing for future growth and preventing incompatible intrusions into existing areas. But though they defined the "interest," they did not define the "public." They noted that individuals would have to sacrifice some private property rights for the good of the whole community but did not really wrestle with the thorny issue of exactly where this "community" was located. Was it part of the city, the whole city, in a suburb, or was it the entire metropolitan region?

When planners spoke of metropolitan growth and regional

planning in the 1920s, their words implied a metropolitan regionwide perspective. At the NCCP in 1923, and again in 1926, Robert Whitten emphasized that regional planning and zoning should go "hand in hand," especially in undeveloped areas. Others noted that regional planning could coordinate the efforts of several cities and towns and prevent in undeveloped areas the same sort of problems existing cities struggled to cure. Studies projecting population growth and land use needs for the whole region decades into the future would guide regional planning and zoning. Observing the need for controlling land use beyond municipal borders, selections in a special issue of the *Annals* of the American Academy of Political and Social Sciences that was devoted to zoning spoke of "regulating land uses in the county" and of "state zoning."[1] Because they saw the logic of and need for a regionwide point of view, planners apparently believed all the region's constituent parts would too.

Zoning proponents knew, of course, that under existing state laws and court opinions a city could not control land beyond its own borders, which is why they emphasized the need for regional planning. But only Edward Bassett explicitly raised the possibility in the early years that some elements of a region might define their own public interest in a way that was inconsistent with the region's. He suggested that some suburbs might try to use zoning like restrictive deed covenants to exclude some uses and people they might find undesirable but that were not in and of themselves harmful to the public health and safety. Still, he doubted that such a use of the police power would be legitimate.[2]

The issue of exclusionary zoning was not tested, however.[3] As metropolitan areas continued to grow with increasing numbers of jurisdictions, each municipality that adopted zoning defined the public interest as it saw fit and based its land use goals on the interest of its own public.

Although land use goals varied among communities, zoning aided their achievement. In his indictment of zoning Bernard Siegan noted that planning and zoning in the suburbs "has been used to accomplish the common objective of suburbanites everywhere of maintaining a single-family character for their community. In this respect, when you've seen one suburban ordinance, you've seen them all."[4] Zoning activity in the seven suburbs examined here only partially supports Siegan's claim. Some communities used zoning to create or maintain residential exclusivity, but others used it to provide for a balanced mix of land uses. Two used zoning to direct new growth and development to achieve a clearly understood goal. Finally, one suburb, despite the presence of a comprehensive zoning ordinance, did not "use" zoning at all but instead allowed ad hoc decision making to substitute for planning. The six communities that effectively used zoning devised ordinances that would effect their goals and they consistently administered those ordinances to that purpose. At the same time, having no clear idea of what it wanted zoning to accomplish, the seventh suburb could not effectively use zoning either to maintain residential exclusivity or to direct future development. Examination of zoning practice in Bexley, Grandview Heights, Marble Cliff, Riverlea, Upper Arlington, Whitehall, and Worthington reveals that zoning could be an effective tool, regardless of community size or goal.[5] Figure 6.1 shows the present configurations of the seven and indicates their populations in 1960, when planning, zoning, and development were occurring simultaneously.

Small and Select: Riverlea and Marble Cliff

It is doubtful that any community ever faced an easier zoning task than the village of Riverlea. Incorporated as a village in 1939, the entire community comprised a single residential subdivision of 102 acres. The village was not adjacent to any developed area initially, and a deep ravine and the Olentangy River, on the south and west, respectively, provided a sense of isolation.

Riverlea's developer had platted the subdivision in 1924 in the midst of a real estate boom. The restrictive covenants he inserted in the deeds were to expire January 1, 1940 (roughly fifteen years after platting), or when superseded by a zoning ordinance. The developer could reasonably have expected in 1924 that the community would be fully developed by 1940, but the Great Depression almost halted construction. Thus in 1939, with deed restrictions set to expire, residents incorporated as a village so they could adopt a zoning ordinance. Deeds had originally limited construction to single-family homes except on High Street, where two-

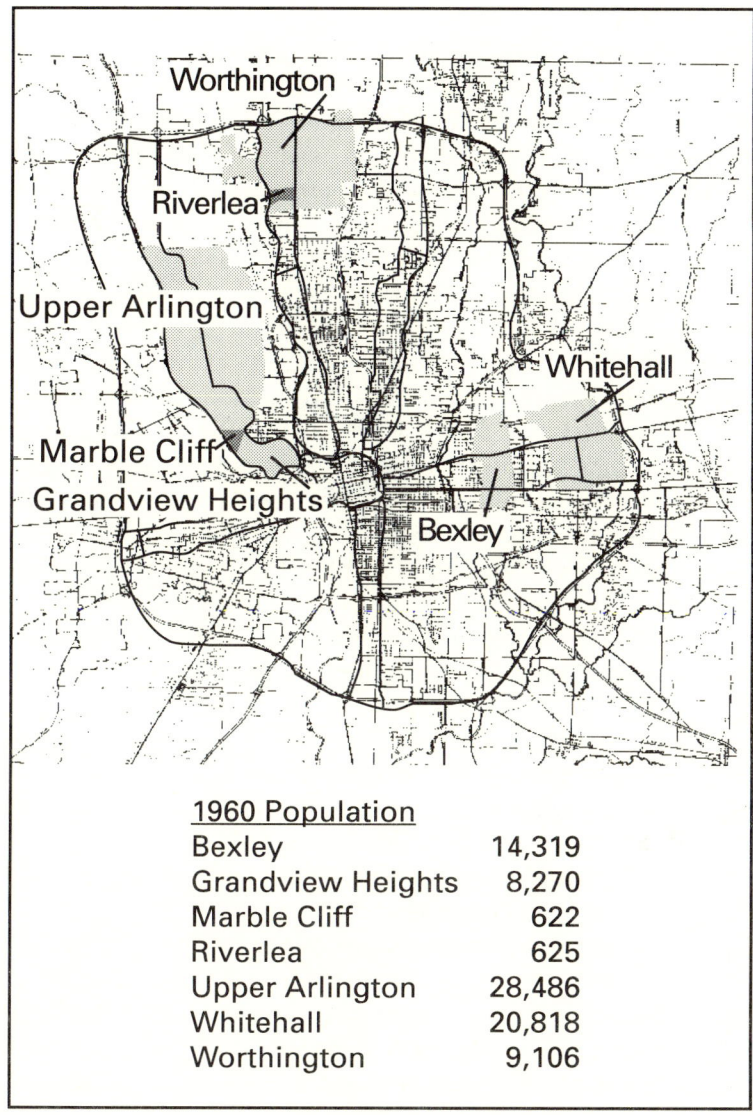

Figure 6.1 The seven suburbs

family dwellings were permitted. When adopted, zoning had merely to preserve the status quo.[6]

However, even before Riverlea's incorporation was recorded in 1939, the village council passed its first ordinance: "to establish zoning ... regulating and restricting the location of dwellings and garages."[7] Zoning would consequently control land use when deed restrictions expired in 1940. Several years later, in 1946, council passed a more thorough zoning ordinance.[8] The 1946 ordinance's preamble noted that since Riverlea was a "residential suburb," whose streets and water and sewer systems had been "designed and constructed for single residences," public facilities would be inadequate to handle more congested development. Residents and council also wished to "preserve the present character of the village."

The zoning ordinance limited all construction to single-family homes, whose architecture and building materials the building inspector would have to approve. The ordinance included specifications for lot size, building height, and front, side, and rear yard building setbacks. Other provisions explicitly prohibited the use of any structure for multiple dwellings or any purpose other than a single residence, as well as activities that might be a "public nuisance."

The ordinance passed in 1946 remained almost unchanged for twenty-five years. In 1949, the council passed amendments specifying floor area minimums both for houses and for any rooms used for sleeping.[9] In addition, all the lots bordering High Street were eventually rezoned to permit construction of two-story four-family dwellings.[10] There were no other use changes or zoning actions through 1970. Thus a tiny residential community remained that way, and public land use controls perpetuated what the original developer had attempted to create.

The village of Marble Cliff was equally successful in maintaining its status quo although it was slightly larger than Riverlea and faced greater challenges.[11] Unlike Riverlea, Marble Cliff contained more than one subdivision and was not physically isolated from its neighbors, Grandview Heights and Upper Arlington. It also included one sizable parcel of undeveloped land at the time it adopted zoning.

Marble Cliff had little variety of land use when it passed its zoning ordinance. The village contained only single-family homes, except on Fifth Avenue, its northern boundary. Two commercial structures on Fifth, in the northeast corner of the village, were an extension of commercial development in neighboring Grandview and were permitted to remain. Otherwise, the ordinance of 1928 permitted only single-family construction. Existing homes in Marble Cliff had been built on large lots and under deed restrictions with fairly high minimum construction costs, and the new ordinance ensured that these high standards would be maintained. No house could be built on a lot smaller than 10,000 square feet, and lots platted in the future would have to be at least 18,000 square feet in area. Size restrictions would thus prevent many from entering the Marble Cliff housing market. Although front yard setbacks varied from street to street, all provided for spacious yards. The zoning ordinance passed in 1928 remained in effect without substantive alteration for twenty-five years.

Changes to the ordinance in 1953 provided more exacting specifications. The village council thought it appropriate to be more explicit in the zoning code and added provisions specifying minimum floor areas for each floor of one, one-and-a-half, and two-story dwellings.[12] These minimums, coupled with the large lot size, ensured continued upper middle income occupancy. Eleven years later council added a provision for multifamily construction, which allowed later development of a small, exclusive condominium complex.[13]

Village officials maintained Marble Cliff's exclusive character when acting on requests for some alteration of the zoning code. Between 1928 and 1970 council acted on twenty requests to alter the application of the zoning ordinance, with half those requests coming in the 1960s and seven others in the 1950s. By special permit, council allowed two churches to be built in the village and gradually expanded the commercial uses along Fifth Avenue. Council strictly regulated the type of commercial activity, however, limiting it to small, neighborhood convenience-type shops or to professional offices. By special permit council also permitted multiple dwellings for no more than four families in areas zoned for professional offices—but only after members had examined and approved detailed site and construction plans. By requiring special permits and plan approval for anything other than single-family homes and by imposing high standards for single-family development, village officials ensured the community's exclusiveness.

Although they maintained the status quo, council members did not try to freeze the village in its 1928 condition. In response to the overall growth and development of the metropolitan area in the

1960s, as well as to increased traffic on Fifth Avenue from adjacent Grandview Heights and Upper Arlington, council did permit the commercial area to expand. It then used the very limited amount of multifamily housing allowed by special permit to serve as a buffer between the single-family homes and the commercial uses. The village also responded to development pressure by allowing a planned residential village to be built in 1965.[14] This was essentially a condominium complex, containing dwellings that were not single-family homes. In its approval of the project, council imposed restrictions requiring a minimum of 10,000 square feet of lot area per unit and the same floor area minimums as for single-family homes. Thus these multiple dwellings would not alter the character of the area. All in all, the changes permitted over forty-two years of zoning did not change Marble Cliff.

Small size was surely an advantage to both Riverlea and Marble Cliff in their efforts to maintain exclusive residential character. Both communities also got a good start because of their initial developers' actions. Deed restrictions had guaranteed middle or upper middle income residency in the dwellings built prior to zoning. By the time each community adopted a zoning ordinance, citizens and council members had a vested interest in the character of their small, select suburbs. Moreover, since there was little growth in either community, zoning had merely to preserve what private developers had created.

Planned Exclusivity: Bexley and Upper Arlington

Bexley and Upper Arlington did on a much grander scale what Riverlea and Marble Cliff accomplished in a small way. They used their zoning codes to perpetuate, and in the case of Upper Arlington to expand, the exclusive residential communities their founders had created. Both carefully controlled developers' activities but allowed residents to alter their homes as they chose, as long as the alteration had no negative impact on the community. When each was still a village and not yet fully developed, municipal officials determined what kind of community residents wanted and each village passed a zoning ordinance to achieve that goal.

Bexley's zoning ordinance was designed to maintain its character. The village adopted its first effective zoning code in October 1923, five years after the last annexation of territory brought the village to its present corporate limits.[15] Many lots were still vacant, particularly in the eastern portion, although almost all land within the village had been platted by this time. The older part of the village, bordering Alum Creek, was home to some of the wealthiest families in Columbus.[16] Impressive homes on large lots gave the village a stately grandeur. Subdivisions platted in the 1910s—some by Charles Johnson—contained restrictions ensuring upper or upper middle income development. The zoning ordinance continued the process. It provided for three use classes: single-family homes, two-family homes, and retail business. There were no apartments or industrial uses. All commercial uses were confined to Main Street and Livingston Avenue, east-west thoroughfares that were streetcar lines where commercial buildings already existed when council passed the ordinance. The two-family districts, which were very small, were in the extreme north and south ends of the village. There they might serve to buffer the village from anticipated development in the City of Columbus. The rest of the village was zoned for single-family use only, with building setbacks and lot areas that would prevent dense development. Also, Bexley's use districts were exclusive, rather than hierarchical, so single-family homes could not be built in two-family areas and no housing of any kind could exist in commercial zones.

The original ordinance had only two substantive changes through 1970. In 1955, a new use district, Apartment-Office, was proposed, detailing specifications for apartments that might be built on the upper floors above businesses. Failing to achieve passage, the proposal was rewritten to provide for some apartment construction but not in conjunction with offices and only when a specific site and construction plan had been approved.[17] In 1957 officials created a University District, which allowed a nonprofit university (i.e., Capital University) to build or remodel structures for its own use, subject to plan approval.[18]

Making few changes in the zoning code's provisions, Bexley officials were equally reluctant to change the use of specific parcels of land. Rezonings or use variances altered the use of only eleven parcels between 1923 and 1970, all to permit either row houses or apartments in or adjacent to the commercial district.[19]

Bexley did not grow in area but it grew in population, and plans for new houses or alterations to old ones presented the zoning board with requests for some change in zoning specifications.[20] In forty-six years the BZA responded to 207 requests, granting 171 of them (82.6 percent). The nature of requests differed considerably from those encountered by the Columbus zoning board; 176 asked for some variance from building setback or yard requirements. These variances involved permission to let fireplace chimneys, bay windows, or door canopies and similar items extend into the setback, or to construct covered walkways between houses and garages or three-car garages rather than the two-car garages allowed by code. The variances requested and granted thus would increase neither density of population nor intensity of land use, but rather would allow residents to build or alter their own homes to suit their tastes or family needs. City Council or the zoning board received just fourteen requests to initiate a nonconforming use, only nine of which were granted. Table 6.1 allows some comparison of zoning activity in Bexley, Upper Arlington, Grandview Heights, Worthington, and Whitehall.

For over forty-five years Bexley officials used their zoning ordinance to maintain the residential exclusivity that the village's early development had created. Property owners could use their property as they chose, provided that such use was a single-family home.

Alone among the suburbs of Columbus Upper Arlington was established to be a wholly planned residential community.[21] A prospectus prepared by developer King Thompson's company indicates Thompson's intent to create an upper class residential suburb that would retain its pleasant spaciousness indefinitely.[22] Under Thompson's direction, the town grew rapidly in both area and population, so that by 1930 more than three thousand people called Upper Arlington home.[23] The city council responded to rapid growth and created a planning commission to draw up a zoning code, which was passed in 1927.[24]

That first zoning ordinance essentially codified King Thompson's plan into law. Those lots in the mall where Thompson's deed restrictions permitted commercial uses were zoned Class III for retail business. Next to them was the Class II district, where multifamily dwellings (housing only two families) could be built.

Table 6.1
Comparison of suburban zoning activity

Suburb	Bexley	Upper Arlington	Grandview Heights	Worthington	Whitehall
1940 population	8705	5370	6960	1569	
1950 population	12378	9024	7659	2131	4877
1960 population	14319	28486	8270	9106	20818
1970 population	14888	38727	8460	15526	25269
Total zoning actions	212	649	297	185	260
Submitted to council	5	67	30	80	158
Percentage granted	100%	75%	100%	55%	94%
Submitted to zoning board	207	582	267	105	102
Percentage granted	83%	80%	83%	77%	74%
Percentage of requests for:					
Setback change	83%	53%	52%	20%	18%
Lot variance		5%	5%	1%	10%
Nonconforming use	7%	4%	11%	1%	25%
Special permit	4%	9%	2%	3%	12%
Fence	1%	11%	16%	18%	

This also matched the provisions Thompson had inserted into deeds. With one small exception (Class IV, a telephone exchange district), the rest of the city was designated Class I, single-family residential. Existing multifamily structures in Class I or II districts were permitted to remain, however, and the zoning board could allow additional four-family houses in the Class II district by special permit.[25] The retail district limited permitted uses to those of a neighborhood convenience type, such as banks, bakeries, restaurants, and gas stations. The ordinance established height, lot area, building setback, and yard specifications for each class that would preserve the open spaciousness of Thompson's original plat. Upper Arlington's use districts were hierarchical rather than exclusive like Bexley's. However, the original Class II and III districts were so small that the likelihood of single-family use in either was negligible. With no provision for industrial or manufacturing use, no apartments, and very limited commercial development, Upper Arlington would remain what Thompson had created, an upper or upper middle income residential suburb.

During the next twenty years, council passed fewer than a dozen amendments to the original code, most of which fine-tuned the language on setback, yard, or frontage provisions. Then in 1949 council amended the Class I provisions to mandate a one-and-a-half-story minimum height for residences, requiring that the second floor be fully finished and contain at least half the floor area of the ground floor. Council created a new residential class, I-a, for one-story houses but zoned relatively little land for it and set higher frontage and lot area minimums for one-story houses than for others. As the city had grown considerably in twenty years, council established a procedure that automatically brought newly annexed land under the zoning code. At this same time, council clarified provisions for the Class III district, listing the specific permitted uses and allowing no others by special permit. Council then added a list of conditional uses, including churches and schools, that could be allowed by special permit in residential areas.[26] In granting such uses, council would attach a list of specific conditions to be met that varied by use. This procedure allowed what might be an innocuous—but otherwise technically nonconforming—use while giving council some control over it.

As the postwar building boom hit Columbus and large-scale tract builders began to operate, Upper Arlington responded by upgrading its minimum floor area, lot area, and frontage standards for single-family districts in the mid-1950s.[27] By this time the city was annexing land not initially platted by Thompson, and it determined to perpetuate his concept of an upper income, residential suburb, using the zoning code to do so. There would be no little "Levittowns" in Upper Arlington. In keeping with the kind of community they were trying to maintain, council members specifically prohibited used car lots or sales as a commercial use and put limitations on commercial signs, prohibiting "pennants, whirligigs or other rotating or moving devices, flashing lights or similar eye-catching devices."[28] As the city had expanded so had the number and size of commercial areas. Council permitted commercial uses at some major intersections and along parts of Riverside Drive (the city's western border and also State Route 33) in addition to the original mall. The limitations on both the uses and their signs ensured that commercial development would not detract from the city's upper income residential character.[29]

Growth clearly posed potential problems for Upper Arlington. Between 1940 and 1960, while the metropolitan area's population increased by 35 percent, Upper Arlington's more than tripled—from 9,024 to 28,486.[30] Like the other suburbs, Upper Arlington belonged to the reconstituted Franklin County Regional Planning Commission, and following the commission's lead used planning funds available under the 1954 Housing Act's Section 701 to commission a comprehensive master plan. For its planning consultant the city commissioned Ladislas Segoe and Associates, who completed their plan in 1962.

The Segoe plan commented on the city's pleasant upper income residential character and credited consistent enforcement of density standards for its even population distribution. For the city to maintain its distinctiveness, the plan said, it should strive for a maximum population between 40,000 and 50,000, with 45,000 being optimum. If it were to remain predominantly residential, the city should annex land only north to Henderson Road. If, on the other hand, the city desired some carefully controlled industrial development for tax base purposes, it should annex farther north to Case Road. The city chose the former option and set Henderson Road as its northern boundary. The Segoe plan recommended maintaining the existing ratios among various land uses, which provided for more than 80 percent owner-occupied, single-family, detached dwellings.[31]

As part of his contract with Upper Arlington, Segoe drew up a new zoning code to replace the original ordinance. The new code, which council adopted in December 1961, reflected the needs of the much larger community but still retained Thompson's original idea of a residential suburb. It created four classes of residential use, including multifamily dwellings for more than four families, but established high enough floor area and lot area requirements per family to ensure upper middle or upper income development. It also still limited most land to single-family use. The land use profile in Segoe's 1962 plan indicated that less than 6 percent of the city's land area contained multifamily or commercial structures. Although the new code created several different types of commercial districts, it strictly limited their location—generally to the intersections of major arterials or along Riverside Drive (State Route 33), the city's western boundary. This matched the proposals of the Segoe plan.[32] Thus, forty-four years after incorporation, Upper Arlington still reflected King Thompson's original goal; and the Segoe plan and its accompanying zoning code provided for a continuation of that ideal.

Upper Arlington's city council and zoning board consistently administered the code to maintain their upper income residential suburb in that state from the time the first zoning code was adopted through 1970.[33] Since Upper Arlington was a larger community than Bexley, as well as an actively growing one, Upper Arlington's municipal officials faced more requests to change land use than their eastside counterparts. Over a forty-three-year period, through rezoning or nonconforming use, Upper Arlington's city council or zoning board changed the use of fifty-six parcels. But like Bexley officials, they made certain the changes did not alter the character of the community. The areas changed to commercial use were either along Riverside Drive or in or adjacent to places that the 1962 Comprehensive Plan had earmarked for neighborhood or community shopping centers. There were no commercial intrusions into established residential areas. The areas rezoned to permit four-family row houses or apartments were adjacent to the existing multifamily structures (some of which predated the 1927 ordinance) or between single-family areas and commercial districts. Thus apartments could serve as buffers. Officials allowed the city to grow and zoning changes met the growing population's needs for more multifamily housing and commercial development, but council and the zoning board strictly controlled the quantity, quality, and site of such development.

Residents of Upper Arlington, like those of Bexley, sometimes found specific provisions of the ordinance limited their enjoyment or use of their property. Thus they presented the zoning board with 582 requests for variances, of which 80.0 percent were granted. Residents sought permission to add rooms, enlarge garages, enclose porches, install swimming pools, and lay tennis courts, proposals which sometimes conflicted with the required yard or setback provisions. Forty-three requests (10.8 percent) involved a variance from some aspect of the zoning code's regulations governing the height and location of fences (Table 6.1). The zoning board generally granted requests if the variance was needed because of some physical irregularity of the lot, or if the change was not contrary to the intent of the code and the plan. At the same time, the board consistently denied lot area variances to construct more or larger multifamily structures than permitted on the parcel in question. Thus the board controlled the actions of developers but did not unduly restrict homeowners, allowing them to alter their dwellings to suit their lifestyle or convenience—as long as such alteration did not impose on the property rights of their neighbors and it maintained the residential character of the upper middle income suburb.

Two controversies arose in Upper Arlington in 1940 that indicated city officials were clearly in tune with citizens' desires.[34] On the advice of the city attorney, early in 1940 zoning officials approved plans for a gasoline service station at the corner of Lane Avenue and Northwest Boulevard on a Class III (retail business) lot. Nearby residents protested and, under provisions of the code, filed a formal appeal from the approval and for a joint meeting of the zoning board and city council to discuss the matter. At that meeting the city attorney confirmed the correctness of the approval, since the land had been zoned for business since 1927 and service stations were an allowable business use. After additional discussion and statements by residents, the zoning board recommended that council rezone the lot in question to either Class I or II, neither of which would allow the service station to be built. Reluctantly, council refused to do so, again acting on the advice of the city attorney, who indicated the city might face an indefensible legal challenge. By not rezoning the land until after the oil company had purchased it (with its retail zoning) and submitted plans, the city could be construed as having "taken" the value of the property in question. Thus, council allowed a legally permitted, though to some unpleasant, commercial use despite residents' displeasure.

The other 1940 controversy also concerned a nonresidential use, but one generally thought of as contributing to the wholesome character of a community—a church. The original zoning ordinance permitted churches only in Class III districts. In January 1940 the Reverend Large, a Lutheran pastor, approached city officials with a request on behalf of his congregation to erect a church in a Class I district. Several members of the congregation lived in Upper Arlington, which had no Lutheran church at the time. The Reverend Large met with city officials and indicated several possible locations for the new church. Two weeks later officials adopted a resolution that churches not be permitted on any Class I parcel as long as Class III land was available. The church continued to pursue the issue, however, which came up again at the joint council-zoning board meeting that had been called on the gas station matter. There the zoning board reaffirmed that Class I districts should remain strictly single-family, with churches prohibited. In early May the Lutherans again came before a joint council-zoning board meeting to request permission to erect a church.

By this time, they had arranged to purchase a particular residential site and obtained statements from several nearby property owners that there were no objections to the proposed church. But other residents objected sharply, saying that churches should be limited to the Class III areas where they were already permitted, and that to allow them in residential areas would decrease property values. A church spokesman responded that the church wanted a "commanding site," which no Class III parcel provided. Also, a large enough piece of Class III land cost more than the church could afford, while a comparably sized residential parcel was within its budget. A member of the zoning board then spoke, saying that the matter had been up before the board several times and should be settled once and for all, adding "that as this village was intended by the Planning Commission to be primarily for residential use, and only enough space was reserved for business purposes to meet the need of and be a convenience to its residents, it is the duty of the Zoning Commission to protect and defend human and property rights by carefully guarding ... Single-Family Resident Properties."[35] The zoning board consequently adopted a resolution to that effect, denying the church. Not until passage of a 1949 amendment to the zoning ordinance were churches permitted in single-family districts, and then only on a conditional basis.[36] Thus, in the future council might allow a church to locate in a residential area but it could require that certain conditions be met.

Like Riverlea and Marble Cliff, Bexley and Upper Arlington had begun with or attained a level of residential exclusivity by the time they adopted zoning ordinances. But although they experienced much more growth and development than their tiny counterparts, they used their zoning codes as effectively to maintain their select residential characters. And their residents heartily approved.

Balance and Diversity:
Grandview Heights and Worthington

Not all suburbs were as exclusive or as determinedly residential as the four discussed above. Both Grandview Heights and Worthington contained a mix of land uses when they adopted zoning, and both used zoning to maintain that mix. Public controls established industrial and commercial districts and allowed them to expand as needed but never to intrude into established neighborhoods. Both suburbs also had a mix of housing types that served different income groups. Each community controlled new residential development to provide for at least a middle income level but neither allowed the residential character of older neighborhoods to deteriorate. Each used its zoning code to preserve the mix of uses while providing a balance among them.

The situation in Grandview was much like that in Bexley. Although the city had nearly attained its present municipal limits by the time it adopted zoning, and almost all the land within its borders had been platted, many lots were still vacant.[37] The principal task of zoning, then, was to maintain what was there and make sure the rest of the village developed in an appropriate manner.

The city's first zoning ordinance, adopted in 1922, did just that.[38] As the eastern end of the village, an area bisected by railroad tracks, already contained some industrial uses, the ordinance zoned that section of the village for industry. A commercial district separated part of the industrial zone from any type of housing. The code also established a second commercial zone, an area where commercial uses already predominated. The ordinance zoned the rest of the village for single-family homes, with one exception—a rather large area zoned for two-family dwellings that separated the single-family homes from the commercial and industrial districts at the east end of town. Though Grandview's use districts were exclusive rather than hierarchical, four-family row houses could be built in the two-family district by special permit.

Lot area, yard requirements, and setback provisions provided for future middle income, but not exclusive, development. The standards set for the two-family district matched those established in King Thompson's Northwest Boulevard subdivisions, portions of which were included in the two-family zone. The industrial zone's factories could not be of a type that would "cause noxious odors, chance of explosions, undue fire hazards, ... or public nuisance." In effect, the zoning ordinance was designed to maintain the mix of uses existing at its adoption and ensure comparable quality for future building.

The ordinance apparently did its job, for there were no substantive alterations to it until council revised the entire code in 1963.[39] The new code was more complex, with multiple classes (varying by floor area and lot size) of residential and apartment zones and different types of commercial areas. It was much like its predecessor in effect and application, however.

Over a period of forty-eight years Grandview officials met the needs of a steadily increasing population by gradually expanding the commercial areas and providing slightly more multifamily housing. Apartments and two-family districts still served as buffers between commercial zones and the single-family areas.[40] But all development was of a low density nature except for a luxury high-rise apartment tower approved in December 1959.[41] Public reaction to the high-rise rezoning was similar to Upper Arlington's response to the church and gas station twenty years earlier. Initially council rezoned an undeveloped tract on the edge of town near a newly annexed industrial parcel. Council approved plans for an eight-story luxury apartment building as part of the rezoning. Before the developer could begin construction, however, a change in his financing arrangements led him to change his plans—three years later he returned for a building permit for a twenty-two story apartment tower. The change from eight to twenty-two stories sparked an outcry and residents claimed that the 1959 rezoning was no longer valid because it had been based on specific plans that were now abandoned. Despite an outside consultant's report that the project would benefit the city, residents continued to resist, claiming that transitory apartment tenants did not contribute to the stability of the community. Nevertheless, council followed the consultant's advice and in 1964 reaffirmed the apartment zoning. To appease residents, they rezoned only that portion of the parcel where the structure was to be built and specified that the remainder of the lot be kept as open space, thus preventing even the appearance of overcrowding.

The zoning board was also responsive to community desires.

Over a forty-eight-year period the zoning board heard 267 requests for some sort of variance and granted 82.8 percent of them.[42] As with the other suburbs, the variances did not increase population density or change the character of the community. More than half (57.3 percent) concerned building or yard setbacks. Residents wanting to erect or alter homes or construct garages where many lots were only fifty feet wide found they needed the board's permission to extend their structures into the setback. An additional 17 percent of the variances involved some aspect of the zoning code's provisions for fences.[43] The variances granted did not really change the city (Table 6.1) although they allowed homeowners to use their property as they chose.

Aware of the growth almost fifty years had brought, Grandview Heights, like Upper Arlington, availed itself of planning funds available under the 1954 Housing Act's Section 701 and contracted with Harland Bartholomew and Associates of St. Louis in the late 1960s to prepare a comprehensive plan. The Bartholomew firm was, of course, familiar with the area from its earlier work for Franklin County and the City of Columbus. The town that Bartholomew found was much like the one that had passed its first zoning ordinance in 1922. Although it had grown up and filled out, it contained the same balanced and diverse mix of uses. Industry provided both a tax base and some employment, commercial development was sufficient to meet the community's needs, and more than one-third of the population lived in two-family or multifamily dwellings (which ranged from modest to luxurious).[44] Zoning had maintained the status quo and Bartholomew's report showed Grandview Heights how to perpetuate it.

Although Worthington grew in both area and population, its experience with zoning was similar. The zoning ordinance the Village of Worthington passed in 1928 was much like that of Grandview Heights.[45] It created the same four use districts: single-family residence, two-family residence, retail, and industrial. The industrial land was at the eastern edge of the village, adjacent to a rail line. The commercial district bordered High Street, south of the original village green. The ordinance zoned the first block of each of the side streets abutting the High Street retail area for two-family residential use but allowed four-family units by special permit. The rest of the village was for single-family homes. The use districts closely matched existing construction and were hierarchical (like those in Columbus and Upper Arlington) rather than exclusive.

For almost three decades the original ordinance sufficed with little alteration, for the town had not yet begun to grow. The only real change occurred in 1942, when a revised zoning ordinance substituted a multiple-residence district for the two-family district.[46] By the mid-1950s, however, the suburban building boom had hit Worthington. Six annexations—all but one of undeveloped farmland—in three years increased the village's area tenfold. Worthington officials were determined to control how that land was developed. In 1955 the village passed new subdivision and platting regulations, revised them in 1956, and then revised the zoning code as well.[47] The new code had three classes of residential use, as well as commercial, industrial, and park or agricultural districts. Lot area, setback, and yard requirements were designed to prevent dense development but did not initially limit new construction to upper income dwellings. A 1959 amendment made use districts exclusive.[48]

Like Upper Arlington, Worthington responded to growth and development by upgrading its single-family residence standards.[49] Rather than maintaining exclusivity, however, this merely increased the mix of income levels in the town, as some of the city's housing was modest to begin with. A totally revised zoning code adopted in 1967 confirmed the mix, with three classes each of single-family and multifamily residence districts.[50] Still, all new development after 1960 was at the higher income levels, and except where council extended the industrial district to the north, it zoned newly annexed land for single-family use.

Worthington's city council found it necessary to rezone relatively little land, and what changes council did make responded to the needs of a growing community. Almost all changes occurred after 1950.[51] Over a twenty-year period, council gradually increased the length of the High Street commercial district and rezoned some single-family lots for multifamily use where they adjoined the expanded commercial or industrial zones.

Worthington City Council still preserved the original village character, though. Through the decades the city had retained the heart of its original plan, a village green laid out at the town's 1803 founding. Council permitted no intense development adjacent to the green, and the lots that faced three of its four quadrants held churches and the town library. To maintain its New England heritage, in 1967 council established the Old Worthington Architectural District. The district included the area of the original 1803 village around the village green (roughly sixteen blocks) plus all the street frontage along High Street and Granville Road (the north-south and east-west arterials, respectively) within the municipal boundary. The district designation did not change the zoned use of any parcel or the lot or density specifications. It did, however, require property owners to get approval from the Municipal Development Commission (Worthington's planning commission) before making any change that would alter the historic character of the district.[52] Though provisions for the Old Worthington Architectural District were not part of the city's zoning code and did not involve the zoning board in their administration, they clearly imposed limitations on the use of private property.

Like its counterparts in the other suburbs, Worthington's zoning board generally granted residents' requests for some variance from the zoning code (77.1 percent); and as in the other suburbs those variances did not really alter the community.[53] A 1958 amendment to the zoning code spelled out the circumstances under which the board could grant a variance request. These involved special circumstances of the land, building, or use peculiar to the lot in question and not affecting those nearby; situations where granting the variance was necessary for the "preservation and enjoyment of substantial property rights"; and occasions where granting the request would not "materially affect adversely the health and safety of neighborhood occupants or be detrimental to the public welfare."[54] Following these guidelines, the board generally allowed portions of homes or garages to extend into the setback, especially on the older narrow lots, or fences taller than the ordinance standard (Table 6.1). At the same time, the board denied more than half the requests of businesses for some exception to the zoning code's sign limitations.[55]

Worthington's officials, like Grandview's, perpetuated the mix of uses already in existence at the time they instituted zoning. They then revised and administered their zoning ordinance to prevent deterioration in the original village and ensure high quality development in new areas. The result was a community whose commercial and industrial districts enjoyed carefully regulated expansion but were not permitted to intrude into residential areas that were mostly, although not exclusively, middle income.

Ad Hoc Incrementalism: The Case of Whitehall

Whitehall's zoning practices were very different from those of the other suburbs. All six discussed above used their zoning codes to maintain or expand their communities with the same character that existed prior to zoning. The relatively few use changes granted were responses to the changed needs of growing towns. Use changes and variances did not substantially alter the communities, although two grew considerably in both area and population. Whitehall, then, presents a contrast. Perhaps the land use provisions of the zoning code did not adequately reflect the needs of the community, or perhaps city officials lacked either a clear conception of the type of community they wanted to maintain or the capacity to achieve their goals. In any event, the nature and number of use changes and variances granted indicate that rather than using their zoning provisions to plan and direct growth and development, officials made every request in essence a spot zoning decision.

The first lots of Whitehall had been platted early in the twentieth century, but the area developed slowly until after World War II. Not until 1947 did the residents incorporate as a village. By 1950 the village population was 4,877. A single annexation in 1952 completed the town's land acquisition. Now growing rapidly, Whitehall became a city in 1956 and by 1960 was home to 20,818 people.[56]

Whitehall's initial zoning code was not appropriate for the village's needs. The first officials took office March 1, 1948, and in June of that year passed a zoning ordinance.[57] That ordinance adopted as the official zoning plan for the village those provisions of the Franklin County Zoning Resolution applicable to land within Whitehall's borders.[58] The Franklin County Regional Planning Commission had proposed the county zoning resolution from the land use perspective of the county as a whole, however, and not from that of Whitehall. The ordinance Whitehall adopted zoned all land fronting the four major arterials for local commercial use, extending to the first alley or street but not beyond three hundred feet. Thus the depth of the commercial zone was irregular. All other land was designated one- and two-family residential, although apartments could be permitted on Main and Broad streets (the east-west arterials otherwise zoned commercial) if approved by the Planning and Zoning Commission. This ordinance remained in effect virtually unchanged for four and one-half years.

Council passed a more comprehensive zoning ordinance in 1952 to bring newly annexed land, some of which contained industrial uses, under the jurisdiction of the zoning code.[59] The new ordinance had six classes of single-family residence districts, with the lowest floor and lot area specifications being the FHA minimums for the time. Because much land in the area was used for truck gardening, there was also a zoning classification labeled Farm Residence. The Farm Residence District required minimum lots of at least five acres and permitted the sale of agricultural products on the property (although not within one hundred feet of the street or road). An Apartment House District allowed for up to four-family dwellings, as well as hotels and nursing homes. Local and General Commercial districts provided for retail and office development of varying intensity, and an Industrial District allowed warehouses and similar uses but prohibited heavy manufacturing. Council amended the ordinance twice, first permitting some specified manufacturing uses in the industrial zone, and then creating two new single-family classes with higher floor and lot area minimums than previously provided. However, the lowest minimums in the code (i.e., the least restrictive single-family districts, which followed FHA minimums) remained unchanged. Also at that time, council added a provision stating that if the setback or lot specifications of deed restrictions differed from those in the zoning code, the deed restrictions would take precedence, as long as they met the minimum zoning code standards.[60] This ordinance remained in effect with only very minor changes through 1970.

Although the structure of the zoning code changed very little, land use under it changed a great deal (Table 6.1). Whitehall officials changed the use of 113 parcels over a period of twenty-three years by rezoning or use variance. These included 48 from row house, apartment, or single-family use to commercial; 30 from commercial or single-family to apartment; and 35 from commercial or apartment to industrial. As all frontage along the city's four arterials was already zoned for commercial use, the rezonings to commercial either extended the depth of the commercial district beyond the first alley or three hundred feet, or allowed commercial intrusions into residential areas. Some of the changes to apartment use were in buffer areas but others were tracts once platted for single-family development and not yet built on or odd infill parcels on single-family streets.

The changes to industrial use, most of which were accomplished by use variance rather than rezoning, largely resulted from a oddity in the zoning code itself. The list of permitted uses in the Local and General Commercial districts did not include any automobile-related activities. Such uses as gasoline service stations, car washes, and new and used car dealerships were classed as industrial and thus not permitted on the major thoroughfares. Rather than amending the code to permit such uses of right in commercial areas, or selecting specified locations along the major streets (where such uses would be convenient to residents but not create traffic or other problems) and rezoning those lots industrial to permit auto-related uses, or even creating a new use classification, council preferred to deal with the requests on a one-by-one basis. Each request granted was thus an instance of spot zoning. Property owners could almost be assured of permission to change the use of their land; of 158 zoning actions heard by council, only 1 failed to pass.[61]

Whitehall's zoning board was less active than the city council on zoning matters, and also less likely to grant property owners' requests. The approval rate was 73.5 percent.[62] The nature of the variances, however, was more important than their number. Almost half the requests concerned extensions into the building setback and one-fourth involved lot specifications. Unlike the situation in the other suburbs, many of the setback requests were not the result of homeowners seeking to build or remodel homes on narrow lots. Instead, they came from business property owners wanting to place their buildings closer to the street than the setback line permitted because other businesses on the street were already in the setback. The board did not view the existing structures as being nonconforming in location and make new ones meet the code; instead, it exempted new structures from conformance as well. The lot specification variances arose in situations where property owners wanted to split an existing lot into two separate lots to create two developable parcels instead of one. In these cases, which were overwhelmingly approved, both new lots were narrower than the minimum specified by the zoning code. Thus, the variances granted were most often to serve the property owners' prosperity rather than because some irregularity of the lot made conformance with code provisions difficult or impossible.

Officials developed the pattern of granting exceptions to zoning provisions governing property use, building setbacks, or lot specifications early in Whitehall's history. In later years they followed their own existing precedent, granting more such exceptions. The result was to increase both the density and intensity of land use but without any consciously thought-out intent to do so. Village officials did not adopt a comprehensive plan indicating what they desired for their community in ten or twenty years' time, although the zoning ordinance of 1952 could have served that purpose had officials followed it more closely.[63] The result was considerable change in the character of the community as it grew. Where once suburban subdivisions had nestled among large and small farms, by 1970 Whitehall was a patchwork of single-family homes (on lots of widely varying dimensions), apartment buildings, and amorphous commercial areas or spot commercial and automobile-related uses. Rather than being planned change, directed at a specific goal, however, Whitehall's change was incremental, occurring in response to an undirected, case-by-case, ad hoc decision-making process.

The Suburban "Status Quo"

The zoning experiences of these seven Columbus suburbs only partially support Siegan's statement about suburban zoning quoted at the beginning of this chapter: "It has been used to accomplish the common objective of suburbanites everywhere of maintaining a single-family character for their community." Four suburbs were overwhelmingly single-family residential communities when they adopted zoning, and all four used zoning to maintain that status. Moreover, one did so while growing in population and another while growing in both population and area.

Two other suburbs, however, had a greater mix of both housing types and land uses when they adopted zoning. Rather than zoning almost all land for upper middle income single-family homes and applying their zoning codes to eliminate other uses gradually, these two expanded their multifamily housing or industrial and commercial districts to maintain the mix. They carefully controlled the expansion of those areas, however, that did not have single-family housing to prevent negative impacts and to preserve the residential quality of the existing neighborhoods. But they did not try to create homogeneous single-family bedroom communities. Thus there was sufficient balance and variety of land uses to meet each city's needs.

The final suburb neither maintained single-family exclusivity nor controlled and directed alternative land use patterns. While the structure of the suburban ordinances did not differ greatly, clearly their administration did. So "when you've seen one suburban ordinance," you have not really seen them all—until you have examined their application to the land.

Whether or not they effectively used zoning to serve community needs, there is no evidence that any of the suburbs used it for explicitly racial purposes. They did not need to for other factors worked to provide near homogeneity of race. A very small community of blacks had lived in Worthington since the Civil War. Similarly, a few black families had farmed land since the mid-nineteenth century that was annexed for development into Upper Arlington in the 1950s. Racial covenants in deeds through 1948, and income restrictions in deeds throughout the development process, effectively kept those two suburban minority populations small and prohibited minority entrance into other suburbs. Fairly high standards for single-family residences in suburban zoning codes perpetuated the income patterns developers had initiated, and relatively few minorities could have afforded the suburban homes built after 1948. Only Whitehall in the 1950s and 1960s had much new development modest enough to permit black homeownership. But that development was geared to the FHA market, and since the FHA did not insure mortgages in racially mixed areas few realtors sold Whitehall homes to blacks. By 1970 less than 1 percent of the entire Franklin County suburban population was nonwhite.

Although their purposes differed somewhat, six suburbs effectively used zoning for a specific purpose. The seventh did not. What accounts for the difference? It was not size, for the smallest and the largest were equally successful, while the one that was less so falls in the middle in terms of size. Nor is the difference explained by timing, whether with respect to when the suburbs adopted zoning or with respect to periods of physical growth. All those suburbs in existence in the 1920s, when the concept of public land use controls achieved its greatest support and adoption, passed zoning ordinances at that time. The other two (Riverlea and Whitehall) adopted zoning ordinances almost coincidentally with municipal incorporation. The two that experienced extensive physical growth after instituting zoning (Upper Arlington and Worthington) used their public controls to direct development in new areas. The one whose zoning was not an effective land use control device grew only slightly after adopting zoning, and four others that used public controls effectively did not grow in area at all.

Moreover, though planning theory would require that effective zoning conform to a comprehensive plan, none of the suburbs had formal plans by 1960 and only two had them a decade later. A formal plan thus cannot explain the difference. However, a well-drafted comprehensive zoning code could function as a plan, and in six communities it did. Officials in six suburbs had a clear vision of their communities' future. Four were to be almost entirely residential, while two others balanced homes with businesses and industries but protected residential areas. All six passed zoning ordinances to effect their visions and administered them consistently. Zoning effectively directed land use patterns in those six. In the seventh, there was apparently neither vision nor direction. Variances and use changes negated the comprehensiveness built into the zoning code. Officials, it seemed, could not see the forest for the trees.

Equally clear is the importance of developers in determining land use patterns. Developers initially established Riverlea, Marble Cliff, Bexley, and Upper Arlington as middle or upper middle income residential suburbs. Public land use controls had merely to perpetuate an established pattern. (This is particularly the case for Riverlea and Upper Arlington, since each was largely the product of a single developer's efforts.) Grandview Heights and Worthington officials adopting zoning faced a pattern of diverse uses that property owners' actions had created. Local public officials determined how those diverse areas could grow, but private actions had created the initial land use pattern. And in Whitehall it was private property owners, whether building businesses of a type or in a place where the zoning code said they should not or building apartments or homes on too small lots, who determined the use of the land. Thus, while public officials played the zoning game, private property owners and developers had prepared the playing field.

SEVEN

Planning for the Private Interest

By 1970 Columbus, Ohio, had grown to several times its turn-of-the-century size. Both the city and its suburbs had adopted public land use controls that affected the metropolitan area's growth and development. But land developers and property owners were also involved; municipalities did not plat lots or build houses. Indeed, developers sometimes also controlled land use. Two sets of controls thus shaped the city's spatial and social structure.

In 1900 Columbus was a city of potential. Stores and offices joined state government downtown, while warehouses and small industries straddled the rivers nearby. But people lived in the city center, too—though infant suburbs were beginning to draw off the well-to-do. Public facilities were inadequate when compared to similar cities, but the *Plan* of 1908 indicated a desire for improvement.

By 1920 major change had occurred. Few people lived downtown anymore, where businesses flourished. Developers had platted subdivisions along the river banks on the northwest, north, and east sides, and some subdivisions had incorporated as suburban municipalities. Other outlying neighborhoods, especially on the northeast side, remained part of the city though far from its center. The south and west sides experienced little change, however.

Columbus's 1923 zoning ordinance clarified existing land use trends by delineating the commercial and industrial areas. It provided for logical expansion of those areas as needed in the future and surrounded them with an apartment zone to house their moderate income and working class employees. Beyond the apartment zone were the two dwelling house districts, with one for only single-family homes. The suburbs also had zoning codes.

These allowed primarily middle and upper income residences although most also allowed enough commercial uses to meet their own residents' needs. Early zoning in the Columbus metropolitan area was in line with contemporary city planning theory about zoning. Incompatible uses were separated, residential areas were protected from incongruous intrusions, and height and area specifications limited population density. In establishing their zoning, however, both city and suburban municipal officials had essentially confirmed developers' actions.

The city expanded physically as its population grew in subsequent decades. To accommodate that growth, developers platted more subdivisions for new homes on the outskirts of either the city or a suburb, but generally before annexation. They concentrated their efforts on the northwest, north, northeast, and east sides, where they and their predecessors had succeeded before. Columbus city policy on water and sewer extensions facilitated the developers' efforts while ensuring the city's growth. Developers determined the nature and level of development for each location by deed restrictions. City or suburban zoning reaffirmed in general terms for large areas what deed restrictions specified for small ones. As middle and upper income households moved to new homes in suburban areas, their old dwellings filtered down to those who could not afford the suburbs or were restricted by racial prejudice.

Examination of seventy years of residential development in and around Columbus, Ohio, illustrates the impact of private property owners' actions. Individual property owners sought their own greatest financial gain; the aggregate of their actions produced the city's spatial structure. Developers seeking to serve upper income households created attractive neighborhoods in the "right" locations into the 1940s and ensured residential exclusivity with restrictive covenants. Later, developers varied the specific provisions of some restrictions to aim development of certain subdivisions at particular (and not just upper income) segments of the home-buying public. Uses or people excluded from restricted subdivisions were forced to locate elsewhere or to remain where they already existed. Thus as the central city became increasingly commercial, middle or upper income people who had once lived nearby relocated to exclusive, new outlying neighborhoods. Denied that option, minorities and low income households moved into the older residential areas just outside the city center, where deeds did not restrict land use and where property owners subdivided existing one- and two-family dwellings to house more households or replaced dwellings with commercial uses. Since many developers imposed restrictions over many years—two on a very large scale—the impact of restrictive covenants on the city form was considerable.

Almost all new development through the 1940s occurred outside municipal boundaries. Thus, private land developers, rather than public officials, decided what land would be developed in what way for what people. The metropolitan area's residential patterns were already set by the time annexations and the application of zoning caught up with the development process. Later, when developers subdivided zoned land, they considered the applicable zoning code when designing their restrictions. However, city and suburban zoning provisions generally maintained or extended to new areas an existing type and level of residential development. Both city and suburban zoning codes reflected patterns the developers had already set as much as they guided future growth. While seeking to increase profits, the land developers had also shaped the city. Theoretically, zoning could have.

Zoning was not without import, however. In both the city and the suburbs zoning maintained the residential quality that developers had provided to middle, upper middle, and upper income neighborhoods. In the two suburbs that grew appreciably after they adopted zoning (Upper Arlington and Worthington), local officials effectively used zoning to determine development in newly annexed land. In older, less exclusive areas—never or no longer protected by deed restrictions—the administration of zoning allowed land use or density changes that substantially altered those areas, diminishing their residential character. This process increased the potential income of property owned by nonresident investors while decreasing the property value and equity of those owning and occupying modest homes. The requests of property owners, instead of the initiative of zoning officials, drove this process of change, however.

The Effectiveness of Zoning

This research set out to examine the role of both private and public land use controls in shaping urban spatial and social structure. With respect to public controls a secondary purpose was to evaluate the effectiveness of zoning, whose earliest proponents had hoped it would serve the public interest (i.e., promote and protect the public health, safety, and welfare) in its broadest sense. The city planners and reformist lawyers who were zoning's earliest proponents had specific goals for public land use controls. Accordingly, they essentially established criteria to be met if zoning was to fulfill its potential. The realtors who allied with the city planners to gain support for zoning had very different goals. By examining the application of zoning against the planners' criteria, one can also see how well it served the realtors' agenda.

The criteria the planners established were necessary not only for zoning to be effective in planning growth and development but also to meet the legal requirement of the police power to serve the public interest. Four things were necessary for zoning to protect the public health, safety, morals, or welfare by limiting the use of private property. First, a zoning ordinance was to be in accordance with a comprehensive plan that would serve as a guide for the ordinance's application. Second, zoning actions had to produce, or strive to produce, a balance of land uses designed to meet all the community's needs. Third, zoning was to prevent the intrusion of incongruous, potentially harmful, uses into existing areas, especially residential neighborhoods. Finally, zoning actions, taken as a whole, were to benefit all income groups. This last had two elements. The early planners hoped zoning would disperse all income levels of population, lessening congestion and preventing further deterioration, rather than sending only the rich to spacious new suburbs while leaving the poor in overcrowded, underserviced, inner city neighborhoods. They did not suggest mixing housing types or income groups within neighborhoods. However, they knew that congestion in tenement and slum districts would be relieved only if multifamily and working class housing were available elsewhere—in outlying areas. Moreover, zoning should protect the existing residential environment of the working and lower classes, who lacked financial resources to protect it themselves—

as the wealthy did through buying restricted exclusivity. If zoning met these four standards it would serve the public interest.

With respect to conformance with the comprehensive plan, early planners and zoning experts such as Harland Bartholomew believed that one way to determine if zoning code design and application conformed to a comprehensive plan was by the number and nature of changes made subsequent to code adoption. Indeed, that was the only way if there was no formally adopted comprehensive plan. A well-drafted ordinance, designed to meet all the community's needs, should require few changes.

The City of Columbus did not adopt a comprehensive plan prior to passing its first zoning ordinance or at any later time. However, Bartholomew's consulting firm performed studies jointly for the city and the regional planning commission for a comprehensive plan in the 1950s. One of those reports revealed problems with zoning in Columbus. Land was zoned for commercial uses far in excess of the amount needed, a large area zoned for industry was almost entirely residential in actual use, and areas occupied by single-family homes and duplexes were zoned for apartments. Nevertheless, over a fifty-year period, the Columbus City Council and the BZA consistently increased the amount of commercial land in older areas of the city when property owners requested a change while commercially zoned land elsewhere lay undeveloped. Council zoned outlying newly annexed land for low density single-family use, then sometimes rezoned it for apartments or commercial development in response to a developer's proposal. The zoning code itself was comprehensive in nature but it was not administered in such a way as to serve as a comprehensive plan. Council and the zoning board responded to the requests of private property owners rather than planning where various land uses ought to be and in what amounts.

The suburbs had greater success. One was begun as a consciously planned community. It and another later commissioned formal plans. In addition, all the suburbs but one essentially administered their zoning ordinances so consistently as to imply the existence of a plan. They allowed few use changes, and those that they approved accommodated growth but did not alter the character of either individual neighborhoods or the community at large. Zoning in the final suburb functioned much as it did in

Columbus, with officials almost giving property owners and developers carte blanche.

Admittedly, the suburbs had a much easier task than did Columbus. They were smaller and more homogeneous. Property owners and developers alike might have felt the pressure of negative public opinion had they requested unpopular zoning changes. The reaction of Upper Arlington residents to the gas station and church controversies, and of Grandview residents to the proposed apartment tower, show that efforts to use land in unpopular ways did not go unnoticed. At the same time, for their part suburban zoning officials did not face the same type of requests as their counterparts in Columbus.[1] Property owners in the suburbs generally did not ask to put commercial uses in residential areas or to build more or larger multifamily buildings than permitted by code (except in Whitehall). The key to that exception may lie in administration. By requiring strict adherence to the code from the beginning and permitting few changes, officials in six suburbs made clear to developers and property owners how requests would be received. Meanwhile, Whitehall officials implicitly told property owners, "Ask and it shall be granted."

All in all, then, six of the eight municipalities essentially followed a comprehensive plan in their zoning activities. But one of the other two is the principal city of the metropolitan area.

Results on the second criterion, a balanced mix of uses, are more diverse. On the face of it, Columbus appears to have done rather well in this respect. Both the initial zoning ordinance and the revision of 1954 provide for industrial, commercial, and residential land uses, with enough different residential classes to house a variety of income groups. The appropriateness of the mix to the city's needs is another matter, however. The Bartholomew report indicated overzoning of both commercial and industrial land, and officials created additional commercial parcels through rezoning or by granting permission for nonconforming uses. So although the mix was there, the balance was not right.

The suburbs present a different situation—by and large they lack the mix. The smallest, Riverlea, is entirely residential. Residential development in Marble Cliff is all upper middle or upper income and covers almost the entire village. Although Bexley and Upper Arlington are much larger, both are also overwhelmingly single-family residential, and predominantly upper middle income or above. Most commercial development in both suburbs is of a scale and type to meet only local neighborhood or community needs. Grandview Heights, Whitehall, and Worthington all have a mix of uses. Commercial and industrial land exists along with a variety of housing types, though in Worthington middle and upper middle income single-family homes predominate. Judged by the balance and mix of uses, then, three suburbs score highest. Four others lack the mix and the city has the mix but not the balance.

With respect to the third criterion—the intrusion of incongruous or incompatible uses—the experience was much the same as with the comprehensive plan. Between the turn of the century and 1920 the central city of Columbus became increasingly commercial as residents moved to new outlying subdivisions or to older neighborhoods just outside the core. The zoning code then designated the downtown as a commercial district and earmarked all nonindustrial areas in the rest of the city—except along major streets—for some type of housing. Through the next fifty years, by single-lot rezoning or by permitting nonconforming uses, zoning officials in the City of Columbus regularly allowed incongruous uses into the older residential areas where, increasingly, minorities and low income persons lived. Neighborhoods developed after the first decade of the century were saved from this fate. However, city officials had much less to do with that than did the developers who had so thoroughly restricted the use of land through covenants in the deeds. The city could not, through a zoning action, negate a private contractual agreement.

In six of the suburbs the situation was quite different. Officials rarely granted nonconforming uses. The few rezonings extended existing commercial or industrial districts but did not permit their intrusion into established neighborhoods, even in older areas. But this is not surprising because it was the older residences that gave such exclusive suburbs as Bexley, Marble Cliff, and Upper Arlington their distinctive character, and Worthington took pride in its historic heritage. Whitehall again is the exception, although not so much as it at first appears. Whitehall rezoned many single parcels for industrial use in commercial districts, which seems to be incongruous. However, these rezonings were to allow gasoline service stations, car dealerships, and other auto-related uses that would have been permitted of right in commercial districts elsewhere. At the same time, rezonings or variances to permit apartments or commercial uses in areas zoned for single-family housing sometimes were intrusions.

Overall, then, most of the suburbs maintained existing areas well and prevented the deterioration that might have accompanied incompatible uses. The city, however, permitted intrusions into older areas but not newer ones, where deeds often already restricted land use.

The final criterion is one of social equity. Early zoning proponents sought to disperse people of all income groups throughout the metropolitan area—though not into mixed-group neighborhoods—to relieve urban congestion. At the same time, they wanted to protect the residential quality of both lower and upper income neighborhoods. Given the governmental structure of the metropolitan area, such a goal was impossible to achieve. Within the area this study examined are eight separate municipal entities, each with its own zoning ordinance and administrative board. No municipality could zone land inside another's borders. Only by having all land in the metropolitan area covered by a single ordinance could the equity standard have been met.

One can, of course, evaluate the actions of each of the eight municipalities with respect to its own land. On this basis, the results for Columbus are mixed. Columbus was in the enviable position of being able to grow out to, and beyond, its suburbs because of its aggressive annexation policies. Theoretically, this allowed zoning officials to provide for some dispersal of all income groups. They could zone outlying land for modest apartments as well as for large homes. The standard practice, however, was to zone newly annexed land for the least dense (and by implication highest income) single-family development. Then, if a developer presented a proposal for an alternative land use and requested a rezoning, the city could grant it. This was the case for several parcels in the northeast part of the city and accounts for the presence of apartments there. However, city officials did not decide ahead of time where different types of housing ought to be built; they responded to the plans of the developers.

On the other half of the equity standard, the city was even less successful. It was the older, pre-1900 residential areas the city initially zoned for apartments that housed most of the working class and lower income individuals. In these same areas city officials allowed increased lot density and intensity of use, thus detracting from the overall residential quality. In middle and upper income areas city officials perpetuated by public land use controls what developers had initiated by private ones. As noted in chapter 5, the lessened residential quality of older neighborhoods caused by commercial intrusions and parking lots effectively lessened population density in areas around the city center. (At the same time, of course, the number of persons living in individual buildings or lots increased as variances permitted more apartment units than the code allowed.) In one sense the city accomplished the theoretically desired deconcentration of population in older districts, but it did so at the expense of the residential quality for those remaining, who had no housing options elsewhere in the city. The hopes of early zoning proponents thus were not met, since relieving area-wide residential congestion did not result in dispersal of the low income population or protection of their neighborhoods from intrusions.

The suburbs, being small by comparison, had no opportunity to disperse their populations, although none had very dense development. In addition, having few or no low income areas, they did not need to protect them. In the spacious suburbs middle and upper income households could seek and find residential sanctuary. Early hopes for social equity, then, were doomed from the start.

How effectively did zoning serve the overall public interest of the metropolitan area? Measured by the hopes of its early proponents the answer is "not well." Columbus made an attempt to serve it by passing a zoning code that was, on its face, comprehensive and that provided for a mix of uses. But the mix was not balanced and code enforcement was inconsistent at best. There was no real effort to use zoning to direct growth and development in a comprehensively planned manner, so the original potential was not realized. Moreover, some residential areas experienced incompatible intrusions. Most of the suburbs, on the other hand, served the interests of their individual publics quite well. They planned their growth and development and protected their residential districts. Consisting largely of upper and upper middle income single-family neighborhoods, the suburbs found it much easier to define—and consequently to serve—their public interests than did the city.

In both city and suburb, however, the interest most clearly being served was that of the property owner. The two types of property owners expected somewhat different things from zoning, but there was no inherent conflict between their expectations. Those who earned their livelihood buying, selling, or developing land, or who rented or leased their property to produce income, wanted zoning to increase the income potential of their land. If platting and building new subdivisions, they wanted zoning provisions that allowed them to target specific markets and that reinforced the provisions of their deed restrictions. Those holding land for investment income wanted profitable apartment or commercial zoning. The zoned "highest and best" use of land for them was what was most profitable. Residential property owners—those who owned and occupied their own single-family homes—had a different goal. They wanted zoning to protect their residential quality and consequently stabilize or increase the market value of their property.

Both Columbus and the suburbs served property owners' interests. They steadfastly protected areas where middle and upper income people owned and occupied their own homes. At the same time, those individuals seeking income from their land had the opportunity to build apartments (sometimes at a greater density than permitted by code) or maintain commercial establishments (sometimes where the code did not allow them). Zoning thus was very successful at protecting property values, even as it limited the right of some individual owners to do as they wished. Early planners had viewed such property-value benefits of zoning as coincidental and secondary to its primary purpose of promoting the public health, safety, and welfare allowed by the police power.[2]

But the two were not inconsistent. Indeed, increasing property values—and everything that is part of them—could be construed as a legitimate element of promoting the public welfare. Justice Sutherland did not mention property values per se in his *Euclid* opinion, but the access of homes to light and air and the "privilege of quiet and open places for [children's] play" he spoke of certainly contributed to them.[3] Almost fifty years later Justice William O. Douglas used similar language when the U.S. Supreme Court upheld another zoning ordinance. "A quiet place where yards are wide, people few, and motor vehicles restricted are legitimate guidelines" for land use regulations that "lay out zones where family values, youth values, and the blessings of quiet seclusion, and clean air make the area a sanctuary for people." Although Douglas did not say it, they can also raise property values. "The police power," he noted, "is not confined to the elimination of filth, stench, and unhealthy places."[4] The police power can protect as well as restrict property rights, as the Columbus zoning experience shows. And if Columbus is typical, the real estate interests who supported zoning have no call to be disappointed.

For their part, the city planners and urban reformers can only hope that the worst land use abuses were prevented. Zoning did not function quite as they wished, but the very existence of land use controls may have dissuaded some from trying to use their land in undesirable ways. Though minimum standards were sometimes lowered, still there *were* minimum standards.

Land Use Controls and Urban Form

Private and public land use controls functioned differently, but both served property interests. How did they affect the city? Have controls determined the spatial and social structure of the metropolitan area?

Private developers determined how land would be used throughout the growing city and its suburbs through their imposition of restrictive covenants in deeds. The developers' covenants also determined who could—and could not—live in newly platted subdivisions. Thus in shaping the city's spatial structure, private controls also shaped its social structure. When they brought restricted lots in exclusive neighborhoods, with the assurance that the neighborhoods would remain exclusive, individual home owners contributed to the developers' prosperity as well as their own, since no unpleasant or unanticipated changes on nearby lots would lessen their property value.

Public land use controls, on the other hand, did not so much shape development as respond to it. Real estate developers, platting subdivisions outside the corporate limits, determined what type of neighborhoods should be where and increasingly protected them through deed restrictions. Local zoning provided another layer of protection when their developments joined the city or a suburb. Public land use controls, then, formalized and perpetuated existing development trends; they did not shape or direct them.

In this sense, zoning was not directly a cause of social stratification or racial segregation. Through restrictive covenants developers determined the income levels of their various subdivisions. Municipal officials zoning land for modest apartments that was deed restricted for large-lot upper income single-family homes would not have created economically mixed communities or provided housing for low or moderate income households in outlying areas. Moreover, using racial covenants during the times of greatest black population growth, developers also determined where minorities would or would not live. Landlords, private individuals, real estate agents, and mortgage lenders (including the FHA) supported and continued discriminatory housing patterns.[5] Zoning affected them only indirectly and primarily to the extent that racial minorities had lower incomes than necessary to live in some single-family areas.

Although zoning did not cause the segregation of people by race and class in Columbus or elsewhere, it certainly encouraged and maintained it. Early zoning proponents never explicitly claimed segregation as one of their goals but they implicitly supported it by mandating separate zones for different land uses and types of housing. As zoning protected residential districts from harmful intrusions, it also protected rich from poor and white from black. The small early twentieth-century black population of Columbus was concentrated on the near east side, in a portion of the band of older housing designated for apartments in 1923. Up through 1948 race restrictions in deeds effectively kept the growing black population confined to that area. After 1948 high housing cost or size minimums in deed restrictions combined with city and suburban zoning provisions for middle or upper income single-family neighborhoods continued the practice, for few blacks could meet the high minimum standards. At the same time, zoning actions affecting land near the central city lessened residential quality, which encouraged the departure of those who could afford it. But race prejudice and discriminatory real estate and mortgage practices limited housing alternatives for blacks regardless of income. By

1970, the Columbus metropolis exhibited a general pattern common to many American urban areas. The city center was given over to business activities and the poor and black lived in declining neighborhoods around it. Wealthy whites lived out in the suburbs. Although early zoning proponents supported dispersal of the population (which depopulation of the Columbus core accomplished), they never suggested that it be dispersed into neighborhoods that mixed people by race and income. Zoning thus furthered the market practices that complicated the efforts of civil rights activists seeking to integrate schools and neighborhoods in the 1960s and 1970s. No, zoning did not cause the illness of segregation; neither did it try to cure it.

Although the private control mechanism of the restrictive covenant had a greater impact on the urban form than publicly imposed zoning, the two were not unrelated. They had no legal connection in tradition or in theory. One was a private contractual matter between two individuals and its purpose was to control land use for the benefit (fiscal or otherwise) of those two individuals. The other was an exercise of the police power to serve the public good: the general welfare of the whole city. Thus there were two separate mechanisms, each controlling land independently of the other.

In fact, as the urban area grew and developed, the two devices exhibited a relationship that was almost reciprocal in nature. Initially, restrictive covenants preceded zoning, since developers platted unincorporated land. But when restricted land was annexed to the city or a suburb and subsequently zoned, the zoning provisions often matched the deed restrictions. In later years, when developers subdivided land outside municipal boundaries, they considered the zoning standards of the municipality they intended to annex their subdivision to and structured the deed restrictions accordingly. Consequently, public controls could potentially shape development (at least to the extent that they set a minimum level or designated use) but in actuality the effect was minimal, as by then the residential patterns of the metropolitan area already had been established.

Zoning thus was only marginally effective as a land use control device to plan and direct growth and development while preventing the deterioration that resulted from uncontrolled land use.

Smaller communities that had a clear idea of what they wanted to become were able to achieve their goals. Generally they sought to maintain the character and level of residential quality that private developers had bequeathed to them. Strict adherence to a zoning ordinance that was based on or reflected a comprehensive plan allowed them to do that. Those communities (one suburb and the major city) that had no plan—either implicit or explicit—were less successful at directing their own growth and development. They faced a multiplicity of interests and lacked a standard against which to measure the impact of serving those interests. The very existence of zoning may have allowed those two communities to avoid the worst impacts of uncontrolled land use, but repeated exceptions and alterations could not prevent those impacts altogether.

Additionally, if public controls were only partially effective at directing growth and controlling land use, they cannot have been solely responsible for the social and spatial structure of American urban areas. Just as individual private land owners, acting independently and seeking their own ends, created the conditions that led city planners and urban reformers to call for the institution of zoning, so those private property owners also created the modern middle and upper income suburbs and the chaos of older residential areas. Zoning, or its misapplication, aided their efforts but the private property owners led the way.

A case study such as this one has obvious limitations. It provides only one example, and other cities may exhibit different patterns. Still, the findings here in part support those of other works. Sam Bass Warner's view, referred to in the introduction, on the role that private individuals played in shaping the city and creating class and racial segregation, proved as valid for a midwestern city that grew and continues to expand in the twentieth century as for eastern cities that filled their borders in the nineteenth.[6] The conclusions of zoning's observers have also been confirmed. Almost from zoning's inception city planners and legal authorities on zoning have bemoaned the gap between the planning theory of zoning and zoning practice. In examining the application of zoning to actual parcels of land, this research confirms that at times (e.g., in Columbus and Whitehall) zoning has not performed as it theoretically should have. Other times (maintaining exclusive suburbs, for example) it performed all too well. Moreover, the study revealed that Columbus exhibited a spatial and social structure common to many U.S. cities studied by historians and social scientists. If private and public land use controls created that structure in Columbus, it is likely that they did elsewhere too.

And what of Jane Jacobs's complaints? She blamed the city planning profession for zoning the "life" out of American cities and for stratifying and segregating their residents, largely because planners did not "understand" how urban areas function. City planners in and around Columbus, Ohio, may or may not have "understood" the city's neighborhoods and their residents. But zoning officials played a much smaller part in separating the city's races and income groups than did the developers who platted and restricted exclusive subdivisions or the property owners who requested land use and density changes in older residential areas just outside the city's core. Moreover, in older parts of Columbus zoning facilitated the variety of land uses Jacobs so praised, but that variety contributed to their demise, not their strength and vitality.

Having examined the application of both private and public controls to actual parcels of land, this work provides another layer of support for the contention that by and large public land use controls have not effectively shaped urban growth and development patterns. One is left to wonder, then, if perhaps the goals its first proponents set for zoning were impossible to achieve. For zoning to direct development in a metropolitan area effectively, there must be either a single code for the entire area or cooperation between and among its constituent municipalities. When several municipalities control only their own land independently of one another, as they did in Columbus and do elsewhere, there can be no comprehensive regional planning and no assurance that all needs will be met. However, having a single jurisdiction large enough to include all metropolitan land increases the number and variety of interests within that jurisdiction who will seek to have zoning serve their own, sometimes conflicting, purposes. Zoning was most effective where the purpose of all involved (developers, residents, local officials) was the same: to preserve the quality of upper and upper middle income residential suburbs. Consequently, creation of a single metropolitan or regional jurisdiction that would be necessary for truly regional land use planning would at the same time create a circumstance where agreement on the goals of that planning would be difficult or impossible to achieve because of the multiplicity of differing interests.

Social equity issues are also problematical. Tenements and slums sparked the early city planners' and reformers' calls for zoning. They wanted to prevent the overcrowding, deterioration, and land speculation that lowered residential quality for the lower and working classes. However, restricting the use of land bids up its price. Indeed, developers who used restrictive covenants to create and maintain exclusive residential areas counted on that. Had the reformist zoners succeeded in so restricting land as to prevent deterioration and raise residential quality, they might also have raised the price of housing to a level the lower and working classes could not pay.[7]

Such theoretical questions as the inherent impossibility of zoning to achieve its goals are beyond the scope of this work. My initial intention was to test its effectiveness as a land use control reform by examining its application to the land, and to determine its impact on urban social and spatial structure. I wanted to find out what happened to American cities because of zoning. The story did not end with New York's ordinance in 1916 or the *Euclid* decision in 1926.

However, I could not examine zoning's impact on the physical and social city without also examining the process of residential real estate development and the private restrictions developers imposed on their land. I discovered two parallel, and sometimes interacting, processes and two primary actors. Through their activities early in the twentieth century, land developers laid the foundation for the growing metropolitan area's spatial and social structure. Through their zoning actions, city and suburban officials confirmed existing patterns and, especially after 1950, encouraged their perpetuation. This is so not only in outlying neighborhoods, where zoning protected middle and upper income residential areas and encouraged or required additional similar development, but also in unrestricted older areas, where Columbus zoning officials' responses to property owners' requests consistently increased the variety, density, and intensity of land use in primarily residential areas. Thus though the two groups — private property owners and public local officials—did not necessarily act together, they also did not act in opposition to each other.

Some researchers have studied the process of zoning in cities and others have studied land development. This research combines the two. Zoning in Columbus functioned much as it did elsewhere and Columbus land developers behaved like their counterparts from New Jersey to California. Moreover, by 1970 Columbus exhibited the same spatial and social patterns—though in less extreme form—as many other U.S. cities. This research shows how private and public land use controls collectively shaped those patterns in Columbus as they may have elsewhere.

The imposition of land use controls—whether private or public—is a form of planning. Whether by design or default those who imposed controls shaped the city. What interest did they serve? Both platters and purchasers of lots in restricted subdivisions benefited from stable or increasing property values. Those owning land whose potential profitability was increased by zoning changes that Columbus and Whitehall city councils and zoning boards allowed also benefited. But the legal justification for publicly restricting private property by zoning was to promote the health, safety, and welfare of all citizens. Indeed, the entire profession of city planning is premised on serving the public interest in its broadest sense. This study shows that, at least in Columbus, Ohio, zoning only partially met the goals its reformist proponents established for it. Moreover, as far as urban spatial and social structure are concerned, public controls did not so much shape land use patterns as perpetuate those that private controls had set. When all was said and done, planning served the private interest.

APPENDIX

Stated in its broadest and most general form, the purpose of this research was to determine how private and public land use controls affected urban spatial and social structure. Secondarily, it was to test the effectiveness of zoning against the goals set for it. The city planners and reformist lawyers who developed and supported zoning hoped it would plan and direct growth and development in new areas while preserving or improving residential quality in existing neighborhoods.

The research thus consisted of two parts. First, it examined the actual process of residential land development to see if the patterns found in cities that developed prior to land use controls also existed in a city whose growth occurred after their adoption. Second, it examined the application of zoning, focusing not on the political or administrative process but on the product—the land itself. It looked at zoning as a planning device to explore its role in determining land use. Together, the two parts explored how the long-term application of land use controls affected urban form as the city grew.

Sources

Public records of actions affecting land use and development were the major sources of information for this study. Real estate and fire insurance atlases, produced at various intervals since the 1880s, gave detailed information about the level and nature of the city's development. Annexation maps and data revealed the physical expansion of Columbus and its suburbs. The Franklin County auditor's and recorder's offices held records on land development. These included subdivision plat maps, maps and petitions for municipal incorporation, and deeds recording property ownership. Deeds indicated any private restrictions or covenants limiting the use or development of land. Municipal records provided detailed information on the legal framework within which land use controls operated, as well as the controls' specific provisions. These included all ordinances (zoning related and otherwise) passed by a city council and actions taken by boards of zoning appeals or adjustment.

Structure of the Study

As noted in the introduction, it was not possible to study the development and zoning actions of the entire metropolitan area in the detail desired because of its size. Consequently, I sampled the city, choosing six linear strips or corridors that stretched from the inner edge of residential development in 1920 to its outer edge in 1970. Examining changes in land use in these linear strips, I could thus observe the advancing fringe of development and see changes in development trends or controls applied within each area. I wanted the areas collectively to produce a picture of the city as a whole, but also to include those places where development occurred first and continued strongest. After examining land use maps from several eras, I delineated study corridors on the north, east, south, west, northwest, and northeast sides.

As the area within the present inner belt was fully developed and largely commercial and industrial by 1920, that freeway (formed by the circular intersection of I-70 and I-71) marked the bottom of each corridor. The outer limit was the present outer belt (I-270). A major transportation artery that had also been a street railway line formed at least one side border of each corridor. These included U.S. 40 (the old "National Road") on the east and west sides of the city and U.S. 23 (which also extends to Ohio's borders) on the north and south sides. The other side border of each corridor was determined by the boundaries of the platted subdivisions within it, and was a second major artery, a river, or (on the northwest and northeast sides) an irregular line.

In Columbus, as in many other cities, development occurred along both sides of major streets. To have defined the study areas with the major arterials in the middle, rather than along one side, would have posed problems, however. I would have had either to double the size of the study to include entire platted subdivisions or to examine only parts of most subdivisions (to keep the total amount of land area studied within manageable limits). Since the subdivision was the basic unit of development, I opted to examine only whole subdivisions and thus restricted my areas to one side of each artery. I chose the following corridors, illustrated in Figure 1, for research: (1) north—the west side of High Street to the Olentangy River; (2) northeast—along Cleveland Avenue; (3) east—between Broad and Main Streets; (4) south—the east side of High Street to Parsons Avenue; (5) west—between Broad Street and Sullivant; (6) northwest—north and east of Goodale Avenue and Dublin Road, paralleling the Scioto River.

I did not confine the study to the municipal limits of Columbus. I examined land within each study corridor that was never annexed to the city as well as land within suburban municipalities. The seven suburbs lying wholly or partially within the corridors are Riverlea and Worthington on the north, Bexley and Whitehall on the east, and Grandview Heights, Marble Cliff, and Upper Arlington on the northwest.

I researched the process and nature of development in each study corridor up through 1970 from what had been the urban fringe in 1920 (before Columbus or any of the suburbs adopted zoning). For each corridor, I defined the fringe as being that point or area below (or within) which almost all land had been subdivided and built upon, at which most land was subdivided and at least half built, and beyond which relatively little was built and much not yet platted. For the land development portion of the study, I collected information on all subdivisions at or beyond the 1920 fringe, regardless of when they were actually platted. Since platting sometimes preceded building by more than twenty years, this included some subdivisions platted before 1900. I examined how zoning was applied to *all* land in each corridor (not just that beyond the fringe), since zoning decisions concerning fully developed land could have implications for land use in developing areas. This also allowed for some comparison of the application of zoning in older developed areas with its application in newer parts of the city.

Data Collection and Processing

The information collected from public records produced two data sets, which I coded for computer processing using the Statistical Package for the Social Sciences (SPSS) program. As development occurred irrespective of municipal boundaries, I had a single development data set that included 335 subdivisions, with the individual subdivision being the case, or unit, of analysis. The zoning information was divided into six data subsets, one each for Columbus and five of the suburbs. (So few actions occurred in Marble Cliff and Riverlea that computerized analysis was not meaningful.) Because each city's zoning ordinance was unique, I had to examine each city's actions in terms of the provisions of its own ordinance. In these data sets, the individual zoning request was the case for analysis. These included 1,858 for Columbus, 212 for Bexley, 297 for Grandview Heights, 649 for Upper Arlington, 260 for Whitehall, and 185 for Worthington. The SPSS functions performed on both data sets were frequencies and crosstabulations. Tables A1 and A2 list the variables for each data set and indicate on which variables frequencies and crosstabulations were performed.

I allowed the observations themselves to determine the organization of the analysis and text, establishing time frames for discussion based on when groups of events actually occurred. This same clustering of events produced the three-mile and six-mile intervals for the discussion of zoning actions in Columbus.

Analysis of the results produced a picture of the residential environment of the metropolitan area as it changed over seventy years, showing where development occurred at different times and the scale and nature of the development. The results also indicated to what extent private development controls through deed restrictions shaped that development and, by extension, the city itself. At the same time, they showed the application of zoning controls to the land. By examining what uses or use changes governmental bodies permitted on different parcels of land, I saw how public land use controls also affected the city. Examining the two processes together, I determined the relative influence of private and public land use controls on the metropolitan area's spatial and social structure.

Table A.1
Subdivision Data Variables and Functions

Number of Cases: 335
Variables:
  Corridor: north, northeast, east, south, west, northwest
  Municipality: none, Columbus, Riverlea, Worthington, Bexley, Whitehall, Marble Cliff, Grandview Heights, Upper Arlington
  Year platted: pre-1901, or actual for 1901–70
  Year annexed: actual
  Distance from city center: actual to 0.5 mile
  Acreage: actual to 0.01 acre
  Number of lots: actual
  Subdivision history: platted once only, replatted, vacated
  Setback: actual building line in deed or plat
  Building type: single family, residential, commercial, and so on
  Minimum building value: actual $ specified
  Minimum building size: actual square feet
  Race restriction: none, Caucasian only, blacks excluded, other ethnic group excluded, combination, association membership required
  Termination date: actual
  Duration: actual number of years
  Era: one of six created by grouping values after examination of frequency results by year
  Lot size: 0.73 acreage divided by the number of lots (73% was computed as the mean amount of land actually platted into building lots after subtracting reserves and streets)
  Acres and lots: recoded from acreage and number of lots, respectively, to create groups of similar size for some analysis
  Density: lots per acre
  Size and value: recoded from minimum building size and minimum building value, respectively, to create groups of similar size for some analysis
Frequencies for variables: corridor, municipality, year, distance, era, acres, lots, setback, building type, building value, building size, race, termination, duration
Crosstabulations for variables:
  era by race, size, distance, acres, lots, setback, density, building value
  municipality by era, lots, acres, density, setback, building type, size, value, race
  corridor by era, lots, acres, density, setback, building type, size, value, race
  building type by lots, acres
  race by lots, acres, building type

Table A.2
Zoning Data Variables and Functions

Number of cases:
  Columbus: 1,858
  Bexley: 212
  Grandview Heights: 297
  Upper Arlington: 649
  Whitehall: 260
  Worthington: 185
Variables:
  Corridor: north, northeast, east, south, west, northwest
  Municipality: Columbus, Worthington, Bexley, Whitehall, Marble Cliff, Grandview, Upper Arlington
  Year of action: actual to 1970
  Actor: city council or zoning board
  Distance from city center: actual to 0.5 mile (for Columbus only)
  Present use zone: single family, apartment, commercial, industrial, and so on
  Requested use zone: single family, apartment, commercial, industrial, and so on
  Setback: variance for main structure, for addition to main structure, for accessory building
  Height: variance from stated maximum
  Lot: variance for area or frontage for main structure, for accessory building
  Floor: variance for floor area for main structure, for accessory building
  Nonconforming use: allow, expand or extend, alter (change from one to another)
  Decision: none recorded, granted, denied, denied on second hearing, granted on second hearing, withdrawn or tabled, vetoed or repealed
  Other action: special permit, fence, sign variance, parking exception, and so on
Frequencies for variables: corridor, year, actor, distance, present use zone, requested use zone, setback, height, lot, floor, nonconforming use, decision, other
Crosstabulations:
  decision by actor, setback, lot, height, floor, nonconforming use, other
  present use zone by requested use zone

All listed crosstabulations were performed on each of the five suburban data sets. For Columbus, the same crosstabulations were performed but for each of nine time frames. Then, a second set of operations crosstabulated corridor by distance for various actions in each time period.

NOTES

Introduction

1. Jane Jacobs, *Death and Life of Great American Cities*; Sam Bass Warner, Jr., *Streetcar Suburbs: The Process of Growth in Boston (1870–1900)*; John Delafons, *Land-Use Controls in the United States*; and Bernard H. Siegan, *Land Use without Zoning*.

2. Roy Lubove, *The Progressives and the Slums: Tenement House Reform in New York City, 1890–1917*.

3. U.S. Department of Commerce, Bureau of Standards, *Zoned Municipalities in the United States*, pp. 10, 16, 19; undated letter from the American Planning Association, Houston Section, received spring 1990 by the Planning Director of the City of Fort Worth, TX. A referendum on zoning failed to pass November 2, 1993, but may be submitted to voters at a later date.

4. Marc Allan Weiss, in *The Rise of the Community Builders: The American Real Estate Industry and Urban Land Planning*, discusses the real estate industry's active role in planning and zoning. However, his work and the comments made by private developers at the National Conference on City Planning throughout the 1910s and 1920s indicate that members of the real estate industry were much less concerned than city planners and reformist lawyers about the public purposes of zoning.

5. In Theodora Kimball Hubbard and Henry Vincent Hubbard, *Our Cities To-Day and To-Morrow: A Survey of Planning and Zoning Progress in the United States*, the authors note that initially Milwaukee zoned for commercial use three times the amount of land in commercial use at that time, and Santa Barbara zoned 91 percent of its land for business and apartments.

6. The research is thus modeled on methods developed by Sam Bass Warner in *Streetcar Suburbs*, his study of metropolitan growth in Boston.

7. The appendix provides a detailed description of the research methodology and delineation of the study areas.

Chapter 1

1. Unless otherwise noted, information in this chapter was derived from decennial reports of the U.S. Bureau of the Census from 1870 through 1970, and from examination of the following maps and atlases: *Caldwell's Atlas of Franklin County and the City of Columbus, Ohio* (Columbus, Ohio: J. A. Caldwell and H. T. Gould, 1872); "Map of Franklin County, Ohio" (Columbus, Ohio: G. J. Brand, 1883); untitled map in *Columbus and Its Attractions* (Columbus, Ohio: Columbus Railway Company, 1901); Topographical Map, quadrant 82'45"–83'15", 39'45"–40'15" (U.S. Geological Survey, 1912); *Baist's Real Estate Atlas of Surveys of Columbus, 1920* (Philadelphia: G. William Baist, 1920); *Insurance Maps of Columbus, Ohio* (New York: Sanborn Map Company, 1922, updated to 1937); *Plat Book of Columbus and Vicinity, Franklin County Ohio* (Philadelphia: Franklin Survey Company, 1937); and "Housing Patterns in Franklin County Ohio," a map prepared by the Housing Opportunity Center of Metropolitan Columbus from 1970 U.S. census data. The author has also relied on her own observation of the city over a period of twenty years' residence.

2. In the 1970s the Leveque tower was surpassed by a state tower housing government offices, and these two have since been joined by other tall office buildings.

3. Thomas Hines, *Burnham of Chicago: Architect and Planner*, includes Union Station in the appendix listing buildings by D. H. Burnham and Company and dates it 1896. The firm also designed two Columbus office buildings in the 1890s. There is nothing to indicate, however, that Burnham was involved in city planning activities in Columbus either then or later. An impressive structure, Union Station was demolished in the 1970s for a convention center-hotel-office complex despite the efforts of preservationists.

4. Columbus's industrial development, which did not begin in earnest until 1870, was later than that in Cincinnati, Cleveland, or other midwestern cities and consequently was slower and of less importance. See Henry L. Hunker, *Industrial Evolution of Columbus, Ohio*, and Eric H. Monkkonen, *The Dangerous Class: Crime and Poverty and Columbus, Ohio, 1860–1885*.

5. Both Monkkonen, *Dangerous Class*, and Hunker, *Industrial Evolution*, date serious industrialization in Columbus from about 1870 and attribute its relatively late start to geographic factors. Central Ohio lacked the extensive mineral deposits found in the southeast part of the state and Columbus's location was not conducive to early industrialization. Wade, in *The Urban Frontier: The Rise of Western Cities, 1790–1830*, has noted that urban and industrial development in the eastern Midwest occurred first in

the Ohio River Valley system and then along the Great Lakes. Midway between the two, Columbus got a late start.

6. Monkkonen, *Dangerous Class*, pp. 113–15. Monkkonnen's case study, which examines the relationships among urbanization, industrialization, poverty, and crime, provides a good picture of the post-Civil War Columbus population.

7. The single most comprehensive work on this era and type of city planning, which focuses on medium-sized cities, is William H. Wilson, *The City Beautiful Movement*. The role of the business community and its relationship to municipal government in city planning are spelled out in Mansel G. Blackford, *The Lost Dream: Businessmen and City Planning on the Pacific Coast, 1890–1920*. The 1909 *Plan* of Chicago and its promotion are the subject of Thomas J. Schlereth, "Burnham's *Plan* and "Moody's *Manual*: City Planning as Progressive Reform."

8. Austin W. Lord, Albert Kelsey, Charles N. Lowrie, Charles Mulford Robinson, and H. A. McNeil, *Plan of the City of Columbus*, introduction.

9. The use of experts from the design fields was typical in this era before the formation of the American City Planning Institute.

10. Lord et al., *Plan*, "Part One: The General Survey."

11. Ibid., "Part Two: Parks, Parkways and Recreation Grounds."

12. Ibid., "Part Three: The Civic Center."

13. Wilson's *City Beautiful Movement* subtly develops this concept of comprehensiveness in city planning, a concept quite different from that reflected in city plans of the 1920s and 1950s.

14. Lord et al., *Plan*, p. 27.

15. Hoyt Landon Warner, *Progressivism in Ohio: 1897–1917*, p. 17.

16. Ibid., pp. 41–44.

17. Ibid., pp. 105–15; letter and sermon by Gladden quoted p. 111.

18. Ibid., pp. 300–307, 312–13.

19. Ibid., pp. 314; 330–32. Warner notes that the strong vote was not indicative of overwhelming support for home rule, however, as many fence straddlers voted in favor of home rule only when they realized supporters had garnered enough votes to assure passage.

20. Ibid., pp. 318–20; 324–25.

21. Ibid., pp. 338–43.

22. In the 1970s Columbus still retained the same basic form of government, with the elected mayor as chief executive or administrator and a seven-member, at-large, council.

23. Warner, *Progressivism in Ohio*, pp. 443–45; 453; 456–60.

24. Wade H. Ellis, *Municipal Code of Ohio*, 5th and 6th eds.

25. Ibid.

26. Columbus *City Bulletin 7*, 25 (1922): 262.

27. Like many cities, Columbus benefited from the same economic prosperity in both the 1920s and 1950s that affected the nation as a whole, which was reflected, in part, by extensive real estate development. As discussed below and in chapter 2, developers often annexed their subdivisions to the city to gain services.

28. A Bexley official indicated that the detachment occurred because one of the residents of this tract wanted to run for mayor of Columbus, which would have required that he be a resident of the city. Rather than move his place of residence, he "moved" the corporate boundary.

29. This process is described in chapters 2 and 4. It is much like that described for other cities in Marc A. Weiss, *The Rise of the Community Builders: The American Real Estate Industry and Urban Land Planning*, and William S. Worley, *J. C. Nichols and the Shaping of Kansas City: Innovation in Planned Residential Communities*.

Chapter 2

1. The terms *restrictive covenants* and *deed restrictions* are used interchangeably throughout this work to refer to those covenants of a restrictive nature inserted into property deeds at the time of transfer.

2. John Delafons, *Land-Use Controls in the United States*, p. 85.

3. Kenneth T. Jackson, in *Crabgrass Frontier: The Suburbanization of the United States*, p. 76, notes that deeds for a subdivision in Brookline, Massachusetts, provided for a thirty-foot building setback and residential construction in 1843. Later in the century they prohibited sales to blacks and the Irish.

4. Helen Monchow, *The Use of Deed Restrictions in Subdivision Development*, pp. 2–5.

5. Ibid., pp. 27–31.

6. Deeds for one of the subdivisions examined in this research prohibited planting of catalpa trees.

7. Monchow, *Deed Restrictions*, p. 32.

8. Ibid., pp 28–38. Monchow's 1928 study found that thirty-nine of eighty-four subdivisions' deeds she examined required construction approval.

9. Ibid., pp. 46–50. In *Shelley* v. *Kramer*, 344 U.S. 1 (1948), racially restrictive covenants were not ruled illegal as such but were held to be not

legally enforceable, as they would be a denial of property rights that individuals would be "willing and financially able to acquire and which the grantors are willing to sell."

10. Monchow, *Deed Restrictions*, pp. 21–24.

11. Ibid., pp. 24–25.

12. Ibid., pp. 56–57. Current practice holds that the rule against perpetual restraints, although applicable to restrictions on the alienation of property, does not apply to covenants affecting use: Urban Land Institute, *The Homes Association Handbook*, p. 335. This point was somewhat ambiguous in the 1920s, however, and as the same set of covenants often addressed both alienation and use, land developers were on the firmest legal ground by specifying a duration.

13. Monchow, *Deed Restrictions*, pp. 58–59.

14. Many deeds recorded since 1950 have automatic extension clauses, which were required by the Federal Housing Administration (FHA) for mortgage insurance. Bernard H. Siegan, *Land Use Without Zoning*, p. 34; Marc A. Weiss, *The Rise of the Community Builders: The American Real Estate Industry and Urban Land Planning*, p. 202.

15. At the time of Monchow's 1928 study there was some question as to whether municipal enforcement would be upheld by law, since the covenants were a private contract. However, in 1973 Ellickson noted that municipal enforcement had been the general rule in Houston; Robert C. Ellickson, "Alternatives to Zoning: Covenants, Nuisance Rules, and Fines as Land Use Controls." Indeed, the Texas state legislature explicitly granted Houston the power to enforce deed restrictions; Diane T. Vague, "The Evolution of Land Use Planning for the City of Houston, Texas: 'Free-Market' Forces Versus Public and Private Controls in the Twentieth Century," p. 33. Houston appears to be the exception in this respect, however.

16. Monchow, *Deed Restrictions*, pp. 62–70. Urban notes that homeowners' associations are sometimes given so much power that they function almost as municipal entities but without the statutory or constitutional checks controlling public bodies. Mark Urban, "An Evaluation of the Applicability of Zoning Principles to the Law of Private Land Use Restrictions."

17. The comment was in a speech Ford made to the eighteenth annual meeting of the National Association of Real Estate Boards, quoted in William S. Worley, *J. C. Nichols and the Shaping of Kansas City: Innovation in Planned Residential Communities*, p. 89.

18. Monchow, *Deed Restrictions*, pp. 8–9, 14–15.

19. Ibid., pp. 17, 20.

20. Ibid., pp. 73–74.

21. Delafons, *Land-Use Controls*, pp. 85–86, 91; Weiss, *Community Builders*, p. 304; Mary Corbin Sies, "American Country House Architecture in Context: The Suburban Ideal in the East and Midwest, 1877–1917," chaps. 5–7; National Conference on City Planning, *Proceedings*, 1916, p. 106.

22. The above discussion has drawn heavily on Helen Monchow's 1928 study of the development of deed restrictions, the most thorough study for its era. She examined deeds in eighty-four subdivisions in the United States and Canada and noted some regional variations in the use of deed restrictions, but she concluded that they were a widely used development device in the 1920s. However, she focused primarily on the technique's development and application and not on its effect on urban structure, a major consideration of this work.

23. In *Streetcar Suburbs: The Process of Urban Growth in Boston (1870–1900)*, Warner explains the "walking city" as one whose radius is no greater than the distance one can comfortably walk within a reasonable length of time — generally a radius of one and one-half to three miles.

24. Unless noted otherwise, information in the remainder of this chapter has been derived from examination of real estate and fire insurance atlases, subdivision plat maps, and recorded deeds. As outlined in the introduction and appendix, this research did not study the entire metropolitan area but examined all subdivisions — a total of more than three hundred — platted beyond the 1920 urban fringe (regardless of when they were platted) in six "corridors."

25. Since all these subdivisions were beyond the urban fringe when platted, they were not within any incorporated municipality. Figure 2, as well as other figures, tables, and all discussion in this study, thus places each subdivision within the municipality to which it was later annexed.

26. Jon C. Teaford, *City and Suburb: The Political Fragmentation of Metropolitan America, 1850–1970*, takes a macroscopic look at this process for the United States as a whole, while Ann Durkin Keating, *Building Chicago: Suburban Developers and the Creation of a Divided Metropolis*, examines it in depth for a single metropolitan area.

27. The remaining half would be annexed to Columbus in the 1920s.

28. Ohio law did not differentiate between incorporated municipalities on the basis of size (i.e., between "cities," with more than five thousand inhabitants, and "villages," with fewer than five thousand) in granting annexation powers. As long as adjacent landholders were agreeable, incipient suburbs like Grandview found it as easy as Columbus did to expand physically.

29. As noted in chapter 1, in 1922 Columbus sought to expand by annexing Bexley, Marble Cliff, Grandview Heights, and Upper Arlington as well but was not successful.

30. Marc Weiss's *Rise of the Community Builders* discusses the land development boom in California during the 1920s, explaining how problems created by the boom and its aftereffects led realtors to become active supporters of the push for municipal zoning ordinances. In *Only Yesterday: An Informal History of the Nineteen-Twenties*, Frederick Lewis Allen describes the Florida land boom and the enormous pressure that real estate speculation put on land values during the 1920s.

31. Given that the proportion of foreign born had been steadily decreasing since 1870 and had dropped to 7 percent by 1930, this last restriction seems unnecessary. Still, the northeast was the logical direction of expansion for the small Italian community.

32. In *Only Yesterday* Allen provides *New York Times* averages for the stock market indicating a 50 percent drop in value between September 3, 1929, and November 13, 1929 (p. 280). The Florida land boom bubble had burst almost as quickly in 1926 (pp. 234–238). The depression-induced drop in building permits in Columbus, Ohio, on the other hand, took months, and the number of permits issued did not reach its ebb until four years after the crash. Meanwhile, land development continued, although at reduced levels, in the suburbs.

33. Otis L. Graham Jr.'s *Toward a Planned Society: From Roosevelt to Nixon* describes the extensive network of government agencies and economic controls set up to mobilize the nation for the war effort. The structure was dismantled almost in its entirety at the war's conclusion (pp. 69–90).

34. For uniformity in time as well as space, it was standard practice for deed restrictions for all lots in a subdivision to have a common expiration date, regardless of when the individual lots sold, and January 1 of a year ending in zero was often chosen. As Riverlea was platted during the boom days of the 1920s, its developer could have reasonably expected that the fifteen-year duration of the restrictions would provide sufficient protection to the development. By that time it could be annexed into the growing Columbus and public land use controls could take over.

35. Monchow, *Deed Restrictions*, p. 72. As indicated in n. 22, Helen Monchow's *The Use of Deed Restrictions in Subdivision Development* examined deeds from eighty-four subdivisions in the United States and Canada. Her study was the first in a series of works that the Institute of Research in Land Economics and Public Utilities, under the direction of economist Richard T. Ely, published as monographs because they were too extensive

to be included in the institute's quarterly journal. Monchow's intent was to examine, from an economic perspective, the impact of deed restrictions on the land and the relations between buyer and seller, which she felt was important given the amount of real estate development during the 1920s.

36. Simeon D. Fess, ed., *Ohio: A Four Volume Reference Library on the History of a Great State*, pp. 142–144.

37. It has often been the norm in the United States for building lots to be noticeably deeper than wide, for in many communities the cost of improvements (e.g., water and sewer lines, street paving and sidewalks) is assessed per foot frontage. Thus, a forty-by-one-hundred-foot lot would have a lower assessment than a fifty-by-eighty-foot one, although both would contain the same amount of acreage.

38. Galen R. Rarick, *Upper Arlington: Glimpses of Its First 50 Years*, p. 3.

39. Ibid., pp. 12–14, 40–41.

40. Ibid., pp. 2–6.

41. This technique could also be used to exclude others on the basis of various group or individual characteristics. The provision mandating civic association membership applied only to the four subdivisions Thompson platted in the 1950s; however, it applied not only to the original purchasers of unimproved lots but also to subsequent purchasers of homes.

42. The Federal Housing Authority (FHA) requirement regarding deed restrictions had no real impact at this time. The FHA, which was established in 1934, required deed restrictions in subdivisions qualifying for government-insured mortgages. But Columbus developers in the 1930s and 1940s were trying to appeal to a higher income group than FHA mortgages were designed to assist. Thus, minimum FHA standards, even into the 1950s, would not have been high enough to serve the developers' purpose.

Chapter 3

1. Peter Hall, *Cities of Tomorrow: An Intellectual History of Urban Planning and Design in the Twentieth Century*, chap. 2; Roy Lubove, *The Progressives and the Slums: Tenement House Reform in New York City, 1890–1917*; William H. Wilson, *The City Beautiful Movement;* and Allen F. Davis, *Spearheads for Reform: The Social Settlements and the Progressive Movement, 1890–1914*, all describe these conditions in detail.

2. Mel Scott, *American City Planning Since 1890*; Donald A. Krueckeberg, ed., *Introduction to Planning History in the United States*.

3. Jon A. Peterson, "The Impact of Sanitary Reform upon American

Urban Planning, 1840–1890," and "The City Beautiful Movement: Forgotten Origins and Lost Meanings," both in Krueckeberg, *Introduction*; Lubove, *Progressives*; Davis, *Spearheads*, and "Playgrounds, Housing, and City Planning," in Krueckeberg, *Introduction*.

4. Seymour I. Toll, *Zoned American*; Lubove, *Progressives*.

5. Wilson, *City Beautiful*; David Schuyler, *The New Urban Landscape: The Redefinition of City Form in Nineteenth-Century America*; Donald A. Krueckeberg, "Introduction to the American Planner," in Krueckeberg, ed., *The American Planner: Biographies and Recollections*; Thomas S. Hines, *Burnham of Chicago: Architect and Planner*.

6. Schuyler, *New Urban Landscape*; Dana F. White, "Frederick Law Olmsted, the Placemaker," in Schaffer, ed., *Two Centuries of American Planning*; Wilson, *City Beautiful*.

7. Hines, *Burnham of Chicago*, chaps. 5–6.

8. Wilson, *City Beautiful*, chap. 3.

9. Wilson, *City Beautiful*; Hall, *Cities of Tomorrow*, chap. 6.

10. Stanley Buder, *Visionaries & Planners: The Garden City Movement and the Modern Community*; Hall, *Cities of Tomorrow*, chap. 4.

11. Buder, *Visionaries*.

12. National Conference on City Planning, *Proceedings* 1909, printed as Senate Doc. 422, 61st Congress, 2d session.

13. Scott, *American City Planning*, pp. 95–100, 163–169; Donald A. Krueckeberg, "The Story of the Planners' Journal"; Eugenie Ladner Birch, "Advancing the Art and Science of Planning: Planners and Their Organizations, 1909–1980"; see also, Don S. Kirschner, *The Paradox of Professionalism: Reform and Public Service in Urban America, 1900–1940*.

14. Krueckeberg, "Planners' Journal."

15. Lubove, *Progressives*, pp. 229–230.

16. Ibid., p. 236; Sam Bass Warner, Jr., *The Private City: Philadelphia in Three Periods of Its Growth*.

17. Lubove, *Progressives*, p. 236.

18. Ibid., p. 245; Seymour I. Toll, *Zoned American*, chap. 4.

19. Thomas H. Logan, "The Americanization of German Zoning."

20. Ibid., p. 378.

21. Ibid., p. 389.

22. John Robert Mullin, "American Perceptions of German City Planning at the Turn of the Century."

23. Ibid.; Senate Doc. 422, 61st Congress, 2d session.

24. Ibid.; Senate Doc. 422, 61st Congress, 2d session.

25. NCCP, *Proceedings* 1909; Senate Doc. 422, 61st Congress, 2d session.
26. Pearl Janet Davies, *Real Estate in American History*, p. 6.
27. Logan, "Americanization," p. 381.
28. Davies, *Real Estate*, pp. 65–67, 78.
29. Sam Bass Warner, Jr., *The Urban Wilderness*, pp. 28–31; Edward M. Bassett, "From the Autobiography of Edward M. Bassett," in Krueckeberg, *American Planner*, p. 102.
30. Bassett, "Autobiography," pp. 112–13.
31. *Village of Euclid* v. *Ambler Realty Co.*, 272 U.S. 365, 47 S.Ct. 114, 71 L. ED 303 (1926).
32. Laurence C. Gerckens, "Bettman of Cincinnati," in Krueckeberg, *American Planner*, pp. 134–35.
33. Laurence C. Gerckens, "Bettman of Cincinnati," in Krueckeberg, *American Planner*.
34. Standard Zoning Enabling Act, U.S. Department of Commerce, rev. ed., 1926; Standard City Planning Enabling Act, U.S. Department of Commerce, rev. ed. 1927.
35. Gordon Whitnall, "History of Zoning," p. 2; Gerckens, "Bettman," in Krueckeberg, *American Planner*, pp. 135–36; Marc A. Weiss, *Rise of the Community Builders: The American Real Estate Industry and Urban Land Planning*, p. 67.
36. The real estate field's interests in planning and zoning are developed at length in Weiss, *Community Builders*.
37. If building codes required windows but did not provide for building setback lines, the first structure on a block could be built to the lot line and use the full land area for construction, but subsequent structures on adjacent lots would only be able to use a portion of their lots in order to allow for windows on side walls.
38. Edward M. Bassett, *Zoning: The Laws, Administration, and Court Decisions During the First Twenty Years*, pp. 7, 23–25, 105, 111.
39. Lubove, *Progressives*, pp. 229–36.
40. Ibid., p. 237.
41. Toll, *Zoned American*, chap. 4; Lubove, *Progressives*, pp. 244–45.
42. Theodorea Kimball Hubbard and Henry Vincent Hubbard, *Our Cities To-Day and To-Morrow: A Survey of Planning and Zoning in the United States*, p. 163.
43. Barbara J. Flint, "Zoning and Residential Segregation: A Social and Physical History, 1910–1940," pp. 21–25, 60–61.
44. NCCP, *Proceedings* 1921, pp. 32–35
45. Ibid., pp. 26–27.

46. Ibid., pp. 28–29.

47. Robert Whitten, "Social Aspects of Zoning."

48. While many works discuss American racial problems in the 1920s, one of the most insightful is Carl Sandburg's *The Chicago Race Riots: July, 1919*. As a reporter, Sandburg had begun investigating the racial situation in Chicago just prior to the outbreak of violence in July. The riots provided impetus to complete his work and led to the publication of his newspaper articles in book form.

49. NCCP, *Proceedings* 1925, pp. 88–90; *Proceedings* 1926, p. 62.

50. Hubbard and Hubbard, *Our Cities*, p. 163.

51. John Delafons, *Land-Use Controls in the United States*, p. 23.

52. Hubbard and Hubbard, *Our Cities*, p. 164.

53. William A. Fischel, *The Economics of Zoning Laws: A Property Rights Approach to American Land Use Controls*, p. 32.

54. It is also referred to as the City Practical and the City Functional.

55. Hall, *Cities of Tomorrow*; Wilson, *City Beautiful*.

56. Scott, *American City Planning*, chap. 3.

57. NCCP, *Proceedings* 1927.

58. Ibid., p. 19.

59. Harlean James, *Land Planning in the United States for the City, State and Nation*, pp. 84–85, 231.

60. Ibid., p. 86.

61. Ibid., p. 86; Toll, *Zoned American*, p. 117.

62. James, *Land Planning*, p. 258.

63. Fischel, *Economics of Zoning*, p. 31.

64. Gerckens, "Bettman," pp. 133–135.

65. ICRPC, *Proceedings* 1925, pp. 414–416; NCCP *Planning Problems of Town, City and Region*, 1926 (proceedings), pp. 57–58.

66. Alfred Bettman, "The Present State of Court Decisions on Zoning," p. 26.

67. Bettman, "Present State," pp. 26–30; Bassett, "Zoning Roundtable," p. 301.

68. James, *Land Planning*, pp. 231–37.

69. Hubbard and Hubbard, *Our Cities*, p. 165.

70. Ibid., p. 165.

71. Charles M. Haar, "In Accordance With a Comprehensive Plan," p. 1157.

72. Ibid., pp. 1158–63.

73. Ibid., pp. 1163–65.

74. Ibid., pp. 1165–66.

75. Ibid., p. 1167.

76. Ibid., pp. 1166–70; Daniel R. Mandelker, "The Role of the Comprehensive Plan in Land Use Regulation."

77. Mandelker, "Comprehensive Plan," p. 971; Gerckens, "Bettman," p. 135.

78. Mandelker, "Comprehensive Plan," p. 971.

79. Toll, *Zoned American*, p. 203; Constance Perin, *Everything in Its Place: Social Order and Land Use in America*, p. 148.

80. Logan, "Americanization," p. 383; Flint, "Zoning and Residential Segregation," p. 21; M. Christine Boyer, *Dreaming the Rational City: The Myth of American City Planning*, p. 94. Realtors', developers', and planners' thoughts on land use controls were all presented at the National Conference on City Planning and are reported in the *Proceedings* of the 1910s and 1920s, especially 1915, 1916, 1921, 1925, 1926, and 1927. The real estate industry's views are also in Weiss, *Community Builders*.

81. Hubbard and Hubbard, *Our Cities*, pp. 176–77, 138–39.

82. Ibid., pp. 188–89; Delafons, *Land-Use Controls*, p. 93.

83. Lubove, *Progressives*, p. 243.

84. Ibid., pp. 237–44.

85. Boyer, *Rational City*, p. 93.

86. Weiss, *Community Builders*, p. 131; Boyer, *Rational City*, pp. 94, 142.

87. Weiss, *Community Builders*, pp. 44–52.

88. Ibid., pp. 208–09.

89. Ibid., pp. 299–304.

90. NCCP, *Proceedings* 915, pp. 75–78; *Proceedings* 1916, pp. 99–104.

91. Hubbard and Hubbard, *Our Cities*, p. 154.

92. Weiss, *Community Builders*; Flint, "Zoning and Residential Segregation," chap. 2.

93. Toll, *Zoned American*, chap. 7.

94. Perin, *Everything in Its Place*, pp. 129–33.

95. Richard F. Babcock, *The Zoning Game: Municipal Practices and Policies*.

96. Perin, *Everything in Its Place*, p. 83.

97. Bassett, *Zoning*, p. 68.

98. Toll, *Zoned American*, chap. 7; Gerckens, "Bettman," pp. 130–35.

99. This same ambiguity of purpose has been noted for economic regu-

lation of business as well. Reformers sought the establishment of agencies such as the Interstate Commerce Commission to serve the public interest while those being regulated often turned the process to their own advantage. See Thomas K. McCraw, "Regulation in America: A Review Article."

100. Weiss, *Community Builders*, pp. 162–163.

101. NCCP, *Proceedings* 1927, p. 203.

102. Boyer, *Rational City*, p. 153.

103. Flint, "Zoning and Residential Segregation," p. 224.

104. Delafons, *Land-Use Controls*, pp. 19–24.

105. Unless otherwise noted, discussion of zoning in Columbus is based on examination and analysis of the actions of City Council and the zoning board as described in the appendix.

106. Ordinance 32417, March 28, 1921.

107. Frank S. So, "Planning Agency Management," in Frank S. So and Judith Getzels, eds., *The Practice of Local Government Planning*, pp. 401–03. In later years, cities created planning departments, with a director who reported to the mayor, city manager, or city council as an element of local government. The planning department (with its paid professional staff) would handle implementation or administration of planning matters, while the independent planning commission (still composed of unpaid citizen volunteers) defined policy and made recommendations to city council. The planning department staff also could provide information and advice to the planning commission on specific planning problems or concerns.

108. Ordinance 34010, August 6, 1923; *Columbus Dispatch*, August 7, 1923, p. 2. Examination of local newspapers from the date the proposed code was first announced until three weeks after its adoption revealed no letters to the editor regarding the code and no articles discussing the public's response.

109. NCCP, *Proceedings* 1941, p. 295.

110. The potential for a parcel to produce income from industrial use is more dependent on external site characteristics such as rail or water access than on zoning designation. Throughout the rest of this work, the planning/zoning framework will be applied, with the single-family home being the highest property use and industrial the lowest. This is appropriate given that one of the initial purposes of zoning was to prevent deterioration of residential areas thought to result from expanding commercial and industrial districts.

111. Unfortunately, the city has few records on Planning Commission rezoning actions, so there is no way to determine how often council either followed or overruled the commission's recommendations. The *City Bulle-*

tin, which published all council actions on a weekly basis and which was the principal record source on rezoning actions for this research, did not indicate Planning Commission recommendations.

112. Ordinance 37138, June 21, 1926.

113. Ordinance 194–48, March 1, 1948.

114. Ordinance 358–49, May 23, 1949.

115. Real estate and fire insurance atlases, prepared between 1920 and 1954, indicate the use of structures on all parcels mapped.

116. Information in this chapter regarding actions of City Council or the zoning board was derived from the results of the frequency and cross-tabulation operations performed on the zoning data set discussed in the appendix. For the City of Columbus, this set included all zoning actions of council in each study area through 1970. It includes all zoning board actions from 1923 through 1970 except for the years 1933 and 1934. The *City Bulletin* recorded requests before the BZA and its decisions regularly though 1932. In the first months of 1933, however, the *City Bulletin* recorded requests but few decisions, then ceased recording BZA actions altogether. The Records Department of the Development Regulations Division has BZA actions on microfiche or in its files beginning with the year 1935. Consequently, there are no extant records of BZA activity for 1933 and 1934. The combined total number of actions taken by both bodies through 1970 is 1,858.

117. Three hundred fifty-one requests were made but decisions have been recorded for only 324. As some decisions involved more than one action (e.g., a property owner might request both a use change and a setback or lot variance), totals for the various types of actions do not equal the number of decisions made.

118. Columbus City Council and Board of Zoning Adjustment actions affected land in the north, northeast, east, south, and west sections of the study. No northwest side land was affected, as none was within the municipal boundaries by 1970 and thus it was not subject to the city's zoning ordinance.

119. Single-family districts would be A area dwelling house zones while row house districts were B area dwelling house zones.

120. One hundred six actions were requested, for which 83 decisions have been recorded.

121. Given that no BZA records exist for 1933 and 1934, the proportion of decisions the board issued was probably even greater.

122. Housing was a permitted use in commercial districts, so a rezoning was not necessary. However, property owners building row houses for

rental may have wanted to make certain that no future tenants engaged in commercial activities, which were prohibited in the dwelling house zone.

123. Harvey A. Kantor, "Charles Dyer Norton and the Origins of the Regional Plan of New York," in Krueckeberg, *American Planner*; David A. Johnson, "Regional Planning for the Great American Metropolis: New York between the World Wars," in Schaffer, *Two Centuries*.

124. Johnson, "Regional Planning," in Schaffer, *Two Centuries*; Roy Lubove, *Community Planning in the 1920's: The Contribution of the Regional Planning Association of America*; Buder, *Visionaries & Planners*; and Hall, *Cities of Tomorrow*, chap. 4.

125. Lubove, *Community Planning*; Howard Gillette, Jr., "The Evolution of Neighborhood Planning: From the Progressive Era to the 1949 Housing Act."

126. Mark I. Gelfand, *A Nation of Cities: The Federal Government and Urban America, 1933–1965*.

127. John Hancock, "The New Deal and American Planning: The 1930s," in Schaffer, *Two Centuries*.

128. Hancock, "New Deal," in Schaffer, *Two Centuries*; Scott, *American City Planning*, pp. 311–16.

129. Joseph L. Arnold, *The New Deal in the Suburbs: A History of the Greenbelt Town Program, 1935–1954*; Joseph A. Eden and Arnold R. Alanen, "Looking Backward at a New Deal Town: Greendale, Wisconsin, 1935–1980"; David Myhra, "Rexford Tugwell: Initiator of America's Greenbelt New Towns, 1935–6," in Krueckeberg, *American Planner*; and Hancock, "New Deal," in Schaffer, *Two Centuries*.

130. Hancock, "New Deal," in Schaffer, *Two Centuries*; Eugenie Ladner Birch, "Woman-made America: The Case of Early Public Housing Policy," in Krueckeberg, *American Planner*.

131. Hancock, "New Deal," in Schaffer, *Two Centuries*; Scott, *American City Planning*, pp. 300–11.

132. Phillip J. Funigiello, "City Planning in World War II: The Experience of the National Resources Planning Board," in Krueckeberg, *Introduction*.

133. John F. Bauman, "Visions of a Post-War City: A Perspective on Urban Planning in Philadelphia and the Nation," in Krueckeberg, *Introduction*.

134. Bauman, "Visions of a Post-War City," in Krueckeberg, *Introduction*; John F. Bauman, "The Paradox of Post-War Urban Planning: Downtown Revitalization versus Decent Housing for All," in Schaffer, *Two*

Centuries; Richard O. Davies, *Housing Reform During the Truman Administration*.

135. Alfred Bettman, "The Fact Basis of Zoning: A Report to the American City Planning Institute," *City Planning* 1 (1925); p. 90.

136. J. Talmadge Woodruff, "Tests of City Planning Efficiency," *City Planning* 4 (1928): 68–74.

137. Wayne D. Heydecker, "What Zoning Ought to Be," *City Planning* 5 (1929): 25–33; Huber Earl Smutz, "Bad Trends in Zoning: A Special Warning to Smaller Communities," *City Planning* 6 (1930): 52–53.

138. Woodruff, "Planning Efficiency," pp. 68–74; NCCP, *Proceedings* 1928, pp. 47–51.

139. NCCP, *Proceedings* 1935, pp. 66–68; *Proceedings* 1940, pp. 70–88; *Proceedings* 1941, pp. 275–87, 294–97.

140. Flavel Shurtleff, "Control of Population Density and Distribution Through Zoning," *Planners' Journal* 4 (1938): 130.

141. NCCP, *Proceedings* 1953, pp. 119–31.

142. *Planning* (formerly NCCP *Proceedings*) 1954, pp. 133–59.

143. Planners' concerns are evident in papers published in NCCP *Proceedings* of 1925, 1927, 1928; in *City Planning* 3 (1927): 231–33; 4 (1928): 83–87; 10 (1934): 36–37; and *Planners' Journal* 4 (1938): 129–31; 7 (1941): 25–30.

Chapter 4

1. Franklin County Regional Planning Commission, *Sewers and Sewage Treatment*, a report for the Metropolitan Columbus Master Plan Study, 1954.

2. Columbus City Planning Commission, *Annual Report*, 1957; Interview with Harmon Merwin, July 19, 1990. (Merwin served with the Mid-Ohio Regional Planning Commission and its predecessors for thirty-five years, beginning in 1951. Unfortunately, few written records other than published reports exist for the commission, as many were misplaced or destroyed when the agency moved a few years ago.)

3. Columbus City Planning Commission, *Annual Report*, 1957.

4. Matthew Edel, Elliot D. Sclar, and Daniel Luria, *Shaky Palaces: Homeownership and Social Mobility in Boston's Suburbanization*, pp. 28–31, present a concise explanation, drawing on both sociology and economics, of how homes have traditionally "filtered" down the income ladder, causing deterioration in some neighborhoods.

5. Barry Checkoway, "Large Builders, Federal Housing Programs, and

Postwar Suburbanization," in William K. Tabb and Larry Sawers, eds., *Marxism and the Metropolis: New Perspectives in Urban Political Economy*; Kenneth T. Jackson, *Crabgrass Frontier: The Suburbanization of the United States*, pp. 234–38.

6. Ned Eichler, *The Merchant Builders*.

7. Kenneth T. Jackson, *Crabgrass Frontier*, p. 241.

8. Ibid., pp. 235–36. Eichler's *Merchant Builders* describes how Levitt and other builders also used design features and amenities such as fireplaces or cedar shakes to appeal to particular market segments.

9. H. E. Bracey, *Neighbours: Subdivision Life in England and the United States*, details results of interviews with and questionnaires completed by twenty households in each of six new subdivisions in the United States and in England. All his U.S. subdivisions were in metropolitan Columbus, Ohio.

10. Ibid., pp. 18–19, 34, 86.

11. Ibid., pp. 29, 12, 35–39.

12. Ibid., pp. 30, 41–42, 81.

13. Ibid., p. 48.

14. Shirley F. Weiss, John E. Smith, Edward J. Kaiser, and Kenneth B. Kenney, *Residential Developer Decisions: A Focused View of the Urban Growth Process*.

15. Ibid., p. 17.

16. Ibid., pp. 31–34.

17. Bernard H. Siegan, *Land Use Without Zoning*, pp. 33–34.

18. John Delafons, *Land-Use Controls in the United States*, pp. 91–92.

19. Siegan, *Land Use Without Zoning*, pp. 78, 83.

20. Warner's *Streetcar Suburbs* clearly shows the connections among transportation, urban growth, and suburban location in Boston. Ann Durking Keating's *Building Chicago* and Michael H. Ebner's *Creating Chicago's North Shore: A Suburban History* make the same point about Chicago, although they focus on other aspects of suburbanization.

21. Peter W. Moore, "Public Services and Residential Development in a Toronto Neighborhood, 1880–1915."

22. Mary Corbin Sies's "American Country House Architecture in Context" discusses the importance of physical amenities and picturesque locations in developing planned exclusive suburban communities.

23. King Thompson Company, "The Country Club District: 1000 Acres Restricted," undated prospectus for Upper Arlington.

24. Ibid.

25. Ibid.

26. The deeds requiring landscaping rarely established specific guidelines, indicating primarily that yards should be planted and maintained. Only one developer, platting subdivisions in the 1920s, imposed the ban on catalpa trees (the pods of which emit a very unpleasant odor after dropping to the ground and beginning to deteriorate). If others found them offensive, they may have believed that no residents would plant the unpleasant trees or that a general prohibition on "noxious" or "offensive" uses, which was standard in many deeds, would provide sufficient protection. To enforce these or other restrictions, a land developer generally either relied on action by neighbors (whose lots, of course, were similarly restricted) or reserved enforcement rights for himself as grantor.

27. Columbus *Dispatch Sunday Magazine*, September 8, 1946; interviews with Howard Wilson (August 2, 1984) and Ruth Kent Wilson (September 4, 1984).

28. Interviews with Howard Wilson (August 2, 1984) and Ruth Kent Wilson (September 4, 1984).

29. In *Rise of the Community Builders*, Marc Weiss indicates that realtors and developers of new residential areas were among zoning's most ardent supporters.

30. There is no indication in available city records of an attempt by either the developers or the city to annex these areas to Columbus.

31. Although the decline in building activity was neither as sharp nor as rapid as the decline in the stock market, its impact was quite evident.

32. Information on the valuation of building permits is taken from the Polk *City Directory* for various years, as the city no longer has such records.

Chapter 5

1. The broadening of focus is discussed in both Mel Scott, *American City Planning Since 1890*, and Peter Hall, *Cities of Tomorrow*.

2. As the provision of housing is not the focus of this work, readers are referred elsewhere for more information on the housing sections of the 1949 act and the planning implications of those sections. Both Hall, *Cities of Tomorrow*, and Scott, *American City Planning*, discuss them in general terms. Case studies of housing and planning activities in Philadelphia and Cincinnati are John Bauman, *Public Housing, Race, and Renewal: Urban Planning in Philadelphia, 1920–1974*, and Robert B. Fairbanks, *Making Better Citizens: Housing Reform and the Community Development Strategy in Cincinnati, 1890–1960*, respectively.

3. Scott, *American City Planning*, pp. 462–67.

4. Ibid., p. 501.

5. Ibid., pp. 462–67, 500–04.

6. Franklin County Regional Planning Commission, *Sewers and Sewage Treatment* (1954); Harmon Merwin, interview (July 19, 1990).

7. Harlean James, *Land Planning in the United States for the City, State and Nation*, p. 252; Theodora Kimball Hubbard and Henry Vincent Hubbard, *Our Cities To-Day and To-Morrow*, pp. 165–68; *Annals* of the American Academy of Social and Political Science, vol. 155, pt. 2.

8. Franklin County Regional Planning Commission, *Sewers*; Columbus City Planning Commission, *Annual Report* (1957); Merwin, interview.

9. Merwin, interview.

10. Frank So and Judith Getzels, eds. *Practice of Local Government Planning*, chap. 13.

11. This was seen as preferable to hiring additional temporary staff or taking existing staff from their regular tasks for the special effort. See Columbus City Planning Commission, *Annual Report* (1957).

12. Merwin, interview.

13. Harland Bartholomew and Associates, *Report Upon Economic Base, Population and General Land Uses* (May 1954); *Report Upon Major Streets and Transit* (n.d.); *Report Upon Schools, Parks, and Recreation* (September 1954); *Report Upon Utilities and Housing* (October 1954); *Report Upon the Central Business District* (April 1955); *Report Upon Housing: A Supplement to the Report on Utilities and Housing* (October 1955); and *Report Upon Transit Facilities* (January 1956) all prepared for the City Planning Commission and the Franklin County Planning Commission.

14. Harland Bartholomew and Associates, *A Summary Report: The Master Plan: Columbus Urban Area* (February 1957).

15. Harland Bartholomew, *Urban Land Uses: Amounts of Land Used and Needed for Various Purposes by Typical American Cities, an Aid to Scientific Zoning Practice*.

16. Ibid., p. 4.

17. Ibid., p. 153.

18. Bartholomew, *Report upon Economic Base*, p. 55.

19. Ibid., p. 56.

20. Ibid., p. 57.

21. Ibid., p. 57.

22. Ordinance 966-54, September 13, 1954.

23. Property owners submitted 659 requests, 16 of which were later withdrawn. City records do not indicate the disposition of the remaining 11.

24. The number of requests was 402, with no decision being recorded for 6 requests.

25. Reflecting increased enrollment in the 1950s and 1960s, Ohio State expanded both north and south with new dormitories. Code provisions were such, however, that land did not need to be rezoned for the dormitories; so the north side's preponderance of requests is not skewed by the university's growth.

26. This procedure benefited the developer financially as residentially zoned land cost less per acre than commercial property.

27. Joyce Thomas, "Bryden Road," unpublished research seminar paper submitted to Professor Richard J. Hopkins, August 1985, indicates that the near east side had begun to deteriorate by the 1920s.

28. Unfortunately, census tract boundaries do not correspond to the study area, or to whole-mile intervals from the city center. However, population figures for those tracts that contain the portions of each side of the city within the three-mile zone reveal a population decline in these older areas. The total 1950 population for all relevant tracts was 75,481 persons; the 1970 population of the same area was 58,230—a drop of 22.92 percent.

29. Barbara J. Flint, "Zoning and Residential Segregation," indicates that zoning was used for explicit racial purposes elsewhere.

30. Housing Opportunity Center of Metropolitan Columbus, "Housing Patterns in Franklin County Ohio," a map prepared from information in the 1970 U.S. Census.

31. Michael O. Sutcliffe, "Neighborhood Activism in Sociohistorical Perspective: Columbus, Ohio, 1900–1980," studies eighty years of neighborhood activism, grouping incidents of such activism into six categories, two of which concern rezonings.

32. Ibid., p. 24.

33. Ibid., pp. 31–32.

34. Ibid., p. 84. This increase is in line with rates of homeownership in the United States overall (Matthew Edel, Elliot D. Sclar, and Daniel Luria, *Shaky Palaces: Homeownership and Social Mobility in Boston's Suburbanization*, pp. 291–95). Changes in mortgage financing and suburban development nationwide, combined with annexations in Columbus, collectively explain the increase.

35. Scott, *American City Planning*, chaps. 6, 7; John Bauman, "Visions of the Postwar City," in Donald A. Krueckeberg, *Introduction to Planning History in the United States*; and "Paradox of Postwar Planning," in Daniel Schaffer, ed., *Two Centuries of American Planning*.

36. Scott, *American City Planning*, chap. 7; Bauman, "Paradox of Postwar Planning," in Schaffer, *Two Centuries*; Bauman, *Public Housing, Race, and Renewal;* Fairbanks, *Making Better Citizens*; Marc A. Weiss, "The Origins and Legacy of Urban Renewal," and Catherine Bauer, "The Dreary Deadlock of Public Housing," both in J. Paul Mitchell, ed., *Federal Housing Policy & Programs: Past and Present.*

37. Kenneth T. Jackson's *Crabgrass Frontier* is probably the best single treatment of suburbanization. See also Hall, *Cities of Tomorrow*, chap. 9. Mark H. Rose, *Interstate: Express Highway Politics, 1941–1956*, discusses both the politics and purposes of the interstate highway system.

38. Scott, *American City Planning*, chap. 7; Hall, *Cities of Tomorrow*, chap. 9.

39. Scott, *American City Planning*, pp. 541–48; Hall, *Cities of Tomorrow*, chap. 10. A good collection of some of the major short works in planning theory, many dating from the 1950s and 1960s, is Andreas Faludi, ed., *A Reader in Planning Theory.*

40. Scott, *American City Planning*, chaps. 7, 8; Hall, *Cities of Tomorrow*, chap. 10. The debate over the nature and scope of city planning, which has continued since the 1960s, is extensive and beyond the scope of this work. Faludi's *Reader in Planning Theory* provides some sense of it, however, as do works by John Friedmann and John Forester.

41. *Planning* 1960, pp. 172–86. In the early 1950s, the American Society of Planning Officials (ASPO) began to publish the proceedings of the annual national planning conference under the title *Planning*, designated by the conference year. References to items from those conference proceedings will thus be cited under that title, followed by the year and pages.

42. *Planning* 1955, pp. 96–102; *Planning* 1960, pp. 187–202.

43. Philip P. Green, Jr., "Is Zoning by Men Replacing Zoning by Law?" *Journal of the American Institute of Planners* 21 (1955): 82–87; Carl Feiss, "Planning Absorbs Zoning," Ibid. 27 (1961): 121–26.

44. *Planning* 1954, pp. 133–59; *Planning* 1960, pp. 196–202.

45. Arnold H. Mays, "Zoning for Mobile Homes," *Journal of the American Institute of Planners* 27 (1961): 204–11; *Planning* 1964, pp. 232–38.

46. *Planning* 1963, pp. 5–14; pp. 62–67.

47. Ibid., pp. 4–14.

48. *Planning* 1964, pp. 56–67.

49. *Planning* 1967, pp. 253–90.

50. Marion Clawson, *Suburban Land Conversion in the United States: An Economic and Governmental Process,* p. 5.

51. The findings of this research thus substantiate the general thrust of

Constance Perin's *Everything in Its Place: Social Order and Land Use in America*. Perin concludes that tenants (which group includes most low income persons and many minorities), lacking property interests, tend to be treated as second-class citizens. Having no fiscal stake in the community (i.e., they do not pay property taxes directly), they also have no voice.

Chapter 6

1. NCCP *Proceedings* 1923, pp. 85–114; *Proceedings* 1926, pp. 57–58; *Proceedings* 1928, pp. 47–48; Harlean James, *Land Planning in the United States for the City, State and Nation*, p. 252; Theodora Kimball Hubbard and Henry Vincent Hubbard, *Our Cities To-Day and To-Morrow*, pp. 165–68; *Annals*, vol. 155, pt. 2 (May 1931).

2. Edward Bassett, *Zoning*, p. 68.

3. Exclusionary zoning did not get major attention in the courts until the 1970s.

4. Bernard H. Siegan, *Land Use Without Zoning*, p. 4.

5. The information in this chapter comes from examination of public records in seven suburbs: the cities of Bexley, Grandview Heights, Upper Arlington, Whitehall, and Worthington, and the villages of Marble Cliff and Riverlea. However, full records do not exist for all seven and variations exist in their governmental structures, making comparisons somewhat difficult. As each community is discussed, a note will indicate what information was available and which administrative board served in which capacity.

6. The village's ordinance books are the only source of information on zoning activity in Riverlea. A wholly residential community of about six hundred people, Riverlea has no municipal offices, and what records exist have been kept in the home of either the mayor or the village clerk. A long-time resident of the village, the clerk at the time of this research indicated that to her knowledge no zoning board or commission has ever functioned in Riverlea. What few variances from zoning provisions might have been requested would have been decided by the building inspector, and there are no records of such actions. However, it is unlikely that many lot area or building setback requests were ever made, as most homes in Riverlea sit on parcels consisting of two or three lots, thus providing spacious yards.

7. Text of Riverlea Ordinance 1, quoted in Ordinance 17. No complete record of Ordinance 1, passed July 18, 1838, remains.

8. Riverlea Ordinance 17, January 25, 1946.

9. Riverlea Ordinance 49, June 24, 1949.

10. Riverlea Ordinance 31, November 14, 1947; Riverlea Ordinance 273, January 15, 1968. In permitting a multifamily dwelling, Ordinance 273 required that each unit contain at least 1,200 square feet of floor space.

11. Like Riverlea, Marble Cliff has a population of about six hundred persons. In contrast, it does have a municipal building where all records are kept. Unfortunately, a fire destroyed records of all actions prior to April 1928. Thus, the text of the village's first zoning ordinance, passed in 1922, is unknown. A new zoning ordinance, 246, was passed June 29, 1928. Information on Marble Cliff zoning activities was drawn from examination of ordinance books. There are no minutes or records of actions by a planning commission or board of zoning appeals or adjustment. Although the 1928 zoning ordinance called for the creation of such a board, in fact council seems to have functioned in that role through the granting of special permits.

12. Marble Cliff Ordinance 450, December 14, 1953.

13. Marble Cliff Ordinance 681, February 17, 1964.

14. Marble Cliff Ordinance 709, September 20, 1965.

15. Bexley Ordinance 456, October 23, 1923. The text of this ordinance refers to a prior zoning ordinance, 415, passed March 27, 1923, which was repealed by the passage of 456, but no record exists of this prior ordinance and its provisions are unknown.

16. Bill Arter, *Columbus Vignettes*, I (1966), II (1967), III (1969), IV (1971), published by the author. The four volumes of Arter's *Vignettes* contain sketches and brief histories of some of the more interesting or important buildings in central Ohio, including several mansions in Bexley, one of which now serves as the official residence of Ohio's governor.

17. Bexley Ordinance 15–55, failed July 15, 1955; rewritten and passed March 27, 1956.

18. Bexley Ordinance 16–57, October 8, 1957.

19. Some of these use changes were rezonings by ordinance passed by City Council. Others were essentially use variances granted either by council or the Zoning Commission. (Zoning Commission is the official title for the board that functioned as Bexley's Board of Zoning Appeals or Adjustment. Since the commission served the same purpose as Columbus's BZA, the terms *BZA* or *zoning board* will be used throughout this discussion.) Information on zoning board actions was drawn from minutes of the board's meetings from 1924 (the first year there were any) through 1970.

20. The village attained status as a city in 1931.

21. Riverlea could be construed as a planned residential suburb, but it

consisted of only a single subdivision, whose developer probably anticipated annexation to a larger entity rather than incorporation. Upper Arlington, on the other hand, contained many subdivisions platted by the same developer to achieve a clearly stated plan and incorporated very shortly after the first lots were developed.

22. "The Country Club District," real estate prospectus prepared by the King Thompson Company, Columbus, Ohio (undated).

23. Ladislas Segoe and Associates, *Comprehensive Master Plan for Upper Arlington, Ohio, 1962*, a report commissioned by the city in 1962. Other population figures in this chapter are from reports of the U.S. Department of Commerce, Bureau of the Census.

24. Upper Arlington Ordinance 198, March 7, 1927; Upper Arlington Ordinance 219, September 13, 1927.

25. The original ordinance created a "Zoning Commission" to function as a board of appeals and hear requests for special permits and variances from the ordinance's provisions. The Zoning Commission functioned in this capacity until 1950, when the Planning Commission began hearing and deciding zoning questions as well as planning matters. Then in 1958 a separate Board of Zoning Appeals was split off from the Planning Commission, separating zoning and planning questions again. For consistency with other jurisdictions and ease of understanding, this research and discussion examines the activities of boards and categorizes them based on function rather than title.

26. Upper Arlington Ordinances 1083, December 6, 1949; and 1097, March 7, 1950.

27. Upper Arlington Ordinances 38–54, July 26, 1954; 19–55, March 14, 1955; and 84–55, September 12, 1955.

28. Upper Arlington Ordinances 16–57, March 11, 1957; and 96–57, November 11, 1957. The sign regulation was aimed at a local fast-food drive-in restaurant chain whose trademark sign was a multicolored neon "whirling satellite."

29. With regard to Riverside Drive (State Route 33), for most of its length in Upper Arlington that city's code applied only to the east frontage. The west side of the road was in either the City of Columbus or unincorporated territory, and much of it was park land along the Scioto River.

30. Segoe and Associates, *Comprehensive Master Plan*, p. 1.

31. Ibid., pp. 1–4, 61.

32. Upper Arlington Ordinance 88–61, December 18, 1961; Segoe and Associates, *Comprehensive Master Plan*.

33. Zoning actions for Upper Arlington studied in detail for this re-

search include all actions of City Council or the zoning board affecting land within the northwest part of the larger metropolitan study area. This portion of Upper Arlington is an irregular strip along the city's western border about one mile in width, which covers almost half the total land area of the city.

34. Information on both issues is contained in minutes of zoning board meetings from January through May of 1940.

35. Minutes of a joint meeting of the Upper Arlington Zoning Commission and City Council, May 6, 1940.

36. Upper Arlington Ordinance 1083, December 6, 1949.

37. The only territorial addition to occur after the zoning ordinance was adopted was a 43-acre industrial parcel annexed in 1958.

38. Grandview Heights Ordinance 292, May 24, 1922.

39. Grandview Heights Ordinance 8–63, April 1, 1963.

40. These changes were accomplished by council rezoning. Late in 1922 the zoning board of Grandview Heights determined that questions involving property *use* were beyond its jurisdiction and would not be dealt with.

41. Grandview Heights Ordinance 53–59.

42. Sorting out zoning board actions in Grandview is a somewhat difficult task. Although the 1922 ordinance created an "Administrative Board" to deal with zoning questions, in 1928 the board's powers were delegated to the Planning Commission by City Council, since the same people sat on both boards. Consequently it was technically the Planning Commission that granted variances, but it did so acting as a board of zoning appeals.

43. The initial code had no fence regulations so all these occurred after the revised code was adopted in 1963.

44. Harland Bartholomew and Associates, *Preliminary Report Upon the Comprehensive Plan, Grandview Heights, Ohio,* June 1969.

45. Worthington Ordinance 240, May 1, 1928. This was not Worthington's first zoning ordinance but it is the earliest available. Records indicate that an earlier ordinance, 088 passed December 28, 1923, contained zoning regulations, but the ordinance book recording 088 is missing and 088's provisions are unknown.

46. Worthington Ordinance 0727, June 1, 1942.

47. Worthington Ordinances 1410, August 29, 1955; 36–56, April 16, 1956; and 79–56, October 1, 1956.

48. Worthington Ordinance 105–59, November 9, 1959.

49. Worthington Ordinances 14–60, March 14, 1960; and 18–62, May 14, 1962.

50. Worthington Ordinance 19–67, April 10, 1967.

51. Annexations and natural growth increased Worthington's population from 2,141 in 1950 to 9,106 by 1960.

52. Worthington Ordinance 5–67, March 20, 1967. Specifically, the ordinance required Municipal Development Commission approval for the following actions: (1) a building to be constructed, remodeled, or enlarged; (2) a sign, wall, or walk to be installed; (3) any demolition or rehabilitation project; and (4) grading, planting, landscaping. Ordinary property maintenance did not require approval if it involved no change in material, design, or arrangement.

53. All zoning board actions concern variances to the 1956 ordinance or its successor. Although the earlier ordinances provided for an administrative board to hear such matters, the city has no records of any zoning board meetings or decisions prior to 1961. Nevertheless, considering how small the town was until well after World War II, it is unlikely that earlier zoning boards faced many requests. From 1961 through 1970, the board heard 105 requests, of which it approved 81.

54. Worthington Ordinance 97–58, November 3, 1958,

55. The 1963 zoning code had very strict limitations on the size and number of signs permitted any business. The board granted only nine of twenty sign variance requests.

56. Information on Whitehall's early history and population growth was compiled by the Whitehall city clerk of council from city records and U.S. census reports.

57. Whitehall Ordinance 19–48, June 30, 1948.

58. In 1947 the county regional planning commission had prepared a zoning resolution for all unincorporated land in the county to serve as a guide for future development. The resolution was advisory only, however, and adoption and enforcement of any of the proposed provisions were matters to be handled by the trustees of each individual township in the county. Whitehall's incorporation negated any provisions that might have been adopted by the township whose land was included within the city's borders.

59. Whitehall Ordinance 135–52, November 5, 1952.

60. Whitehall Ordinances 209–53, November 4, 1953; and 225–53, December 30, 1953.

61. Whitehall also presents a contrast to the other six suburbs in the proportion of zoning actions submitted to council rather than the zoning

board. Council decided half again as many as the zoning board in Whitehall, while elsewhere the zoning board heard several times more cases than city council.

62. This is compared to rates ranging from 77 to 83 percent for the other communities. Under Whitehall's zoning code, the Planning and Zoning Commission heard variance requests; however, that commission also reviewed plats, approved lot splits, and made nonbinding recommendations to council regarding rezonings and special permits. Effective January 1967 Whitehall split the commission into two distinct administrative boards, with the Board of Zoning Appeals being responsible for variance requests and lot splits. For consistency, the term *zoning board* is used here for the board handling variance and lot split actions, regardless of the proper title of the board deciding the matter when each particular case was heard.

63. None of the other suburbs adopted comprehensive plans either, until the 1960s. However, each followed its zoning ordinance much more closely, using the ordinance to guide future growth and development.

Chapter 7

1. Some parts of Columbus reflect the same pattern as the suburbs, with few use changes either requested or granted. These are generally outlying middle and upper middle income residential areas developed with restrictive deed covenants.

2. Theodora Kimball Hubbard and Henry Vincent Hubbard, *Our Cities To-Day and To-Morrow*, p. 164.

3. *Village of Euclid* v. *Ambler Realty Co.*, 272 U.S. 365, 47 S.Ct. 114, 71 L.ED 303 (1926).

4. *Village of Belle Terre* v. *Borass*, 416 U.S. 1, 94 S.Ct. 1536, 39 L.ED 797 (1974).

5. Drawing on a large body of research, Kenneth T. Jackson's *Crabgrass Frontier* presents a good overview of the history of housing discrimination.

6. This work also agrees with the larger theme of William S. Worley, *J. C. Nichols and the Shaping of Kansas City: Innovation in Planned Residential Communities*. This is not to imply that private individuals bear sole responsibility, in Columbus or elsewhere. Research on other cities has shown that land development, though carried out by private property owners, often occurred where a municipality extended water and sewer lines or granted a streetcar franchise to operate. In Columbus, however, the city liberally allowed outlying developments to hook up to its water and

sewer lines irrespective of their locations. Thus water and sewer policy (at least until the 1950s) responded to rather than directed developers' activities.

7. This is essentially the principle on which those practicing exclusionary zoning base their actions. William A. Fischel, *Economics of Zoning Laws: A Property Rights Approach to American Land Use Controls*, blames part of zoning's "failure" on the planners' inability to view it in economic terms and consider its effect on land market values.

BIBLIOGRAPHY

In addition to those cited specifically in the text, many other works informed this research. They are consequently included in this bibliography.

Abbott, Carl. *Portland: Planning, Politics and Growth in a Twentieth-Century City.* Lincoln: University of Nebraska Press, 1983.

Allen, Frederick Lewis. *Only Yesterday: An Informal History of the Nineteen-Twenties.* New York: Harper and Row, 1931.

Annals of the American Academy of Political and Social Science. Special Issue: Zoning in the United States. vol. 155, pt. II (May 1931).

Arnold, Joseph L. *The New Deal in the Suburbs: A History of the Greenbelt Town Program, 1935–1954.* Columbus: Ohio State University Press, 1971.

Arter, Bill. *Columbus Vignettes*, volumes 1–4. Columbus, OH: the author, vol. 1: 1966, vol. 2: 1967, vol. 3: 1969, vol. 4: 1971.

Babcock, Richard F. *The Zoning Game: Municipal Practices and Policies.* Madison, Milwaukee, and London: University of Wisconsin Press, 1966.

Banfield, Edward C. *The Unheavenly City Revisited.* Boston and Toronto: Little Brown and Company, 1974.

Bartholomew, Harland. *Urban Land Use: Amount of Land Used and Needed for Various Uses by Typical American Cities—An Aid to Scientific Zoning Practice.* Cambridge: Harvard University Press, 1932.

Bartholomew, Harland and Associates. *Preliminary Report Upon the Comprehensive Plan, Grandview Heights, Ohio*, June 1969.

———. *A Report Upon Economic Base, Population, and General Land Uses*, prepared for the City Planning Commission and Franklin County Regional Planning Commission, May 1954.

———. *A Summary Report: The Master Plan: Columbus Urban Area*, prepared for the City Planning Commission and Franklin County Regional Planning Commission, February 1957.

Bassett, Edward M. "From the Autobiography of Edward M. Bassett" (intro. Donald A. Krueckeberg). In *The American Planner: Biographies and Recollections*, edited by Donald A. Krueckeberg. New York and London: Methuen, 1983.

———. "Zoning Roundtable." *City Planning* 2, no. 1 (1926): 59–60; 2, no. 4 (1926): 299–301.

———. *Zoning: The Laws, Administration, and Court Decisions During the First Twenty Years*. New York: Russell Sage Foundation, 1940.

Bauer, Catherine. "The Dreary Deadlock of Public Housing." In *Federal Housing Policy & Programs: Past and Present*, edited by J. Paul Mitchell. New Brunswick, NJ: Center for Urban Policy Research, 1990.

Bauman, John F. "The Paradox of Post-War Urban Planning: Downtown Revitalization Versus Decent Housing for All." In *Two Centuries of American Planning*, edited by Daniel Schaffer. Baltimore: Johns Hopkins University Press, 1988.

———. *Public Housing, Race, and Renewal: Urban Planning in Philadelphia, 1920–1974*. Philadelphia: Temple University Press, 1987.

———. "Visions of a Post-War City: A Perspective on Urban Planning in Philadelphia and the Nation, 1942–1945." In *Introduction to Planning History in the United States*, edited by Donald A. Krueckeberg. New Brunswick, NJ: Center for Urban Policy Research, Rutgers University, 1983.

Bender, Thomas. *Toward an Urban Vision: Ideas and Institutions in Nineteenth Century America*. Baltimore and London: Johns Hopkins University Press, 1975.

Berger, Bennett M. *Working-Class Suburb: A Study of Auto Workers in Suburbia*. Berkeley and Los Angeles: University of California Press, 1968.

Bettman, Alfred. "The Fact Basis of Zoning: A Report to the American City Planning Institute." *City Planning* 1 (1925): 86–90.

———. "The Present State of Court Decisions on Zoning." *City Planning* 2, no. 1 (1926): 24–31.

Birch, Eugenie Ladner. "Advancing the Art and Science of Planning: Planners and their Organizations, 1909–1980." *Journal of the American Planning Asociation* 46, no. 1 (1980): 22–49.

———. "Radburn and the American Planning Movement: The Persistence of an Idea." *Journal of the American Planning Association* 46, no. 4 (1980): 424–439.

———. "Woman-made America: The Case of Early Public Housing Policy." In *The American Planner: Biographies and Recollections*, edited by Donald A. Krueckeberg. New York and London: Methuen, 1983.

Blackford, Mansel G. "Civic Groups, Political Action, and City Planning in Seattle, 1892–1915." *Pacific Historical Review* 49, no. 4 (1980): 557–580.

———. "The Lost Dream: Businessmen and City Planning in Portland, Oregon, 1903–1914." *Western Historical Quarterly* (January 1984): 39–56.

———. *The Lost Dream: Businessmen and City Planning on the Pacific Coast, 1890–1920*. Columbus: Ohio State University Press, 1992.

Boyer, M. Christine. *Dreaming the Rational City: The Myth of American City Planning*. Cambridge and London: MIT Press, 1983.

Bracey, H. E. *Neighbours: Subdivision Life in England and the United States*. Baton Rouge: Louisiana State University Press, 1964.

Bremner, Robert H. *From the Depths: The Discovery of Poverty in the United States*. New York: New York University Press, 1956.

Bridenbaugh, Carl. *Cities in Revolt: Urban Life in America, 1743–1776*. New York: Alfred A. Knopf, 1968.

———. *Cities in the Wilderness: The First Century of Urban Life in America, 1625–1742*. New York: The Ronald Press Company, 1938.

Brownell, Blaine A. *The Urban Ethos in the South, 1920–1930*. Baton Rouge: Louisiana State University Press, 1975.

———. "Urban Planning, the Planning Profession, and the Motor Vehicle in Early Twentieth-Century America." In *Shaping an Urban World*, edited by Gordon E. Cherry. London: Mansell, 1980.

Bryant, R. W. G. *Land: Private Property, Public Control*. Montreal: Harvest House, Ltd., 1972.

Buder, Stanley. "The Model Town of Pullman: Town Planning and Social Control in the Gilded Age." *Journal of the American Institute of Planners* 33 (1967): 2–10.

———. *Visionaries & Planners: The Garden City Movement and the Modern Community*. New York and Oxford: Oxford University Press, 1990.

Buenker, John D., John C. Burnham, and Robert M. Crunden. *Progressivism*. Cambridge, MA: Schenkman Publishing, 1977.

Burnham, Robert. "Pulling Together for Pluralism: Politics, Planning and Government in Cincinnati, 1924–1959." Ph.D. dissertation, History, University of Cincinnati, 1990.

Checkoway, Barry. "Large Builders, Federal Housing Programs, and Postwar Suburbanization." In *Marxism and the Metropolis: New Perspectives in Urban Political Economy*, edited by William K. Tabb and Larry Sawers. New York and Oxford: Oxford University Press, 1984.

Cherry, Gordon E., ed. *Shaping an Urban World*. London: Mansell, 1980.

Christensen, Carol A. *The American Garden City and the New Towns Movement*. Ann Arbor: UMI Research Press, 1986.

Chudacoff, Howard P. *Mobile Americans: Residential and Social Mobility in Omaha, 1880–1920*. New York: Oxford University Press, 1972.

Churchill, Henry. "Henry Wright: 1878–1936." In *The American Planner: Biographies and Recollections*, edited by Donald A. Krueckeberg. New York and London: Methuen, 1983.

Clawson, Marion. *Suburban Land Conversion in the United States: An Economic and Governmental Process*. Baltimore and London: Johns Hopkins Press for Resources for the Future, 1971.

Conzen, Kathleen Neils. "Patterns of Residence in Early Milwaukee." In *The New Urban History: Quantitative Explorations by American Historians*, edited by Leo F. Schnore. Princeton: Princeton University Press, 1975.

Davies, Pearl Janet. *Real Estate in American History*. Washington, DC: Public Affairs Press, 1958.

Davies, Richard O. *Housing Reform During the Truman Administration*. Columbia: University of Missouri Press, 1966.

Davis, Allen F. "Playgrounds, Housing, and City Planning." In *Introduction to Planning History in the United States*, edited by Donald A. Krueckeberg. New Brunswick, NJ: Center for Urban Policy Research, Rutgers University, 1983.

———. *Spearheads for Reform: The Social Settlements and the Progressive Movement, 1890–1914*. New York: Oxford University Press, 1967.

Delafons, John. *Land-Use Controls in the United States*. 2nd ed. Cambridge and London: MIT Press, 1969.

Ebner, Michael. H. *Creating Chicago's North Shore: A Suburban History*. Chicago and London: University of Chicago Press, 1988.

Edel, Matthew, Elliot D. Sclar, and Daniel Luria. *Shaky Palaces: Homeownership and Social Mobility in Boston's Suburbanization*. New York: Columbia University Press, 1984.

Eden, Joseph A. and Arnold R. Alanen. "Looking Backward at a New Deal Town: Greendale, Wisconsin, 1935–1980." *Journal of the American Planning Association* 49, no. 1 (1983): 40–58.

Eichler, Ned. *The Merchant Builders*. Cambridge and London: MIT Press, 1982.

Ellickson, Robert C. "Alternatives to Zoning: Covenants, Nuisance Rules, and Fines as Land Use Controls." *University of Chicago Law Review* 40, no. 4 (1973): 681–781.

Ellis, Wade H. *Municipal Code of Ohio*. 5th ed. Cincinnati: W. H. Anderson, 1912.

———. *Municipal Code of Ohio*. 6th ed. Cincinnati: W. H. Anderson, 1922.

Fairbanks, Robert B. *Making Better Citizens: Housing Reform and the Community Development Strategy in Cincinnati, 1890–1960*. Urbana and Chicago: University of Illinois Press, 1988.

Faludi, Andreas, ed. *A Reader in Planning Theory*. Oxford: Pergamon Press, 1973.

Fess, Simeon D., ed. *Ohio: A Four Volume Reference Library on the History of a Great State*, vol. 5, suppl. biog. vol. Chicago and New York: Lewis Publishing, 1937.

Fischel, William A. *The Economics of Zoning Laws: A Property Rights Approach to American Land Use Controls*. Baltimore and London: Johns Hopkins University Press, 1985.

Fisher, Ernest M. and Robert M. Fisher. *Urban Real Estate*. New York: Henry Holt, 1954.

Fisher, Irving D. *Frederick Law Olmsted and the City Planning Movement in the United States*. Ann Arbor: UMI Research Press, 1986.

Fishman, Robert L. "American Suburbs/English Suburbs: A Transatlantic Comparison." *Journal of Urban History* 13, no. 3 (1987): 237–51.

———. *Bourgeois Utopias: The Rise and Fall of Suburbia*. New York: Basic Books, Inc., 1987.

Flint, Barbara J. "Zoning and Residential Segregation: A Social and Physical History, 1910–1940." Ph.D. dissertation, History, University of Chicago, 1977.

Foster, Mark S. *From Streetcar to Superhighway: American City Planners and Urban Transportation, 1900–1940*. Philadelphia: Temple University Press, 1981.

Friedman, Lawrence. *Government and Slum Housing: A Century of Frustration*. Chicago: Rand McNally, 1968.

Funigiello, Philip. *The Challenge to Urban Liberalism: Federal City Relations During World War II*. Knoxville: University of Tennessee Press, 1978.

———. "City Planning in World War II: The Experience of the National Resources Planning Board." In *Introduction to Planning History in the United States*, edited by Donald A. Krueckeberg. New Brunswick, NJ: Center for Urban Policy Research, Rutgers University, 1983.

Gardner, Deborah S., ed. "The Early Years of Public Housing." Special issue of *Journal of Urban History* 12, no. 4 (1986).

Gelfand, Mark I. *A Nation of Cities: The Federal Government and Urban America, 1933–1965*. New York: Oxford University Press, 1975.

Gerckens, Laurence C. "Bettman of Cincinnati." In *The American Planner: Biographies and Recollections*, edited by Donald A. Krueckeberg. New York and London: Methuen, 1983.

Gillette, Howard, Jr. "The Evolution of Neighborhood Planning: From the Progressive Era to the 1949 Housing Act." *Journal of Urban History* 9, no. 4 (1983): 421–444.

Goldfield, David and Blaine A. Brownell. *Urban America: From Downtown to No Town*. Boston: Houghton Mifflin, 1979.

Gould, Lewis L. *Reform and Regulation: American Politics from Roosevelt to Wilson*. New York: Alfred A. Knopf, 1986.

Graham, Otis L., Jr. *Toward a Planned Society: From Roosevelt to Nixon*. London, Oxford, New York: Oxford University Press, 1976.

Griffen, Clyde and Sally Griffen. *Natives and Newcomers: The Ordering of Opportunity in Mid-Nineteenth Century Poughkeepsie*. Cambridge and London: Harvard University Press, 1978.

Haar, Charles M. "In Accordance With a Comprehensive Plan." *Harvard Law Review* 68 (1955): 1154–1175.

———. *Land-Use Planning: A Casebook on the Use, Misuse, and Re-use of Urban Land*. 3d ed. Boston and Toronto: Little, Brown, 1976.

Hall, Peter. *Cities of Tomorrow: An Intellectual History of Urban Planning and Design in the Twentieth Century*. Oxford: Basil Blackwell, 1988.

Hancock, John. "The New Deal and American Planning: The 1930s." In *Two Centuries of American Planning*, edited by Daniel Schaffer. Baltimore: Johns Hopkins University Press, 1988.

———. "Planners in the Changing American City, 1900–1940." *Journal of the American Institute of Planners* 33 (1967): 290–304.

Hays, Samuel P. *Conservation and the Gospel of Efficiency: The Progressive Conservation Movement, 1890–1920*. Cambridge: Harvard University Press, 1959.

———. "The Politics of Reform in Municipal Government in the Progressive Era." In *American Political History as Social Analysis*. Knoxville: University of Tennessee Press, 1980.

Hines, Thomas S. *Burnham of Chicago: Architect and Planner*. Chicago and London: University of Chicago Press, 1979.

Hopkins, Richard J. "Status, Mobility, and the Dimensions of Change in a Southern City: Atlanta, 1870–1910." In *Cities in American History*, edited by Kenneth T. Jackson and Stanley K. Schultz. New York: Alfred

A. Knopf, 1972.

Howe, Frederic C. *Confessions of a Reformer*. Kent, OH: Kent State University Press, 1988.

Hoyt, Homer. *One Hundred Years of Land Values in Chicago: The Relationship of the Growth of Chicago to the Rise in Its Land Values, 1830–1933*. Chicago: University of Chicago Press, 1933.

———. *Where the Rich and the Poor People Live: The Location of Residential Areas Occupied by the Highest and Lowest Income Families in American Cities*. Washington, DC: Urban Land Institute, 1966.

Hubbard, Theodora Kimball and Henry Vincent Hubbard. *Our Cities Today and To-morrow: A Survey of Planning and Zoning Progress in the United States*. Cambridge: Harvard University Press, 1929.

Hunker, Henry L. *Industrial Evolution of Columbus, Ohio*. Columbus: Ohio State University, 1958.

International City and Regional Planning Conference. *Planning Problems of Town, City and Region*. Papers and discussions at the conference, New York City, April 20–25, 1925. Baltimore: Norman Remington, 1925.

Jackson, Anthony. *A Place Called Home: A Century of Low-Cost Housing in Manhattan*. Cambridge: MIT Press, 1976.

Jackson, Kenneth T. *Crabgrass Frontier: The Suburbanization of the United States*. New York and Oxford: Oxford University Press, 1985.

———. "Urban Deconcentration in the Nineteenth Century: A Statistical Inquiry." In *The New Urban History: Quantitative Explorations by American Historians*, edited by Leo F. Schnore. Princeton: Princeton University Press, 1975.

Jacobs, Jane. *The Death and Life of Great American Cities*. New York: Random House, 1961.

James, Harlean. *Land Planning in the United States for the City, State and Nation*. New York: Macmillan, 1926.

Johnson, David A. "Norris, Tennessee on the Occasion of Its Fiftieth Anniversary." *Planning History Bulletin* 6, no. 1 (1984): 32–42.

———. "Regional Planning for the Great American Metropolis: New York between the World Wars." In *Two Centuries of American Planning*, edited by Daniel Schaffer. Baltimore: Johns Hopkins University Press, 1988.

Kantor, Harvey A. "Charles Dyer Norton and the Origins of the Regional Plan of New York." In *The American Planner: Biographies and Recollections*, edited by Donald A. Krueckeberg. New York and London: Methuen, 1983.

Keating, Ann Durkin. *Building Chicago: Suburban Developers and the Creation of a Divided Metropolis*. Columbus: Ohio State University Press, 1988.

King, Andrew J. *Law and Land Use in Chicago: A Prehistory of Modern Zoning*. New York and London: Garland Publishing, 1986.

Kirschner, Don S. *The Paradox of Professionalism: Reform and Public Service in Urban America, 1900–1940*. New York, Westport, CT, and London: Greenwood Press, 1986.

Kolko, Gabriel. *The Triumph of Conservatism: A Reinterpretation of American History, 1900–1916*. New York: Macmillan, 1963.

Krueckeberg, Donald A., ed. *The American Planner: Biographies and Recollections*. New York and London: Methuen, 1983.

———. *Introduction to Planning History in the United States*. New Brunswick, NJ: Center for Urban Policy Research, Rutgers University, 1983.

———. "The Story of the Planner's Journal, 1915–1980." *Journal of the American Planning Association* 46, no. 1 (1980): 5–21.

Linteau, Paul-André. "Canadian Suburbanization in a North American Context: Does the Border Make a Difference?" *Journal of Urban History* 13, no. 3 (1987): 252–274.

Logan, Thomas H. "The Americanization of German Zoning." *Journal of the American Institute of Planners* 42 (1976): 377–385.

Lord, Austin W., Albert Kelsey, Charles N. Lowrie, Charles Mulford Robinson, and H. A. McNeil (Plan Commission). *The Plan of the City of Columbus: Report Made to the Honorable Charles A. Bond, Mayor, to the Honorable Board of Public Service, and to the Honorable City Council, February 1908*.

Lubove, Roy. *Community Planning in the 1920's: The Contribution of the Regional Planning Association of America*. Pittsburgh: University of Pittsburgh Press, 1963.

———. *The Progressives and the Slums: Tenement House Reform in New York City, 1890–1917*. Pittsburgh: University of Pittsburgh Press, 1962.

———. "The Urbanization Process: An Approach to Historical Research." *Journal of the American Institute of Planners* 33 (1967): 33–39.

McCraw, Thomas K. *Prophets of Regulation: Charles Francis Adams, Louis D. Brandeis, James M. Landis, and Alfred E. Kahn*. Cambridge and London: Belknap Press of Harvard University Press, 1984.

———. "Regulation in America: A Review Article." *Business History Review* 49, no. 2 (1975): 159–183.

McKelvey, Blake. *The Emergence of Metropolitan America, 1915–1966*. New Brunswick, NJ: Rutgers University Press, 1968.

———. *The Urbanization of America (1860–1915)*. New Brunswick, NJ: Rutgers University Press, 1963.

Makielski, S. J., Jr. *The Politics of Zoning*. New York and London: Columbia University Press, 1966.

Mandelker, Daniel R. "The Role of the Comprehensive Plan in Land Use Regulation." *Michigan Law Review* 74 (1976): 899–975.

Marcuse, Peter. "Housing Policy and City Planning: The Puzzling Split in the United States, 1893–1931." In *Shaping an Urban World*, edited by Gordon E. Cherry. London: Mansell, 1980.

Meck, Stuart and Edith M. Netter. *A Planner's Guide to Land Use Law*. Washington, DC, and Chicago: Planners Press, American Planning Association, 1983.

Miller, Zane L. *Suburb: Neighborhood and Community in Forest Park, Ohio, 1935–1976*. Knoxville: University of Tennessee Press, 1981.

———. "Urban Blacks in the South, 1865–1920: An Analysis of Some Quantitative Data on Richmond, Savannah, New Orleans, Louisville, and Birmingham." In *The New Urban History: Quantitative Explorations by American Historians*, edited by Leo F. Schnore. Princeton: Princeton University Press, 1975.

Mitchell, J. Paul, ed. *Federal Housing Policy & Programs: Past and Present*. New Brunswick, NJ: Center for Urban Policy Research, 1990.

Mixon, John. "Jane Jacobs and the Law—Zoning for Diversity Examined." *Northwestern University Law Review* 62, no. 3 (1967): 314–356.

Mohl, Raymond A. and Neil Betten. "The Failure of Industrial City Planning: Gary, Indiana, 1906–1910." *Journal of the American Institute of Planners* 38 (1972): 203–215.

Monchow, Helen. *The Use of Deed Restrictions in Subdivision Development*. Chicago: Institute for Research in Land Economics and Public Utilities, 1928.

Monkkonen, Eric H. *The Dangerous Class: Crime and Poverty in Columbus, Ohio, 1860–1885*. Cambridge, MA, and London: Harvard University Press, 1975.

Moore, Peter W. "Public Services and Residential Development in a Toronto Neighborhood, 1880–1915." *Journal of Urban History* 9, no. 4 (1983): 445–471.

Mullin, John Robert. "American Perceptions of German City Planning at the Turn of the Century." *Urbanism Past and Present* 3 (1976–77): 5–15.

Myhra, David. "Rexford Guy Tugwell: Initiator of America's Greenbelt New Towns, 1935–6." In *The American Planner: Biographies and Recollections*, edited by Donald A. Krueckeberg. New York and London: Methuen, 1983.

National Conference on City Planning. *Planning Problems of Town, City and Region*. Papers and discussions at the eighteenth conference, St. Petersburg and Palm Beach, March 29–April 1, 1926. Philadelphia: William F. Fell, 1926.

———. *Planning Problems of Town, City and Region*. Papers and discussions at the nineteenth conference, Washington, DC, May 9–11, 1927. Philadelphia: William F. Fell, 1927.

———. *Proceedings* of the seventh conference, Detroit, June 7–9, 1915. Cambridge: University Press, 1915.

———. *Proceedings* of the eighth conference, Cleveland, June 5–7, 1916. New York: [n.a.], 1916

Nelson, Robert H. *Zoning and Property Rights: An Analysis of the American System of Land-Use Regulation*. Cambridge and London: MIT Press, 1977.

Orser, W. Edward. "Secondhand Suburbs: Black Pioneers in Baltimore's Edmondson Village, 1955–1980." *Journal of Urban History* 16, no. 3 (May 1990): 227–262.

Perin, Constance. *Everything in Its Place: Social Order and Land Use in America*. Princeton: Princeton University Press, 1977.

Peterson, Jon A. "The City Beautiful Movement: Forgotten Origins and Lost Meanings." In *Introduction to Planning History in the United States*, edited by Donald A. Krueckeberg. New Brunswick, NJ: Center for Urban Policy Research, Rutgers University, 1983.

———. "The Impact of Sanitary Reform upon American Urban Planning, 1840–1890." In *Introduction to Planning History in the United States*, edited by Donald A. Krueckeberg. New Brunswick, NJ: Center for Urban Policy Research, Rutgers University, 1983.

Pred, Allan R. *The Spatial Dynamics of U.S. Urban-Industrial Growth, 1800–1914: Interpretive and Theoretical Essays*. Cambridge: MIT Press, 1966.

Proceedings of the Thirteenth Annual Conference on City Planning, Pittsburgh, May 9–11, 1921 [no publication information given].

Rarick, Galen R. *Upper Arlington: Glimpses of Its First 50 Years*. Upper Arlington, OH: privately published in observance of the fiftieth anniversary of the city's founding, 1968.

Reps, John W. *Cities of the American West: A History of Frontier Urban*

Planning. Princeton: Princeton University Press, 1979.

———. *The Making of Urban America: A History of City Planning in the United States.* Princeton: Princeton University Press, 1965.

———. *Monumental Washington: The Planning and Development of the Capital Center.* Princeton: Princeton University Press, 1967.

———. *Town Planning in Frontier America.* Princeton: Princeton University Press, 1969.

Rose, Mark H. *Interstate, Express Highway Politics, 1941–1956.* Lawrence: Regents Press of Kansas, 1979.

Samuelson, Robert E., et al. *Architecture—Columbus.* Columbus: Foundation of the Columbus Chapter of the American Institute of Architects, 1976.

Sandburg, Carl. *The Chicago Race Riots: July, 1919.* New York: Harcourt, Brace, and Howe, 1919.

Schaffer, Daniel, ed. *Two Centuries of American Planning.* Baltimore: Johns Hopkins University Press, 1988.

Schlereth, Thomas J. "Burnham's *Plan* and Moody's *Manual*: City Planning as Progressive Reform." *Journal of the American Planning Association* 47 (1981): 70–82.

Schnore, Leo F., ed. *The New Urban History: Quantitative Explorations by American Historians.* Princeton: Princeton University Press, 1975.

Schultz, Stanley K. *Constructing Urban Culture: American Cities and City Planning, 1800–1920.* Philadelphia: Temple University Press, 1989.

Schuyler, David. *The New Urban Landscape: The Redefinition of City Form in Nineteenth-Century America.* Baltimore and London: Johns Hopkins University Press, 1986.

Schwartz, Seymour I., and Robert A. Johnston. "Inclusionary Housing Programs." *Journal of the American Planning Association* 49, no. 1 (1983): 3–21.

Scott, Mel. *American City Planning Since 1890.* Berkeley and Los Angeles: University of California Press, 1969.

Seely, Bruce E. *Building the American Highway System: Engineers as Policy Makers.* Philadelphia: Temple University Press, 1987.

Segoe, Ladislas, and Associates. *Comprehensive Plan for Upper Arlington, Ohio, 1962.*

Siegan, Bernard H. *Land Use without Zoning.* Lexington, MA: D. C. Heath, 1972.

Sies, Mary Corbin. "American Country House Architecture in Context: The Suburban Ideal in the East and Midwest, 1877–1917." Ph.D. dissertation, American Studies, University of Michigan, 1987.

Silver, Christopher. "American Planners and the Changing City Center." *Planning History Bulletin* 5, no. 2 (1983): 29–40.

———. "The Ordeal of City Planning in Postwar Richmond, Virginia: A Quest for Greatness." *Journal of Urban History* 10, no. 1 (1983): 33–60.

———. *Twentieth-Century Richmond: Planning, Politics, and Race.* Knoxville: University of Tennessee Press, 1984.

So, Frank S. and Judith Getzels, eds. *The Practice of Local Government Planning*, 2d ed. Washington: International City Management Association, 1988.

Sutcliffe, Michael O. "Neighborhood Activism in Sociohistorical Perspective: Columbus, Ohio, 1900–1980." Ph.D. dissertation, Geography, Ohio State University, 1985.

Teaford, Jon C. *City and Suburb: The Political Fragmentation of Metropolitan America, 1850–1970.* Baltimore and London: Johns Hopkins University Press, 1979.

Thernstrom, Stephan. *Poverty and Progress: Social Mobility in a Nineteenth Century City.* Cambridge: Harvard University Press, 1964.

Toews, John C. "Validity Rules Concerning Public Zoning and Private Covenants: A Comparison and Critique." *Southern California Law Review* 39 (1966): 409–437.

Toll, Seymour I. *Zoned Amercian.* New York: Grossman Publishers, 1969.

Urban Land Institute. *The Homes Association Handbook.* Rev. ed. ULI Technical Bulletin 50. Washington: Urban Land Institute, 1964.

Urban, Mark. "An Evaluation of the Applicability of Zoning Principles to the Law of Private Land Use Restrictions." *UCLA Law Review* 21 (1974): 1655–1689.

U.S. Department of Commerce, Bureau of Standards. *Zoned Municipalities in the United States.* Report prepared by Norman L. Knauss of the Division of Building and Housing. Letter Circular LC-374, May 5, 1933.

Vague, Diane T. "The Evolution of Land Use Planning for the City of Houston, Texas: 'Free-Market' Forces versus Public and Private Controls in the Twentieth Century." Masters project, School of Urban and Public Affairs, University of Texas at Arlington, 1991.

Wade, Richard. *The Urban Frontier: The Rise of Western Cities, 1790–1830.* Cambridge: Harvard University Press, 1959.

Warner, Hoyt Landon. *Progressivism in Ohio, 1897–1917.* Columbus: Ohio State University Press for the Ohio Historical Society, 1964.

Warner, Sam Bass, Jr. *The Private City: Philadelphia in Three Periods of Its*

Growth. Philadelphia: University of Pennsylvania Press, 1968.

———. *Streetcar Suburbs: The Process of Growth in Boston (1870–1900)*. Cambridge: Harvard University Press, 1962.

———. *The Urban Wilderness*. New York: Harper and Row, Publishers, 1972.

Weaver, Clifford L. and Richard F. Babcock. *City Zoning: The Once and Future Frontier*. Chicago and Washington: American Planning Association, Planners Press, 1979.

Weibe, Robert H. *The Search for Order, 1877–1920*. New York: Hill and Wang, 1967.

Weiss, Marc A. "The Origins and Legacy of Urban Renewal." In *Federal Housing Policy & Programs: Past and Present*, J. Paul Mitchell, editor. New Brunswick, NJ: Center for Urban Policy Research, 1990.

———. *The Rise of the Community Builders: The American Real Estate Industry and Urban Land Planning*. New York: Columbia University Press, 1987.

Weiss, Shirley, John E. Smith, Edward J. Kaiser, and Kenneth B. Kenney. *Residential Developer Decisions: A Focused View of the Urban Growth Process*. Chapel Hill: Center for Urban and Regional Studies, Institute for Research in Social Science, University of North Carolina, 1966.

White, Dana F. "Frederick Law Olmsted, the Placemaker." In *Two Centuries of American Planning*, edited by Daniel Schaffer. Baltimore: Johns Hopkins University Press, 1988.

Whitnall, Gordon. "History of Zoning," *Annals* of the American Academy of Political and Social Science 155, no. 2 (May 1931): 1–14.

Whitten, Robert. "Social Aspects of Zoning." *Survey* (June 15, 1922): 418–419.

Wilson, William H. *The City Beautiful Movement*. Baltimore and London: Johns Hopkins University Press, 1989.

Worley, William S. *J. C. Nichols and the Shaping of Kansas City: Innovation in Planned Residential Communities*. Columbia and London: University of Missouri Press, 1990.

Wright, Gwendolyn. *Building the Dream: A Social History of Housing in America*. New York: Pantheon Books, 1981.

INDEX

Adams, Thomas, 78, 98
Advisory Committee on Zoning, 66
American City Planning Institute (ACPI), 62, 65, 78
Annexation, benefits of, 26–27, 106; in Columbus suburbs, 38, 106–7, 178; process in Ohio, 25–27, 216–17n; and real estate development, 27, 49, 57, 104, 214n
Ardmore (Bexley), 54

Babcock, Richard, 101
Bartholomew, Harland, 73, 100, 135, 153, 191–92
Bartholomew, Harland, and Associates, 134–36, 177
Bassett, Edward, 65–67, 77–78, 161
Bauer, Catherine, 98
Beechwold (Columbus), 54
Berkeley, California, 34
Bettman, Alfred, 65–66, 73, 75, 78
Bexley, 10, 13, 15, 16, 26, 35, 37, 38, 49, 54, 103, 106, 121, 122, 136, 151, 185, 192–96, 214n; zoning in, 166–68
Blucher, Walter, 156
Burnham, Daniel Hudson, 12, 61, 68, 212n

Charity Organization Society, New York, 63
City Beautiful movement, 61, 71
City Efficient movement, 71
City Planning, 62
City planning, purposes of, 78
City planning profession: design background of, 61; early accomplishments of, 71–72; early development of, 59–63; education for, 154–55; friction in, 155, 231n; growth and development of, 97–99; and postwar development, 153–56; as public employees, 134, 153, 223n, 229n; suburban development and, 154; underlying beliefs of, 62; and zoning, 68–73, 99–101, 155–58
Civic associations. *See* Community associations
Columbus:
annexation, 7, 43, 103–4, 106, 116, 121
blacks in, 15–16, 152, 184, 198–99
blacks in suburbs of, 184–85
Board of Zoning Adjustment, 83, 84, 85
city charter, 25, 133, 213n
city planning department, 134
ethnic minorities in, 16, 217n
growth of city of, 7, 8, 116, 188–89
Plan Commission, 20
Plan of the City of Columbus (1908), 19–22, 120–21
planning commission, 80, 84, 133–34, 223n
population: decline in, 230n; (1870), 17; (1900), 19; (1970), 17
social structure of, 120–24, 188–89; and land development, 52; (1870), 18–19; (1900–1945), 58; (1970), 14–16
spatial form of, 40, 120–24, 188–89; (1870), 17–18; (1900–1945), 58; (1945–60), 107; (1970), 11–13; zoning and, 147, 149–52
study area, 8, 10, 206–7
suburbs of, 7, 13, 35, 38, 49–51, 103, 106–7, 116, 122–24 (*see also under specific suburbs*)
zoning: apartment, 86–87, 146–47;

253

application, 148–49, 190; application (1923–30), 85–88; application (1931–35), 88–90; application (1936–45), 91–92; application (1946–55), 92–95; application (1956–65), 139–43; application (1966–70), 144–47; commercial, 85, 90, 92, 95, 96, 143–44, 146–47, 148, 149, 191; and comprehensive plan, 85; industrial, 86; parking provisions under, 141, 145–46; public reaction to, 152–53; residential, 86, 97, 141–43, 146–47, 148–53; rezonings, 152–53; rezonings (1923–30), 87–88; rezonings (1931–35), 92; rezonings (1936–45), 92; rezonings (1946–55), 93–95; rezonings (1956–65), 141–44; rezonings (1966–70), 143, 146–47; variances (1923–30), 87–88; variances (1931–35), 89–90, 92; variances (1936–45), 92; variances (1946–55), 93–95; variances (1956–65), 140–42; variances (1966–70), 143, 145–46
zoning code, 6, 135; administration of, 83–84; first, 80–85; revised (1954), 136–40; variances from, 83, 84
Columbus Country Club, 55, 122
Columbus Lands Company, 56
Committee on the Congestion of the Population, New York, 62, 63
Community associations, 57, 215n, 218n
Comprehensive planning, 66, 71, 72–73, 100, 157, 213n
Country Club District: Kansas City, 32–33, 56–57; Upper Arlington, 57, 122–23
Craig, David, 156

Davis Estate (Worthington), 55
Death and Life of Great American Cities, 2
Deed restrictions, 30–35, 65, 214n, 217n
  on alienation, 31
  annexation and, 127–28
  automatic renewal of, 116
  building cost and, 31; in Columbus, 36–37, 40–41, 45, 46–48, 52, 53–58, 111, 113–14, 118, 123, 126
  building location, 31
  building materials, 31
  building size, 31; in Columbus, 41–42, 46–48, 52, 53–58, 111, 113–14, 118, 123, 126
  in Columbus, extent of, 123–24; impact on, 124; (pre-1900), 36; (1900–1920), 40–43; (1920s), 45–48; (1930–45), 52; (1945–60), 107–14; (1960s), 118
  developer's taste and, 125–26
  duration, 32–33, 127–28, 215n, 217n; in Columbus, 116
  enforcement, 32–33, 215n
  insertion of, 105
  land development and, 3, 30, 33, 188–89
  legal basis for, 33–34
  limitations on effectiveness of, 126–28
  market demand and, 55–56, 104, 114–15, 118–19, 120
  minorities and, 31; in Columbus, 41–42, 45, 46–48, 52, 53–58, 112–13, 118, 123, 124, 126; in Columbus suburbs, 184
  for neighborhood character, 34; in Columbus, 37, 45, 46–48, 51, 52, 53–58, 123
  nuisance prevention and, 31, 228n
  on occupancy, 31
  property value and, 34, 119, 120, 188–89
  purposes of, 30–31
  residential, 31; in Columbus, 41–45, 46–48, 51, 53–58, 109, 113–14, 118, 123, 126
  on setback line, 31; in Columbus, 37, 40–41, 45, 46–48, 51, 53–58, 107, 108, 112, 118, 123, 126
  on trees, 31, 125, 228n
  zoning and, 104–5, 116, 127, 188–89, 197, 199–200, 202–3; in Columbus, 118, 124; in Columbus suburbs, 181
Douglas, William O., 196–97

Eastcleft (Upper Arlington), 54
Eastmoor (Columbus), 55

Fairway (Whitehall), 55, 107
Federal Housing Administration, 113, 154, 181, 184, 218n
Ford, George B., 33
Franklin County Department of Sanitary Engineering, 103
Franklin County Regional Planning Commission, 132–36, 171, 180, 236n

Garden City concept, 61–62, 98
German urban land reform, 63–64
German Village (Columbus), 14
Gladden, Washington, 23, 24
Grandview Heights, Ohio, 10, 13, 15, 26, 35, 37, 38, 49, 56, 57, 103, 106, 118, 121, 122, 186, 192–96; zoning in, 175–77, 235n
Greenbelt town program, 98

Haar, Charles, 101
"Highest and best" use of land, 81, 119
Home rule, in Ohio, 23–25
Hoover, Herbert, 66
Horack, Frank, 156
Housing and Home Finance Agency, 131
Housing problems, 131, 153–54, 228n
Houston, 4, 158, 211n; deed restrictions in, 119–20
Howard, Ebenezer, 61–62

Jacobs, Jane, 2, 201
Johnson, Charles F., 56, 122, 124, 167; and land development and use of deed restrictions, 53–56
Johnson, Charles F., Inc., 53
Johnson, Tom, 23, 24
Jones, Samuel "Golden Rule," 23

Kelsey, Albert, 20
Kenilworth, Illinois, 34
Kenworth Place (Columbus), 53

Land development:
  in Columbus (pre-1900), 35–37; (1900–1920), 37–43; (1920s), 43–49; (1930–45), 49–52; (postwar), 102–15; (1946–60), 106–15; (1960s), 116–20
  financing of, 105
  Great Depression and, 217n; in Columbus, 49, 128–29
  growth and, 199
  location and, 121–23
  natural amenities and, 121–23
  planning and, 33
  professional, in Columbus, 48–49
  staggered, 105
  water and sewer service and, 103, 121, 237n
  zoning and, 189
  See also Deed restrictions: land development and
Land speculation, 63, 68
Land use: balance of, 5, 73, 135, 190–93, 211n; balance of, in Columbus suburbs, 175, 177; hierarchy of, 81–82, 137–38, 223n; incompatible, 5, 62, 66, 138, 182, 190, 193–94; survey, 135
Levitt and Sons, 104, 119, 154
Levittown, 114
Linden Heights, 26, 35, 37, 38
Lord, Austin W., 20
Lowrie, Charles N., 20
Lubove, Roy, 2

MacNeil, H. A., 20
Marble Cliff, 10, 13, 26, 35, 37, 38, 57, 103, 106, 118, 121, 122, 185, 192–96, 233n; zoning in, 164–66
Marsh, Benjamin, 62, 64
Master Plan: Columbus Urban Area, (The Summary Report), 134–35
Medick, Frank, 51; and land development and use of deed restrictions, 125–26
Medick Estates (Worthington), 125
Merriam, Charles, 68–69
Miller, James, 57
Monchow, Helen, 216n

256 • Index

Morganthau, Henry, 68
Mumford, Lewis, 98

National Association of Real Estate Boards (NAREB), 67, 78
National Conference on City Planning (NCCP), 62, 63, 64, 66
National Resources Planning Board, 99
Neighborhood character, 114–15. *See also* Deed restrictions: for neighborhood character; Zoning: neighborhood character and
Nichols, Jesse Clyde, 32–33, 56–57, 77, 116
Nolen, John, 68, 71–72, 153
Northwest Boulevard Company, 56

Ohio State University: expansion of, and zoning, 230n; in 1908 *Plan*, 20, 21
Old Worthington, and zoning for historic district, 179
Olmsted, Frederick Law, 61
Olmsted, Frederick Law, Jr., 64
Our Cities: Their Role in the National Economy, 99

Perry, Clarence, and the Neighborhood Unit concept, 98
Police power, 1, 197
Pomeroy, Hugh, 100, 156
Population congestion, 62, 63, 190
Progressives and the Slums, The, 2
Public interest, 2, 3, 100, 155, 156–57, 160; zoning and, 71, 190–91, 195–97, 201–2, 203

Real estate development. *See* Land development
Redevelopment, 131–32, 154, 155; planning requirements for, 131–32
Regional Plan for New York and Its Environs, 98
Regional planning, 131–36, 157, 160–61; in Columbus, 132–36

Regional Planning Association of America (RPAA), 98
Report Upon Economic Base, Population, and General Land Use, 135–36
Reps, John, 157–58
Residential location, consumers' choice of, in Columbus, 115
Residential satisfaction, 114–15
Restrictive covenants. *See* Deed restrictions
Riverlea, 10, 13, 51, 103, 162, 185–86, 192–96, 232n; zoning in, 51, 162–64
Riverside, Illinois, 30
Robinson, Charles Mulford, 20
Roland Park (Baltimore), 32, 34
Russell Sage Foundation, 98

St. Martins (Philadelphia), 34
Section 701, 131, 134, 171, 177. *See also* Regional planning
Segoe, Ladislas, and Associates, 171
Segregation, 201
 class, 2, 113–14; in Columbus, 124, 188–89
 racial, 2, 112–13, 221n; in Columbus, 124, 188–89; in Columbus suburbs, 184–85
 zoning and, 2, 152, 198–99
Shaker Heights, Ohio, 32, 35
Shelley v. *Kraemer*, 32, 112, 124, 214n
Short Hills, New Jersey, 34
Shurtleff, Flavel, 100
Siegan, Bernard, 161, 183
Social structure, land use controls and, 197–99
Spatial form, land use controls and, 197–99, 237n
Standard City Planning Enabling Act, 66–67
Standard Zoning Enabling Act, 66–67
Stein, Clarence, 78–79
Subdivision lot density, in Columbus: (pre-1900), 35; (1900–1920), 40; (1920s), 43–45; (1930–45), 51; (postwar), 105; (1945–60), 107, 109; (1960s), 116–17
Subdivision size, in Columbus: (pre-1900), 35; (1900–1920), 40; (1920s), 43; (1930–45), 51; (post-

war), 105; (1945–60), 107–8; (1960s), 117
Suburbs, class structure and, 114
Sutherland, George, 66, 196

Tennessee Valley Authority (TVA), 98
Thompson, Ben, 38, 53
Thompson, King, 38, 53, 106, 112–13, 122, 123, 128, 168; and real estate development and use of deed restrictions, 56–58
Thompson-Johnson-and-Thompson Realty Company, 56
Tugwell, Rexford, 98

U.S. Housing Act: of 1937, 99; of 1949, 99, 131; of 1954, 99, 131
U.S. Senate Committee on the District of Columbia, 62, 64
Upper Arlington, 10, 13, 26, 38, 49, 57, 103, 106, 112, 114, 116, 122, 123, 125, 128, 136, 151, 166, 184, 185–86, 192–96, 234n; zoning in, 168–74, 234n
Urban deterioration, 60, 99, 153–54; in Columbus, 195
Urban Land Uses, 135
Urban reform, 60
Urban renewal. *See* Redevelopment

Variance, use, 182. *See also* Zoning: variances
Village of Euclid v. Ambler Realty Company, 65–66

Warner, Sam Bass, Jr., 2, 200, 211n
Water and sewer service, 103, 121; and annexation, 103
Webster Park (Columbus), 53
Weiss, Marc Allan, 211n
"White City." *See* Worlds' Columbian Exposition
Whitehall, 10, 13, 15, 49, 103, 107, 114, 116, 136, 184, 185–86, 192–96; zoning in, 180–83, 236–37n
Whitten, Robert, 69–70, 73, 81, 161

Windermere (Upper Arlington), 54
Woodruff, J. Talmadge, 100
Worlds' Columbian Exposition, 61
Worthington, 10, 13, 16, 18, 50–51, 103, 106, 114, 115, 125, 175, 184, 185–86, 193–96; Old, 179, 236n; zoning in, 177–80, 236n

Zoning:
  agricultural, in Columbus suburbs, 181
  of automotive uses in Whitehall, 182
  Board of Adjustment or Appeals, 67, 101
  business community and, 76
  churches and, in Upper Arlington, 173–74
  in Columbus. *See under* Columbus
  commercial, in Columbus suburbs, 164, 166, 167, 170, 172, 175, 177–78, 181, 182
  commission, 67
  comprehensive plan and, 4, 67, 72–75, 100, 136, 156, 190–92; in Columbus suburbs, 171–72, 183, 185
  controversies, in Columbus suburbs, 173–74, 176, 192
  deed restrictions and, 95–96, 104–5, 116, 148–49, 193, 197, 199–200, 202–3; in Columbus suburbs, 181, 185
  effects of, 1, 2, 190–97, 199–200, 201–3; in Columbus, 96–97, 147–53, 158–59; in Columbus suburbs, 183–86
  equity, 5, 69, 77, 101, 156–57, 190, 194–95, 202
  exclusionary, 161
  exclusive uses of, 138, 167, 175, 178
  German model, 63–64
  goals, 4–6, 63, 67, 69–71, 79, 156, 190–97, 201–3
  growth and, 73, 161, 194; in Columbus suburbs, 170–72, 176, 178, 185
  for historic preservation, in Worthington, 179

home occupations and, in Columbus, 82
home owners' interests and, 77–78, 196–97; in Columbus, 153
industrial, in Columbus suburbs, 175–76, 177, 181, 193
judicial interpretation of, 73–75
jurisdiction over, 3, 161, 194
land development and, in Columbus, 116, 130
land speculation and, 68
legal profession and, 65
neighborhood character and, 161, 189, 200; in Columbus, 148–53; in Columbus suburbs, 166, 168, 172, 173–74, 177, 178–80, 183–84
New York City (1916), 63, 71, 76
nonconforming uses and, 137; in Columbus, 82, 87–88, 89–90, 141, 143, 146
nonexclusive, 82; in Columbus, 84; in Columbus suburbs, 169
outside municipal boundaries, 132–33
planning theory of, 72–75, 157–58, 188, 200
power of, 66, 157, 190
precedents, 64–65
as preventative, 68
property value and, 70–71, 75–79, 101, 156, 196–97; in Columbus, 95–97, 144, 147, 150–53; in Columbus suburbs, 183
purposes of, 1, 2, 7, 59, 70–71, 78–79, 100–101, 155–58, 160
race and, 70, 198–99; in Columbus, 152; in Columbus suburbs, 184–85
real estate support for, 75–79, 190, 197, 211n
regional, 132, 161, 180
separation of land uses and, 81
spot, 74–75, 180; in Whitehall, 182
spread, 4, 67, 77
success, 190–97, 199–200, 201–3, 238n; in Columbus suburbs, 185–86
upgrading, in Columbus suburbs, 170
variances, 101; in Columbus suburbs, 168, 172–73, 177, 179, 181–83.
See also City planning profession; Columbus; Segregation